# Classical Ballet Technique

University Press of Florida
Florida A&M University, Tallahassee
Florida Atlantic University, Boca Raton
Florida Gulf Coast University, Ft. Myers
Florida International University, Miami
Florida State University, Tallahassee
New College of Florida, Sarasota
University of Central Florida, Orlando
University of Florida, Gainesville
University of North Florida, Jacksonville
University of South Florida, Tampa
University of West Florida, Pensacola

# Classical Ballet

## Gretchen Ward Warren

**University Press of Florida**

Gainesville  Tallahassee  Tampa  Boca Raton  Pensacola  Orlando  Miami  Jacksonville  Ft. Myers  Sarasota

# _____ _Technique_

_Photographs by Susan Cook_

_Foreword by Robert Joffrey_

16   15   14   13   12        17   16   15   14   13

Library of Congress Cataloging-in-Publication
Warren, Gretchen.
Classical ballet technique / Gretchen Warren; photographs by Susan Cook.
p. cm.
Bibliography: p.
Includes index.
ISBN 978-0-8130-0895-0 (cloth)
ISBN 978-0-8130-0945-2 (paperback)
1. Ballet dancing. 2. Ballet dancing–Pictorial works.
I. Cook, Susan, 1948–.        II. Title.
GV1788.W37 1989
792.8'2–dc19    89-31141

The University Press of Florida is the scholarly publishing agency for the
State University System of Florida, comprising Florida A&M University,
Florida Atlantic University, Florida Gulf Coast University, Florida Inter-
national University, Florida State University, New College of Florida,
University of Central Florida, University of Florida, University of North
Florida, University of South Florida, and University of West Florida.

University Press of Florida
15 Northwest 15th Street
Gainesville, FL 32611
www.upf.com

Printed in China

*For Emily, Herman, and Margery*

*and for all my students, past, present, and future*

# Contents

## Part I. Theory and Tradition

### Chapter 1. Basic Concepts  5

### Chapter 2. The Ideal Body Structure and Proportions for Classical Ballet Dancers  64

### Chapter 3. The Ballet Class: Notes for Teachers  71

## Part II. The Movements of Classical Ballet

### Chapter 4. Exercises at the Barre  86

## Chapter 13. Batterie 320

## Chapter 14. Pointe Work 349

## Chapter 15. Révérence 366

Robert Joffrey conducting class. Photo by Herbert Migdoll.

# *Foreword* _____

## *by Robert Joffrey*

Most young dancers know what it takes to earn a place in a professional company—good physical proportions, coordination, technical facility, musicality. But many of them do not realize how important it is to be fully trained when they get there. Once in the company, they will be learning the repertoire, practicing, and preparing for performances, and there will be little time to make up for incomplete training. Ideally, dancers should be so well trained that in their first professional performances they could confidently undertake soloist roles.

Fundamental to their complete dance education is the mastery of classical ballet technique. Young dancers typically have learned their technique in the classroom and through a kind of oral tradition passed down over the years from teacher to student, from classroom to classroom. This tradition seems to have worked rather well if we judge by the evolution of American ballet training over the last twenty years: today's dancers are more versatile and better trained than ever. Many have studied with former professional dancers of some repute who were able to pass on a wealth of knowledge and experience to their students. However, considerable stylistic versatility and technical virtuosity is now expected of professionals in ballet companies, and dancers need to continue exploring as many avenues as possible in mastering classical technique.

One way to do this is to supplement the oral tradition with a written one. With this book Gretchen Warren has made a valuable contribution to such a tradition. She analyzes all the steps in the vocabulary of classical ballet, showing through words and photographs the correct execution of the most basic to the most advanced forms of each step. Someone once said that there is nothing more intoxicating than watching a dancer perform an adagio at the barre. In this book one can find a detailed analysis of all the movements in this and many other exercises, beautifully illustrated by some of America's finest young dancers. Aware of the stylistic and technical versatility demanded of dancers today, Warren includes, along with steps already familiar to us, useful movements found only in the Soviet syllabus, which she studied first-hand in the U.S.S.R. She also notes Danish and English variations.

Of course, a complete dance education is a continuing, growing experience incorporating mind, body, and spirit. Understanding the technical components of the art is but a beginning, and aspiring dancers should move outside the ballet classroom to explore other elements of their craft. The history and development of dance and music, an appreciation for various cultural styles, a grounding in sound acting techniques—all must be part of a dancer's education. Perhaps most important is for dancers to learn, through musical training, how to appreciate and analyze a variety of musical forms and to understand their rhythms.

To master the art of ballet, a dancer serves a long apprenticeship. The best dancers remain inquisitive about their art throughout their careers and are always willing to explore new areas of growth and discovery. Whether they are at the beginning of their apprenticeship or well into it, this book is for those dancers.

# _Acknowledgments_

All of the instructional photographic sequences in this book were taken by Susan Cook, without whom this book would not have been possible. The live-action photographs of ballet dancers in performance were taken by Myra Armstrong, Juri Barikin, Steven Caras, Paul B. Goode, and J. Tomas Lopez. I thank them all for their irreplaceable contributions to this effort.

As a dancer, and later as a teacher-in-training, I have been privileged to participate in the classes of many remarkable teachers. They inspired me and gave me the background necessary to write this book. In particular, I am grateful to John Barker, Maggie Black, Jeremy Blanton, Edward Caton, Gabriella Darvash, Olga Evreinoff, Barbara Fallis, Maria Fay, Barbara Fewster, Mila Gibbons, Benjamin Harkarvy, Frano Jelincic, Thalia Mara, Ann Parson, Robert Rodham, Margarita de Saa, Jurgen Schneider, Lupe Serrano, Erling Sunde, Maria Swoboda, Richard Thomas, and John White.

I owe an enormous debt of gratitude to all the wonderful dancers who posed tirelessly and patiently for the studio photographs. I thank them for believing in the project and for giving so generously of their time and talent.

In addition, I would like to thank the following people and organizations for their assistance in many ways, large and small, throughout the five years it took to bring this book to fruition: American Ballet Theatre; Bill and Stephanie Adams; Jonathan Arkin; Gwen Ashton; Ballet Barres, Inc., Arcadia, Florida; Gil Boggs; Charles Brooks; Robert Calvo; Rima Corben; Robert Fitzgerald; Homer Garza; Marrie Hadfield; Deborah Hamilton; Ken Hanks; Connie Hardinge; Betty Ann Hawkins; Laurie Horn; Jeff Jones; Julia Jones; Jill Johnston; Marc W. Katz; Martine Lamy; Diana Larsen; Victoria Leigh; Robert McCormick; Herbert Migdoll; Ellen Parker-Chayes; Sandra Robinson; Galina Shlyapina: Michael Sikes; Bonnie and Stephen Simon; Lloyd Sobel; Martha Swope Studio; the Tampa Ballet; David Telford; Tenley Taylor; Alexander Trohatchev; the University of South Florida Department of Dance; Jeffrie Wall; Herman and Margery Ward; Spencer Wertheimer; Richard Wielette; and especially Marilyn Hawkridge; Cynthia Gold; Silvia Ruffo-Fiore; and my editor, Deidre Bryan, the production editor, Nicola Sorenson, and the book's designer, Larry Leshan.

I am particularly grateful to the late Robert Joffrey for his support and encouragement, and for the foreword that begins this book.

Soviet ballerina Galina Shlyapina in *Giselle*, Act II, U.S.S.R. Photo: Juri Barikin.

# Introduction

This book is for teachers and students of ballet, for dance professionals, and for all who marvel at the beauty and strength of the classically trained dancer. It grew out of my desire to document material passed on to me by many remarkable teachers, as well as to share valuable information distilled from my own twenty years of teaching in the professional ballet world. My purpose has been to define and clarify the entire vocabulary of classical ballet and to comment in detail upon the manner in which it ought to be taught.

For the sake of accuracy, I felt it essential that the book employ photographs instead of drawings. *Classical Ballet Technique* contains more than 2,600 pictures by dance photographer Susan Cook, in which twenty of America's finest ballet professionals expertly demonstrate the poses and exercises that are the foundation of ballet technique. For the young dancer struggling to master these movements, the book offers advice and encouragement and answers many of the questions most often raised by parents of aspiring dancers. For teachers and other dance professionals, it is a comprehensive reference source; indeed, many aspects of classical training that have often been considered "gray" areas, or avoided by teachers as areas of controversy, are frankly and sensibly confronted here. Finally, for balletomanes everywhere, it offers a complete pictorial survey of the behind-the-scenes process that produces classical ballet dancers.

A dancer's ultimate goal, after spending years of training for a career in professional ballet, is to be able to use the body as an expressive instrument of communication. To do so, the dancer must master a movement vocabulary as precise as that of any verbal language. This "language" of classical ballet was first systematized in the Académie Royale de Musique et de Danse, founded by Louis XIV in 1661. To this day, the elegant carriage cultivated by the dancers of his court remains the primary stylistic characteristic of classical ballet.

During the eighteenth century, several prominent dancer-teachers, most notably France's Auguste Vestris and Italy's Carlo Blasis, continued developing and refining the ballet vocabulary. The change in social mores at the end of the French Revolution directly affected this development. Reflecting trends in fashion, ballerinas' costumes became shorter and lighter, permitting a greater range and variety of movements, particularly jumps and turns. Flimsier fabrics permitted greater visibility of the dancer's silhouette, and a new emphasis was placed on "line" (i.e., the shape and positioning of the dancer's limbs in space). In addition, the practice of dancing en pointe, or on the toes, was initiated.

In its basic forms and premises, ballet technique has changed little since that time. The scope of the vocabulary, however, as well as its level of difficulty, has greatly increased. More and more complex movements have been added to the vocabulary, and dancers all over the world have been influenced by the particular demands of each other's styles and techniques. Today's dancer must be prepared to dance an extremely diverse repertoire of dances by widely differing classical and contemporary choreographers. Each piece requires not only specific stylistic differences, but individual technical strengths as well. How does today's dancer prepare to meet these challenges?

I believe that it is no longer sufficient to have been trained exclusively within one school (Soviet, French, Italian, Balanchine/American, English, or Danish). To be adequately prepared for a professional career today, dancers need some exposure to the considerably varying technical demands of **all** the schools of classical ballet. Students will be better able to meet the variety of challenges that await them if the unique, strength-building aspects of the programs (i.e., syllabi) taught by each of the existing schools are integrated into their daily ballet classes. All of these special movements, including particularly useful ones from the Soviet and Danish schools, are described in this book; many are illustrated here for the first time anywhere.

Classical Ballet Technique is divided into two parts. Part I begins with a pictorial chapter devoted to important basic concepts of classical ballet training. It reflects in detail those traditions and theories upheld in my own classes, but I emphasize that these theories are not my personal inventions. I have compiled them after years of observing master teachers throughout the world and have put them to use in my own classes only after considerable thought and discussion with my colleagues in the profession. They reflect the methodology I have found to be most logical, effective, and aesthetically desirable.

Also included in Part I is a chapter devoted to the analysis and illustration of the natural physical characteristics that are considered prerequisite for men and women desiring to pursue a professional career in ballet. Part I concludes with a chapter entitled "The Ballet Class: Notes for Teachers," featuring key aspects of the preparation, content, and structure of a successful ballet class.

In Part II, sequential photographs illustrate the step-by-step technical execution of the entire range of movements in the classical ballet vocabulary. This part of the book was designed to help the reader fully understand all the components of each ballet step. At least one form of every movement in the classical vocabulary, from the most basic to the most advanced, is pictured in this section. The twenty models for these photographs are all members of major American ballet companies, including the American Ballet Theatre and the Joffrey Ballet. Dressed in simple practice attire, they demonstrate clearly and precisely how each movement is ideally performed.

Part II also clarifies the use of standard French ballet terminology, the traditional, internationally used method for designating classical ballet steps. A pronunciation guide with English phonetic transcription and a glossary of common dance terms are included at the end of the book.

Accompanying many of the captions for each photographic sequence are notes with additional information about rhythm, style, national and historical derivation, usefulness, and correct technical execution. These notes are intended not only to help the student or teacher understand **how** to do a step, but also to point out other considerations—for example, **why** a step is important to the development of a strong classical technique; at what point the step ought to be practiced within the structure of a ballet class; whether the step is for advanced dancers only; and whether the step is traditionally restricted to male or female dancers.

As a teacher, I am certainly aware of the fact that photographs and words are limited in their ability to communicate several important aspects of dance training. Emotional expressiveness, musical nuance, and the rhythmical characteristics that differentiate one movement from another (or, more simply, the rhythmical nature of movements in general) are almost impossible to convey in still pictures. To learn these essential aspects of technique, dancers must observe and imitate other dancers in motion. Therefore, this book is intended for use by students **only** in conjunction with the traditional form of classroom study; it should never be used in lieu of the classroom. Ballet technique, whose essence is movement, must be learned in the dance studio, where "hands-on" assistance and the physical example set by the teacher are available. This book was designed to complement and facilitate that process. However, the expertly demonstrated movements in the photographs have one important advantage over dance in motion: in the studio, the observation of movements is fleeting; here, the movements are frozen on the page, giving students the luxury of examining the multitude of details in each of them. The understanding and successful execution of these details is essential to mastering the art of ballet.

For young dancers and teachers, and for all who love ballet, I hope this book will provide an illuminating overview of the complex process involved in the transformation of the human body from its natural state into a wondrous and expressive instrument of classical grace and strength.

# Part I

## Theory and Tradition

In Tbilisi, U.S.S.R., a teacher instructs a second-year student about how to stand correctly in 5th position. Photo: G. Warren.

# 1 ∽ Basic Concepts

## Correct Stance

Correct stance is essential to the study of classical ballet and should be mastered within the first year of training. Failure to achieve it will result in technical weakness (often leading to injury) and will prevent the dancer from attaining technical control and freedom of movement.

**INCORRECT**

**INCORRECT**

The weight of the body is correctly centered over the feet, with the armpit and hipbone vertically aligned.

"Swaybacked": stomach muscles are released, and shoulders are in back of the hips.

"Tucked under": pelvis is thrust forward, upper back is rounded, and the weight of the body is back on the heels.

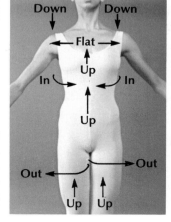
**INCORRECT**

Using the central muscles at the base of the ribcage, the dancer correctly holds the ribs "in and flat." Thus she is able to control the lower back and stabilize the vertical placement of the torso directly on top of the supporting leg(s).

When the ribs are inflated and thrust forward, the result is a swayed back. This artificial placement of the torso is anatomically unhealthy and will prohibit freedom of movement.

**MUSCULAR SENSATIONS WHILE MAINTAINING CORRECT STANCE**

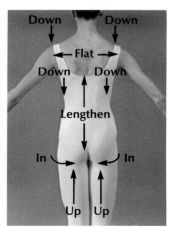

The directional arrows show the complex combination of muscular functions, including both contraction and extension, that results in correct ballet stance. Repeating the directions verbally is helpful for the student. Through constant practice, this posture eventually becomes automatic for the dancer.

# Correct Stance on the Supporting Leg

Standing correctly "on top of" the supporting leg in a turned-out position is one of the most difficult and fundamental challenges of classical ballet. The center of the dancer's weight must fall in a straight line from the navel down through the leg to the center of the supporting foot (see p. 20). The torso must appear to be lifted upward "out of" the hips. The thigh, abdominal, and buttocks muscles must all be strongly engaged to maintain this position. Knowledge of how to maintain the body centered on this vertical axis is particularly essential for the study of pirouettes.

(see p. 20)

INCORRECT  INCORRECT

  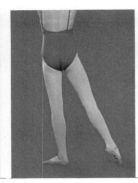 

| | | | |
|---|---|---|---|
| Front view. Correct placement "on top of" the supporting leg. | Incorrect placement. The weight of the body has been shifted off the center of support and out toward the working leg. | Back view. Correct placement "on top of" the supporting leg. Note the lift of the buttocks muscles at the top of the leg. | The dancer is "sitting" into the supporting hip. The buttocks and abdominal muscles are not being used. The torso is not lifted up "out of the hips." The upper thigh is not rotated (i.e., turned-out). |

INCORRECT  INCORRECT

| | | |
|---|---|---|
| Profile view. Correct placement "on top of" the supporting leg. Note the lift in the abdominal muscles and up the back of the leg underneath the buttocks. | The abdominals have been relaxed, allowing the pelvis to tilt back. The buttocks muscles are not being used. The weight has been shifted backward, putting unsafe pressure on the supporting knee. Maximum turnout of the upper thigh has been lost. | The dancer is tensing the buttocks muscles excessively, which thrusts the pelvis forward and throws the weight of the upper body backward. |

# The Correct Way To Hold the Barre

The barre is used to help the dancer maintain stability while performing exercises "turned-out." Almost all movements (including jumps and turns) are first studied at the barre. For the advanced dancer, the barre acts as a warm-up tool. It should **never** be relied upon to hold the dancer upright or to compensate for a lack of correct placement (i.e., body weight centered over, and supported by, the legs and feet). It is essential that both the arm and the hand on the barre side remain relaxed at all times.

Correct distance from the barre, with the elbow **down** and relaxed.

The hand is placed lightly on top of the barre with the wrist **down** and relaxed.

Facing the barre, the hands are in line with the shoulders. The elbows and wrists are dropped.

The hand is placed slightly in front of the body.

INCORRECT

INCORRECT

INCORRECT

INCORRECT

The elbow of the arm on the barre should never remain or rotate up in the air.

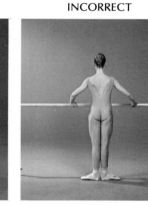

If the dancer is too close to the barre, the inside shoulder will lift, ruining the placement of the upper back.

The hands are too far out to the side, the elbows are lifted, and there is too much tension in the arms.

## *Readjusting the hand forward for arabesque positions*

INCORRECT

The hand must move forward along the barre whenever the leg is raised to the back above the level of 45°. Failure to make this readjustment will result in pinched, uncomfortable positions of the upper back and the arm on the barre.

# Turn-out

## The correct use of turn-out

All movements in the classical ballet vocabulary are performed with the legs turned-out, or rotated outward from the hips. The degree to which the legs can be rotated outward without causing injury varies according to each dancer's natural facility for turn-out. Although primarily activated by the six deep rotator muscles in the hip, turn-out is not completely confined to the hip joint. Rather, it is the sum total of the leg's external rotation: hip, knee, tibia, ankle, and foot (Hamilton, *Physical Prerequisites,* p. 64).

The ideal 90° (per leg) of outward rotation demanded of professional ballet dancers is usually achieved with 60°–70° of external rotation coming from above the knee and 20°–30° from below (Hardaker et al., *Pathogenesis,* p. 21). It cannot be overemphasized, however, that the force for turn-out of the legs must come from the hip down and not from the floor up. If the turn-out does not originate from the hip, it will be forced from the knee; and the knee, being a hinge rather than a rotary joint, is not designed to rotate. Forcing turn-out from the knees and feet usually results in injury; correct ballet training therefore stresses turn-out from the hips.

Legs rotated outward in 1st position.

DEVANT      À LA SECONDE      DERRIÈRE

 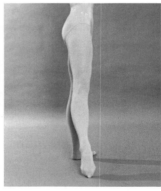 

Correct turn-out in extended positions.

DEVANT      À LA SECONDE      DERRIÈRE

Unrotated, or parallel, positions of the leg.

# Common errors in turn-out

Unequal rotation of the legs in 5th position. The legs should be equally turned-out at all times.

Tucking the pelvis under in an effort to increase turn-out. This distorts the alignment of the spine and throws the weight of the body backward.

Forcing turn-out by sacrificing the correct placement of the torso. (The hips are not vertically aligned under the shoulders, and the lower back is swayed.)

It is often incorrectly assumed that turn-out is maintained by contracting the buttocks muscles. **The hip rotator muscles — not the gluteus muscles — rotate the legs outward.** However, the buttocks muscles are often used to stabilize the body in the turned-out position and can help the dancer to feel and control turn-out. These muscles should not be overused. The sensation of tightening should be felt at the top of the back of the legs—more underneath the buttocks than on top of them. **Never** pinch the buttocks together so that the pelvis is thrust forward (i.e., tucked under).

Turned-out from the feet instead of from the hips. Note bent knees and rolled-over feet. Working in this position is unstable and can cause a knee injury.

The knees are not aligned over the feet. It would be safer to work with the feet less turned-out.

Unequal rotation of the legs, with the hips twisted in an effort to force a greater degree of turn-out in the working leg.

# Body structure and natural capacity for turn-out

The following photographs illustrate a simple posture useful for ascertaining an individual's degree of natural turn-out in the hip joints. Children auditioning for professional ballet schools are often asked to assume this position so that their turn-out, an important aspect of their anatomical suitability for classical ballet, can be evaluated. Only a few human bodies possess the "recommended" degree of rotation pictured below.

The individual lies on his or her back on the floor with both legs bent and drawn up as close as possible to the torso. The soles of the feet are then pressed together, with the knees dropped sideways, outward toward the floor. Most important, the lower back must be pressed firmly against the floor. In this position, the closer the knees are to the floor, the greater the degree of natural turn-out in the hip joints.

RECOMMENDEDACCEPTABLE

The degree of natural rotation in the hip shown by both of these dancers will facilitate the study of classical ballet.

UNACCEPTABLE

The study of classical ballet will be difficult and possibly injurious for a person with such limited flexibility.

There is a great deal of controversy in the ballet world regarding proper turn-out. Research has shown that with children between the ages of eight and eleven (the recommended period for beginning serious ballet training), it is sometimes possible to increase slightly the degree of natural turn-out in the hip (i.e., that amount with which an individual is born). The bone structure of children in this age group is still malleable, and the repeated practice of ballet exercises in the turned-out position seems to produce a torsional deformity of the femur (where it inserts into the hip socket) which results in a permanently increased degree of rotation (Hamilton, *Physical Parameters*). For this reason many serious professional ballet academies, such as those in the Soviet Union, require that beginning students force their legs almost immediately into the 180° turned-out position. This is considered imperative to their future development as classical dancers, and is probably not harmful to these students, whose extreme natural flexibility has been ascertained in the careful physical screening they have undergone before being accepted for training. Moreover, these beginner students practice daily in small classes in a painstakingly slow manner, facing the barre, under the careful tutelage of teachers who are constantly on the lookout for any sign of incorrect placement.

In the West, where commercial teachers are often faced with large beginner classes that do not meet on a daily basis and may contain many youngsters whose bodies are less than ideally flexible, the approach toward turn-out tends to be somewhat more conservative. In such situations, forcing turn-out can be physically harmful and certainly should never be advocated for beginners who are over twelve years old. A more gradual, less severe method of developing good rotation is recommended.

My personal belief is that each student must be treated individually. Students who demonstrate the recommended degree of turn-out on page 10 should be asked to use the maximum degree of rotation possible for their bodies, **provided** that the training goes slowly and that careful attention is paid to all aspects of correct placement. Students with less flexibility should be taught to know their limitations and to work within them. Remember that it is generally impossible, beyond the age of eleven, to increase the degree of outward rotation in the hip joint. However, most dancers can learn to make the most of what they have, in such a way as to camouflage a less-than-perfect degree of natural turn-out.

Very few human bodies possess the capacity for perfect turn-out. Students should remember that they are trying to achieve more than the ability simply to turn their legs outward. Their goal must be to develop the muscular strength to **control** and **maintain** their own maximum degree of turn-out **at all times** while they are dancing.

In a contemporary pas de deux, Soviet ballerina Galina Shlyapina demonstrates her perfect natural facility for turnout. Photo: Juri Barikin.

# Footwear for Ballet Class

Two special types of shoes are used by ballet dancers: "soft" ballet slippers and "hard," blocked pointe shoes, or toe shoes. All beginning students, male and female, wear the soft-soled slippers, which are made of either leather or canvas. Male dancers continue to wear these pliable, snug-fitting slippers throughout their careers. Women, however, must also learn to dance in pointe shoes. When their legs and feet are strong enough, they begin to study pointe work. Later, as advanced dancers, they may opt to wear old, "broken-in" pointe shoes for their regular nonpointe classes, instead of soft ballet slippers. It takes considerably more strength in the plantar muscles underneath the foot to bend or point a pointe shoe than it does to bend the lighter, softer, much more flexible ballet slipper. In order to maintain and increase the strength in their feet, many female dancers prefer to challenge themselves by wearing old pointe shoes for class. However, **only** advanced dancers should engage in this practice.

All ballet shoes must fit snugly. Beginning students should be fitted at reputable dancewear shops and should take their new shoes, before wearing them, to their teacher for approval. A shoe that fits improperly will be both uncomfortable and unattractive. Since foot structure is a highly individual matter, all advanced and professional dancers rely upon custom-made footwear, an expensive but absolutely essential element of their success as dancers.

*The correct way to tie the ribbons of a pointe shoe*

Draw the ribbon from the inside of the foot diagonally up and across to the other side of the ankle.

Wrap it one-and-a-half times around the ankle, above the ankle bone, finishing on the inside of the ankle.

Lift the other (outside) ribbon diagonally across the first ribbon and wrap it once around the ankle on top of the first ribbon.

Tie both ribbons together at the **inside** of the ankle and tuck the ends securely under the ribbons around the ankle, pushing the knot to the inside so that it is completely hidden.

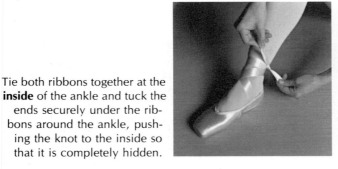 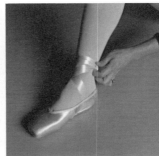 

It can be harmful to the Achilles tendon to tie pointe shoe ribbons at the back of the ankle. There is a small indentation just in back of the inside ankle bone where the knot can be hidden under the ribbons; in this spot it is both comfortable and invisible.

A small amount of protective material such as lamb's wool or brown paper may be placed inside the shoe around the toes. Elastic may be added to secure the shoe at the heel.

# The Positions of the Feet

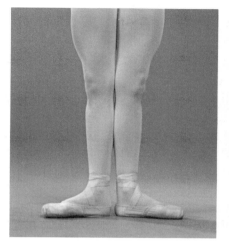

1st position.

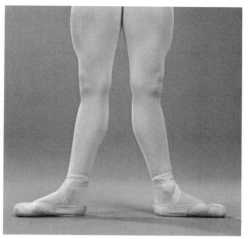

2nd position. (The distance between the feet should be approximately one-and-a-half times the length of one of the dancer's feet.)

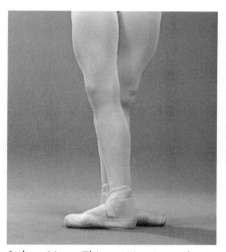

3rd position. (This position is used primarily in character and historical dances.)

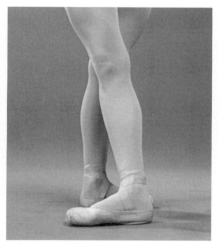

4th position. (The distance between the feet should be approximately the length of one of the dancer's feet.)

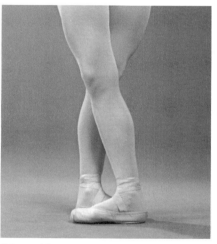

5th position.

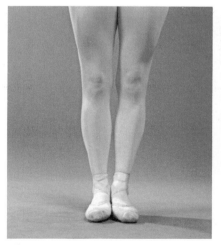

6th position.

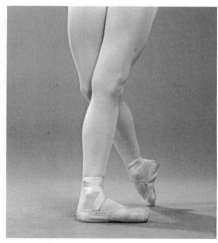

"B+" (also called attitude à terre), a common preparatory pose. Note that knees are **together.**

# The Use of the Foot

## The foot extended, fully pointed

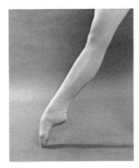

Correctly extended, or pointed, foot in 2nd.

Correctly pointed foot in a shoe.

Weight is incorrectly resting on the toes.

INCORRECT

INCORRECT

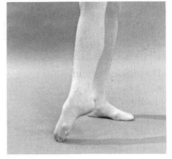

Correctly pointed foot devant.

"Sickled" foot devant.

Pronated foot caused by slight flexing of ankle.

INCORRECT

INCORRECT

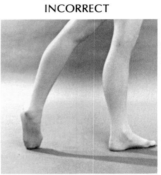
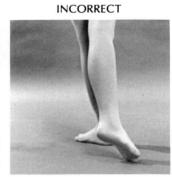

Correctly pointed derrière; no weight on big toe.

"Sickled" foot derrière.

Beveled foot caused by slight flexing of ankle.

## The foot en demi-pointe

INCORRECT

INCORRECT

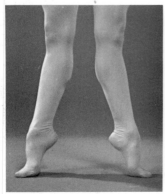
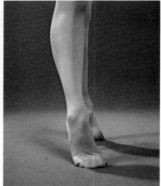
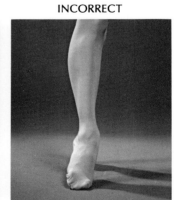

Three-quarter position demi-pointe. This position requires hyper-mobility in the ankle and instep joints. (See note, p. 70.) The use of the quarter or half demi-pointe positions is rare today.

"Sickling out."

"Rolling in."

# The foot en pointe

Pointe work is traditionally performed only by female dancers. The study of elementary pointe exercises is begun **only after correct stance has been achieved and the student has demonstrated considerable strength in the feet and legs en demi-pointe.** It is generally considered unadvisable for pointe work to be attempted by children younger than ten years old, since malformation of the immature bones of the feet could result.

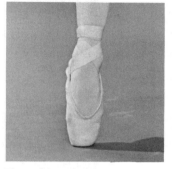
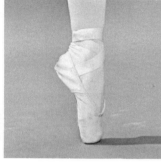

INCORRECT

INCORRECT

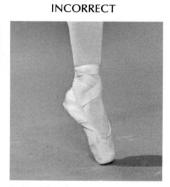

The ankle is held strongly in the vertical position without any sickling. The toes are straight and the feeling is one of "pulling up out of the shoe."

"Knuckled" over.

Pulled back.

# Moving from the whole foot onto pointe or demi-pointe

Relevé is executed in one smooth, continuous motion (at any speed) by first straightening the knees and then lifting the heels from the floor. (It is incorrect to lift the heels before straightening the knees.) It is also possible to rise on straight legs to the demi-pointe or pointe without a preceding plié, in which case the movement is termed "elevé." In either case, the dancer must maintain the maximum degree of turn-out when the heels are released from the floor.

Piqué is a step directly onto a straight leg en demi-pointe (or pointe). It requires a strong transfer of weight from one leg (in plié) to the other.

RELEVÉ

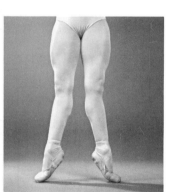

PIQUÉ

Piqué en avant to attitude derrière en pointe.

# Opening and Closing the Foot from 5th Position

### Correct

  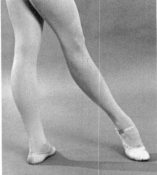 

From 5th—

Slide to a small 4th position, keeping the working heel on the floor.

Release the heel, keeping it pressed well forward.

Slide the toe outward to the fully stretched position.

### Incorrect

  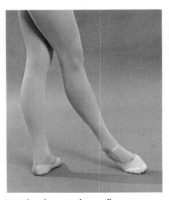 

From 5th—

Toes lead out.

Heel releases from floor too soon.

Heel is not pressed forward.

### Incomplete closing of the foot in 5th position in back

These two errors are common when executing a series of fast battements to the side.

INCORRECT          INCORRECT

Not crossed enough.

Heel not on floor.

 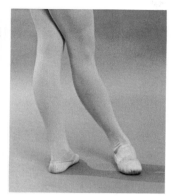 

Release the ankle, bringing the toe back toward the heel.

Lower into a small 4th position.

Slide the foot into 5th, maintaining the turn-out.

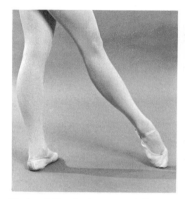 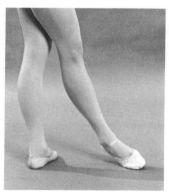 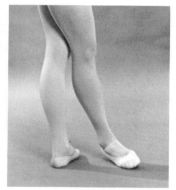 

Only at the last moment (too late) does the heel press forward into the fully stretched pointe tendue.

Heel drops, toes trail behind as foot draws in.

Heel closes with foot in unturned-out position.

Toes flip back into 5th.

## Lowering the Foot from Pointe Tendue to 4th Position

The distance between the feet in 4th position is approximately the length of the dancer's foot.

Pointe tendue devant.

Pull toes back in line with heel.

Lower heel into 4th position.

If toes are left in place and heel is pushed forward to lower into 4th, the result will be a too-wide 4th position in which it is impossible to maintain turn-out of the upper leg.

# The Positions sur le Cou-de-pied

There are two positions sur le cou-de-pied devant. The "fully pointed" position is used when executing fondus and développés; "wrapped" is for frappés and petits battements. There is only one position sur le cou-de-pied derrière.

## "Fully pointed" position devant
### ("conditional" cou-de-pied in Soviet syllabus)

## "Wrapped" position devant

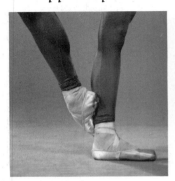

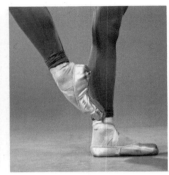

Fully stretched ankle, heel in front of ankle, toes pulled around behind.

Side view. In order for fully stretched foot to fit around the ankle, knee must be firmly pressed to the side.

Toes placed above ankle.

Note space between heel and supporting leg.

## "Fully pointed" position derrière

## "Fully pointed"
### (with the supporting leg in fondu)

Heel placed in back of ankle, toes away.

An acceptable alternate placement of the foot in cou-de-pied in fondu. The toe of the working foot is placed above the ankle in the center of the supporting leg so that the heel is **outside** of, rather than against, the supporting leg. This placement allows maximum use of turn-out (especially for dancers with very deep demi-pliés) and insures that the pointed toe will never rest on the top of the supporting foot.

## Common errors in cou-de-pied

INCORRECT

INCORRECT

INCORRECT

INCORRECT

Heel is too low, causing ankle to flex and toes to touch floor.

"Cupped" foot is pointed everywhere **except** ankle!

"Sickled" foot devant.

"Sickled" foot derrière.

# Trajectory of the Leg Opening and Closing from 5th Position

## From 5th position opening devant

   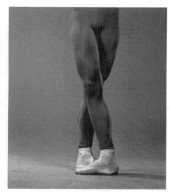

The foot slides from 5th forward through a small 4th position.

Fully extended, the toes are in line with the hip; the heel is in line with the navel.

Returning, the toes readjust outward, lowering through a small 4th position.

The foot slides back into 5th position.

## From 5th position opening derrière

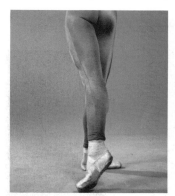  

Slide the toes backward, keeping heel firmly pressed down.

Fully stretched, the toes are in line with the hip.

Return, lowering the foot through a small 4th position and sliding it into 5th.

## Opening to the side

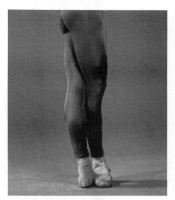  

From 5th position, the foot slides through 1st to a small 2nd position, at which point the heel releases and the toes stretch and slide out à la seconde. Keep the heels in line.

Take care to prevent the leg from inscribing a small circle (instead of a straight line through 1st) when moving in and out à la seconde.

# Weight Distribution

## Weight distribution over both feet

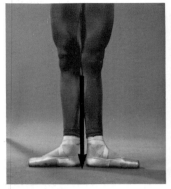   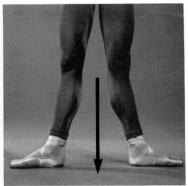

Center of weight in 1st position.

Center of weight in 5th position.

Center of weight in 4th position.

Center of weight in 2nd position.

## Weight distribution over the supporting foot

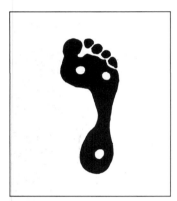 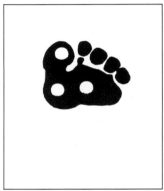  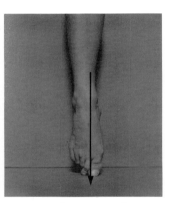

On the whole foot the weight is distributed equally between the three dots.

En demi-pointe the weight is equally distributed between the three dots.

En demi-pointe the center of weight falls between the first and second toes.

En pointe the center of weight falls primarily on the first and slightly on the second toe.

## Shift of the center of weight over the supporting foot at various levels

**ON THE WHOLE FOOT**  **EN DEMI-PLIÉ**  **EN DEMI-POINTE**  **EN POINTE**

The vertical line indicates where the center of weight was **when the dancer was standing on two feet in 1st position.** Note the shift of the center of weight away from this line at the various levels. On one leg, the dancer's weight must fall in a similar direct vertical line from the nose, through the navel, to the center of the supporting foot.

# Degree of Pelvic Tilt in Extensions

*Placement of the hips in extensions to the side*

With the leg pointed à terre, there is no tilt of the pelvis. This is also true with the leg lifted to the 45° level.

At approximately 90°, there is a visible tilt of the pelvis. Note that shoulders remain parallel to the floor at all levels of the extension.

At 120°, not only is the pelvis tilted, but there is a **slight,** permissible displacement of the rib cage.

INCORRECT

"Sitting" into the supporting hip.

INCORRECT

Overly displaced rib cage.

*Placement of the hips in extensions to the front*

INCORRECT

Both hips are in line. Note small curve in lower back, which indicates a correctly placed pelvis.

The pelvis is tucked under, flattening lower back and causing supporting knee to bend slightly.

In **very high** extensions to the front, it is usually necessary for hip of lifted leg to go forward.

High attitude croisée devant, in which hip of working leg is lifted forward.

**In both the above cases, take care to maintain as much turn-out in the lifted leg as possible.**

# Placement of the Torso in Grand Rond de Jambe

Grand rond de jambe is performed at all levels (à terre, 45°, 90°, and above) and with the working leg bent in attitude.

EN DEHORS

From the extension devant, demi-rond the leg à la seconde **without leaning toward the barre** or "sitting" into the supporting hip. **Maintain height of working leg.** Never allow it to drop between positions.

EN DEDANS

From the extension derrière, slightly penché the body forward and immediately begin to bring the heel under as the leg moves à la seconde. This transition from arabesque to 2nd must be made **as quickly as possible** because the body moves through in an extremely unflattering position.

*Common errors in grand rond de jambe en dehors*

CORRECT

INCORRECT

As the leg moves toward the back from 2nd, the dancer must lengthen the working side forward from the shoulder to the hip to accommodate the rotation to arabesque. Arching back against the leg at this moment will cause the leg to drop. The dancer will appear awkward and feel uncomfortable.

From à la seconde, keeping the thigh turned-out, press the working leg as far back as possible behind the hip and shoulder (1–6 inches) until that point when the thigh must begin to rotate under to assume the arabesque line. **The upper body must adjust forward as the leg goes back.** Take care to prevent the hip from lifting and the upper body from leaning toward the barre during this difficult adjustment.

The leg should arrive in 2nd completely turned-out. From there, the heel immediately begins to rotate under as the leg comes devant. Keep the shoulders parallel to the floor and take care to prevent the hip from lifting and the upper body from leaning toward the barre.

INCORRECT  INCORRECT

Lifting the hip and leaning toward the barre.

Rotating the heel under too soon as the leg moves en dehors from 2nd to arabesque.

# Facial Expressions

Eyes en face are slightly lifted.

In profile.

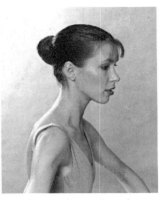

Eyes lowered at 45° angle.

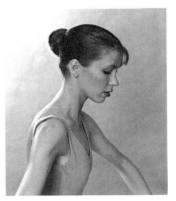

Eyes too low.

A well-placed gaze gives the dancer a look of self-confidence and authority, and can lend important emotional connotations to a movement. Dancers may look toward the direction in which they are traveling, or at the audience, or at another performer with whom they are dancing, but the eyes must be alive and focused at all times, as well as dramatically communicative. Blank, unseeing stares are unsettling to the audience, and a dancer with downcast or shifty eyes communicates a feeling of insecurity. A strong focus also helps the dancer maintain balance, especially when "spotting" in turns.

The "dead" classroom expression, with facial muscles dropped.

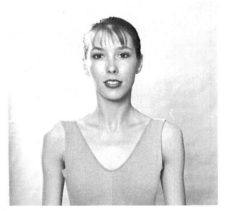

The vital classroom expression, with facial muscles lifted.

## Expressions to avoid

The "glued-on" smile.

"Suffering."

Eyebrows lifted.

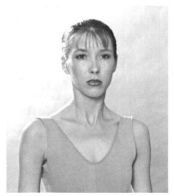

Intense concentration.

# The Positions of the Head

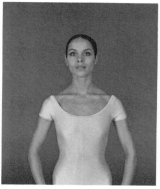

Straight front en face (or de face).

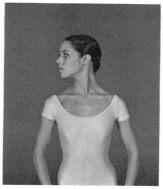

Turned in full profile.

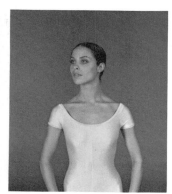

On 45° diagonal.

Inclined (turned at 45° and tilted).

Inclined (tilted) with eyes down.

Turned in profile, looking up.

Turned in profile, looking down.

Looking up 45°.

Lookng down 45°.

**INCORRECT**

Chin lowered too far.

**INCORRECT**

Chin lifted too far.

**The importance of correctly coordinating the head and eyes with the port de bras cannot be overemphasized.** Failure to do so will result in unharmonious poses in which the dancer may appear awkward or disoriented. In particular, never lower the chin to rest on the chest (when looking down), nor drop the head all the way back on the neck (when looking up). When the head is improperly positioned, the audience loses sight of the dancer's face, seeing instead only the top of the head or the underside of the chin.

# Épaulement

 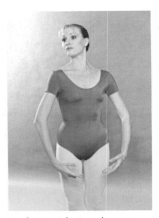 

En face without épaulement. En face with épaulement. Profile with épaulement.

Épaulement, or shouldering, gives a more dimensional, stylized look to the body, particularly in movements executed en face. The dancer slightly twists the upper torso and the face toward the leg that either (1) is placed in front in 3rd, 4th, or 5th position or (2) is in movement but is **about** to be placed in front in 3rd, 4th, or 5th. The head turns (not tilts) toward the shoulder that is pressed forward at a 45° angle, halfway between en face and profile. It is important that both sides of the face always remain visible to the audience and that the gaze relate to the new direction of the nose (i.e., en diagonale).

Common errors in épaulement are (1) twisting the hips, which should always remain squarely en face, and (2) leaving the eyes toward the front as the chin turns en diagonale, instead of moving them in line with the direction of the nose.

WORDS OF CAUTION: It is not advisable to introduce the use of shouldering to beginning students until they have acquired a certain amount of stability away from the barre. However, the groundwork for learning épaulement may be laid almost from the beginning of training, by telling students to turn the head toward the front foot when executing the preparatory and final poses of exercises at the barre. This practice reinforces the correct head-to-front-leg coordination long before the twist of the torso is added.

Grand assemblé volé without épaulement.

With épaulement. Note how the inclusion of épaulement increases the illusion of height in the jump.

## Épaulement with the arms in low 3rd

Note relationship of nose and elbow. They are in line.

Correct gaze. The eyes follow the same line of direction as the nose.

Incorrect gaze. The eyes are focused backward instead of being in line with nose.

Épaulement greatly enhances the effect of all movements with which it is used. It is most often employed in demi-caractère or character variations, such as the Hungarian Princess's solo from *Raymonda,* pictured here. For a well-trained dancer, the use of épaulement is second nature.

Magali Messac poses in 5th en pointe with épaulement, in American Ballet Theatre's production of *Raymonda.* Photo: Mira.

# The Positions of the Arms

1st position. (In the Cecchetti method this is called 5th position en avant.)

2nd position.

2nd in profile.

Demi-seconde (palms up). Note lifted elbows.

Demi-seconde (palms down).

NOTE: In a commonly used version of 3rd position low in the Soviet syllabus, both arms are placed lower (at the level of demi-seconde) rather than at the traditional level, as pictured below.

3rd position low. (In the Soviet syllabus this is called "small pose.")

3rd position high. (In the Soviet syllabus this is called "big pose.")

4th position.

4th in profile.

5th position en haut. (In the Soviet syllabus this is called 3rd position.) The distance between the hands is equal to the length of the dancer's little finger.

5th position en bas (shown in croisé). (In the Soviet syllabus this is called "preparatory position.")

5th position en bas in the Bournonville style. The fingertips are outside the thighs.

5th position en haut, in the style of the Romantic period.

# Common errors in positioning the arms

In classical port de bras, the elbows must always remain outside the shoulders, never coming close to the sides of the torso.

## The arms in 1st and 5th

INCORRECT

CORRECT

5th position. Shoulders appear narrow and lifted. Arms are too close to ears.

Elbows are well outside shoulders.

INCORRECT

CORRECT

INCORRECT

CORRECT

1st position. Upper arm too close to torso.

Hands are level with base of rib cage.

5th position en bas. Elbows too straight and too close to torso.

Elbows are correctly rounded.

## The arms in arabesque

INCORRECT

CORRECT

INCORRECT

CORRECT

In arabesque at 90°, the back arm should be lifted well off the arabesque leg.

Elbow hyper-extended.

Arabesque arms en face. Note lifted elbows.

## Isolating arm movements from the shoulders

As the arms move from position to position, **never** allow the bones in the front of the shoulders to move forward or up. The integrity of the upper back position must be constantly maintained and isolated from any movement of the arms.

| INCORRECT | CORRECT | INCORRECT | CORRECT |
|---|---|---|---|

   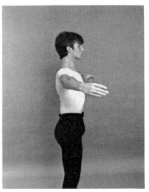

As the arms moved to 1st, the shoulder bones were allowed to move forward, rounding the upper back.

In 1st position, the shoulder bones stay pressed back. The front of the upper chest is flat all the way across. The movement of the arms to this position is totally isolated from the shoulders.

The shoulder bones are forward and the arms are too far in front of the torso in 2nd position. The pose has a "closed," hunched look.

In 2nd, the shoulder bones are pressed back flat in line with the chest, giving a wide, open appearance to the pose.

# The Classical Position of the Hand

**The hand must appear relaxed at all times,** with the fingers beautifully arranged in a natural, unmannered fashion. There must be space between each of the fingers, and all of them should extend in the same general direction—following the line of the arm.

In 2nd position, palm facing en face, fingers are arranged with thumb inside hand and pointing toward middle finger.

From the side, the wrist and fingers complete the curve of the arm.

In arabesque the palm faces the floor and the fingers lift slightly, flattening the curve in the hand.

# The Arm in Motion

## Closing the arm from 2nd to 1st position

The upper arm starts to come forward into the body.

The wrist bends slightly and the fingers trail behind.

Halfway in, the upper arm stops moving and the lower arm continues across body.

The fingers are the last to curve in, as the arm finishes moving into 1st position.

## Lifting the arm from 2nd to 5th position en haut

The fingers extend outward, flattening the curve in the wrist.

Halfway up, the upper arm stops moving and the inner wrist leads the forearm as it continues to curve upward.

The forearm completes the oval shape with the fingers being last to curve into position.

## Opening the arm from 5th en haut to 2nd

The dancer should think of drawing an imaginary diagonal line with the little finger of the arm that is lowering to 2nd. The elbow is kept lifted and rotated throughout the movement, so that the arm arrives in the rounded 2nd position **without any need for readjustment.**

## Half port de bras (with introductory "breath" arm movement)

From 5th en bas, on the upbeat, the arms open sideways to a small demi-seconde with a breath. The head follows the "leading" arm. On the count, the arms re-close to 5th en bas.

## Full port de bras en dehors

The arms lift from 5th en bas through 1st to 5th en haut.

## Full port de bras en dedans (also called "reverse" port de bras)

Open the arms outward from 5th en bas, lifting to 2nd with palms downward.

The arms lift to 1st, with the head inclining to one shoulder and the eyes looking into the palm of the leading hand.

The arms open from 1st to 2nd, with the head turning toward the leading arm.

From 5th en haut, with the eyes following the "leading" arm, the arms open to 2nd, then lower to 5th en bas, palms down.

Continue lifting the arms to 5th en haut, then lower through 1st position to 5th en bas. The eyes follow the "leading" hand throughout.

# The Concepts of En Dehors and En Dedans

En dehors = movement **away** from the supporting leg.
En dedans = movement **toward** the supporting leg.

## Floor pattern of the leg in rond de jambe par terre

EN DEHORS

EN DEDANS

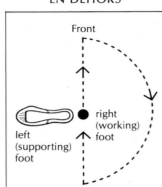 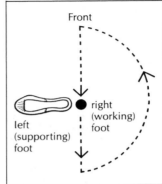

From 1st (or 5th) position, the working leg stretches to the front, opens to the side, continues circling to the back, then passes in a straight line forward through 1st position.

From 1st (or 5th) position, the working leg stretches to the back, opens to the side, continues circling to the front, then passes backward in a straight line through 1st position.

## Movement pattern of the leg in rond de jambe en l'air

**EN DEHORS**

From à la seconde, the working leg circles in toward the back, passes the side of the supporting leg, circles out toward the front, and re-straightens to 2nd.

**EN DEDANS**

From à la seconde, the working leg circles in toward the front, passes the side of the supporting leg, circles out toward the back, and re-straightens to 2nd.

# Examples of turns en dehors and en dedans

## Pirouette en dehors from 5th position

The turn is away from the back (supporting) leg. The front leg is lifted in retiré devant.

## Pirouette en dedans from 5th position

The turn is toward the front (supporting) leg. The back leg executes a passé.

## Soutenu en tournant en dedans at the barre

Close the extended leg in front, turning toward the original supporting leg.

## Half-turn en dehors at 90° devant at the barre

Relevé in the devant position, turning away from the supporting leg (outward from the barre).

# The Use of the Arms in Turns

The standard preparatory pose of the arms for pirouettes is low 3rd position. The palm of the hand in 1st position may be either rounded (in the correct 1st pose) or allongé (turned to the floor) in a low arabesque position (for women only).

## Pirouettes en dehors with the arms in 1st

On the upbeat, as the preparatory plié deepens, the front arm opens from 1st halfway out to the side. On the relevé retiré, both arms close quickly and simultaneously to 1st position, where they remain for the duration of the turn.

## Pirouettes en dehors taking the arms to 5th en haut through 1st

On the upbeat, as the preparatory plié deepens, the front arm opens from 1st halfway out to the side. On the relevé retiré, both arms close simultaneously to 1st and continue to lift to 5th position en haut without hesitation.

## Turning away from the barre

As the preparatory plié deepens, the front arm opens slightly to the side and the torso begins to twist outward. **Simultaneously** with the relevé, the inside arm releases from the barre, joining the other arm in 1st position.

## Pirouettes en dedans with the arms in 1st

As the preparatory plié deepens, the torso twists slightly toward the front leg and the arm opens halfway out to the side. **Simultaneously** with the relevé, both arms close to 1st position, where they remain for the duration of the turn.

## Pirouettes en dedans taking the arms to 5th en haut through 2nd

As the preparatory plié deepens, the torso twists toward the front leg and the arm opens fully à la seconde. **Simultaneously** with the relevé, both arms lift from 2nd directly up to 5th, where they remain for the duration of the turn.

## Incorrect use of the arms in turning away from the barre

The arm must not remain on the barre at the moment of relevé. If it does (as shown), the force of the turn will be lost and the torso and arms will not be correctly aligned above the hips during the turn.

# The Use of the Head in Turns

In order not to become dizzy while turning, dancers learn a special coordination technique called "spotting." Focusing the eyes on a point in space, the dancer whips the head around quickly in order to re-focus the eyes on this point at the completion of each turn. Focusing and re-focusing the eyes prevents the room from "spinning" and enables the dancer to maintain vertical stability throughout a series of turns. Spotting should be used in the execution of all turns and pirouettes in classical ballet, with one possible exception (grande pirouette in arabesque).

When first studying spotting, students can practice without doing pirouettes, simply by pivoting around in place on two feet, whipping the head around and re-focusing the eyes. A fast spotting technique can be developed only if a dancer learns to release all tension in the neck. Some dancers find that the fast whipping motion of the head knocks them off balance; this is usually caused by excessive neck tension. Relaxing and allowing the head to move freely in isolation from the rest of the upper body usually improves their stability. Dancers with vision problems can also have difficulty spotting; corrective lenses often solve this problem.

Students should never be allowed to get into the bad habit of turning without spotting. Such a habit will severely inhibit their potential to develop speed in turning and to perform multiple pirouettes. It is also unsafe. A dancer who becomes dizzy or disoriented because his or her eyes are not focused will not be able to execute a secure and confident finish at the end of turns and may have difficulty making a graceful transition into the next movement.

## "Spotting" a pirouette

The chin must be kept level at all times when spotting; i.e., there should be no inclination of the head. If there is, the head will appear to roll around instead of whip, and both the speed and stability of the turn will be adversely affected.

In the preparatory pose, focus the eyes on a particular object or point in space, slightly above eye level.

As the turn begins, look back over the shoulder as long as possible at the chosen point in space.

At the last possible moment, as the body faces upstage, quickly whip the head around and re-focus the eyes over the downstage shoulder at the point in space.

As the body completes the turn, focus the eyes strongly on the point in space.

# Positions of the Head at the Barre

| DEVANT | À LA SECONDE | DERRIÈRE | DERRIÈRE |
|---|---|---|---|

Head turned at a 45° angle, chin slightly lifted, eyes gaze upward on a diagonal, in line with nose.

Head faces directly front, chin slightly lifted, eyes gaze upward on a diagonal.

Head slightly inclined forward and turned, with eyes looking into palm of hand in 2nd. Note straight diagonal line from head to pointed foot in back.

Head may also be turned toward the barre in the derrière position, following the rule of "head to the front foot." In this case, the head is simply turned 45° to the inside shoulder without inclination forward.

Preparatory pose upon beginning an exercise, **and** upon finishing an exercise if the outside leg finishes closed in front in 5th.

Two final poses for exercises finishing with the leg closed in back in 5th position. The head may be turned either toward or away from the barre at a 45° angle.

## *Additional head and arm positions from the Soviet syllabus*

Note the slight inclination of the torso forward or backward in the positions below, as well as the relationship of the eyes to the hand.

Inclined forward with elbow curved and lifted à la seconde.

Inclined forward with elbow and wrist dropped à la seconde.

Inclined backward with palm up and elbow dropped à la seconde.

Inclined backward with palm down.

# The Nine Directions of the Body

The positioning of the legs and torso and the direction of the head and eyes **in relation to the audience** differentiate the nine directions of classical ballet. At the discretion of the teacher, the arms can be placed in a variety of classical positions, several of which are pictured on the following pages.

SHOWN WITH ARMS
IN 5TH EN BAS

Croisé devant.

À la quatrième devant.

Effacé devant.

Croisé derrière.

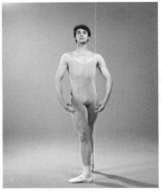

À la quatrième derrière.

Effacé derrière.

Écarté devant.

À la seconde.

Écarté derrière.

# Using the directions of the body at the barre

Port de bras may vary at the discretion of the teacher.

## Working with the outside leg

Devant en face.

Croisé devant.

Effacé devant.

Soviet effacé devant with head turned toward the working leg (shown with arm 5th en haut).

À la seconde.

Croisé derrière.

Derrière.

Effacé derrière.

Écarté devant.

Écarté derrière.

## Working with the inside leg

The effacé and écarté positions are rarely used when working with the inside leg.

Croisé devant.

Croisé derrière.

# Port de Bras Variations with the Directions of the Body

## Croisé devant

### Standard poses

Croisé devant with arms in high 3rd in opposition to working leg.

Croisé devant with arms in high 3rd, "looking under" the downstage arm.

### Common variations

Croisé devant with arms in low 3rd in opposition.

Croisé devant with arms in low 3rd, a standard preparatory pose.

Croisé devant with arms in low 3rd in opposition, looking over front arm.

Croisé devant with low 3rd arabesque arms, looking over front arm.

Croisé devant with arms in "Spanish" 4th position (note profile head and full twist of upper body).

Croisé devant with arms in Romantic-style 4th position.

Croisé devant with arms in high 3rd allongé in opposition.

Croisé devant with arms in arabesque à deux bras in Romantic style.

# Croisé derrière

*Standard poses*

Croisé derrière, arms in high 3rd.

Croisé derrière, arms in opposition, "looking under" the downstage arm.

*Common variations*

Croisé derrière with arms in low 3rd in opposition, a standard preparatory pose.

Croisé derrière with arms in low 3rd, looking over front hand.

Croisé derrière with low 3rd arabesque arms.

Croisé derrière with Soviet 3rd arabesque arms.

Croisé derrière with arms in high 3rd allongé.

Croisé derrière Spanish pose with full épaulement.

Croisé derrière with arms in high 3rd, looking up to top hand, with full épaulement.

Croisé derrière with arms in 4th position in opposition, with slight backbend and torso turned downstage.

# Effacé devant

The standard effacé poses are the strongest of the nine directions of the body. **An upright head** is essential to achieving the correct, proud feeling of these poses. Any tilting or inclination of the head will weaken this effect.

*Standard pose*

Note the inverted "S" curve formed by the arm and the back.

The strong curve in the dancer's back is lost if the torso is twisted downstage in this pose.

*Common variations*

Effacé devant with arms in low 3rd in opposition.

Effacé devant with arms in low 3rd, leaning over front arm.

Révérence position effacé devant, with the body twisted upstage and leaning over the front leg.

Effacé devant with arms in high 3rd in opposition, with a full twist of the body upstage.

Slavic character-style effacé devant, with one hand on hip.

Effacé devant with arms in 4th in opposition, with a slight backbend and twist of the body downstage.

# Effacé derrière

## Standard pose

**Épaulé,** an alternate form of effacé derriere from the Cecchetti syllabus. The dancer stands in 2nd arabesque with the torso twisted to reveal the back to the audience. The gaze follows the front arm, which is lifted slightly above shoulder level. The arms are extended in a long diagonal line.

## Common variations

Effacé derrière with downstage hand on hip (typical men's pose).

Effacé derrière with arms in low 3rd with "Spanish" épaulement.

Effacé derrière with arms in high 3rd allongé, with eyes looking up at downstage arm.

Effacé derrière with arms in high 3rd allongé in opposition.

Demi-caractère effacé derrière.

Effacé derrière with arms in Romantic-style arabesque à deux bras.

Effacé derrière with arms crossed in front of body in Romantic style.

Effacé derrière in the "listening" pose from Romantic period ballets.

# Écarté

In the standard écarté poses, the shoulders tilt diagonally. The eyes follow the diagonal direction: upward and out past the lifted elbow in écarté devant, and down over the hand in écarté derrière. The line of the arm à la seconde reflects the tilt of the shoulders.

*Standard poses*

Écarté devant.　　　　　　　　　Écarté derrière.

*Common variations*

Cecchetti écarté, used in Romantic period ballets.　　　Écarté devant allongé.　　　Écarté derrière allongé.

Écarté devant with arms in low 3rd.　　　Écarté derrière with arms in low 3rd.

# The Fixed Points of the Stage or Studio

Knowledge of the fixed points helps students to orient themselves in space and facilitates speedy communication between teacher and students (particularly when new enchaînements are being taught). Most teachers find the Soviet system of designating the points of the room to be the easiest for students to assimilate and remember.

## Soviet system

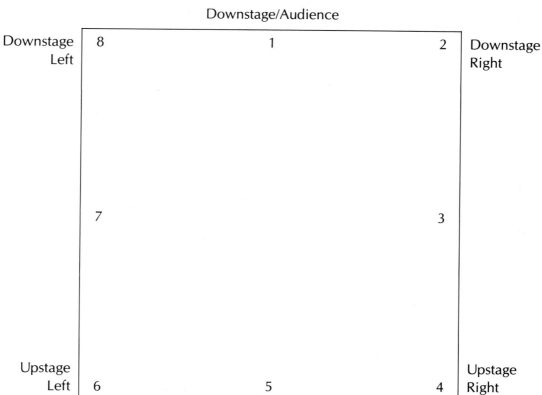

Downstage/Audience

| Downstage Left | 8 | 1 | 2 | Downstage Right |

7 · 3

| Upstage Left | 6 | 5 | 4 | Upstage Right |

| MOVEMENT DIRECTION | STATIC EQUIVALENT |
|---|---|
| En avant (traveling forward) | Devant (in front) |
| En arrière (traveling backward) | Derrière (in back) |
| De côté (traveling sideways) | À la seconde (to the side) |

## Cecchetti system

Audience

| 2 | 5 | 1 |

6 · 8

| 3 | 7 | 4 |

# Arabesque

### Placement of the shoulders in relation to the hips (in arabesque and attitude derrière)

Note that the shoulders are **always** in front of the hips when the leg is lifted to the back.

At 45° (and also in pointe tendue derrière).

At 90°.

At 120° (arabesque allongée).

Attitude derrière at 45° (in plié).

At 90°.

High "Russian" attitude.

### Maintaining the arch in the upper back

The strong arch in the upper back must always be maintained at all levels of arabesque. The shoulders must not be allowed to hunch forward, nor the chest to cave in, in striving to increase the height of the leg. Never shorten the long line at the back of the neck by lifting the chin and throwing the head backward.

At 90°.

At 120°.

In penchée.

# The arabesque positions *(Soviet syllabus)*

1st arabesque in profile. The arm to the side is pressed **slightly** in back of the shoulder.

2nd arabesque in profile. Note continous curve (indicated by dotted line), which includes head.

3rd arabesque. The position of the body is identical to that of 2nd arabesque, except it is in croisé alignment.

4th arabesque. Note the full twist of the upper torso, which reveals the full back to the audience, with the head turned downstage over the front shoulder.

4th Arabesque, front view. Keep the shoulders parallel to the floor, to avoid tilting the body toward the supporting side.

Arabesque à deux bras (also called Cecchetti 3rd arabesque).

**CORRECT**

1st arabesque, front view. Note the "T" placement of the shoulders in relation to the supporting leg. Both sides of the body are equally long, and the collarbone is parallel to the floor.

**INCORRECT**

A common error in all arabesques is tilting the torso so that one shoulder is higher than the other (shown in 2nd arabesque).

Ross Stretton partners Cynthia Harvey in 1st arabesque penchée in American Ballet Theatre's production of *La Bayadère*. Photo: Mira.

## *Several variations of arabesque*

1st arabesque penchée, with arms crossed in front of body (as in *Giselle*).

"Balanchine" 1st arabesque, with torso twisted open and side arm pressed back.

The 1st arabesque made famous by the Royal Ballet's Margot Fonteyn (leg lower, body more upright).

High 1st arabesque, a bravura movement.

Demi-caractère arabesques.

Arabesque with arms in 5th position allongé en haut.

High 3rd arabesque.

Romantic-style arabesque à deux bras.

Arabesque with arms pressed back (like wings).

# Bends of the Body

## Cambré forward and backward

The combination of this bend forward and backward with a full port de bras en dehors is called the 3rd port de bras in the Soviet syllabus.

During the backbend, it is considered more aesthetic to turn the face outward toward the lifted arm. This keeps the dancer's face visible to the audience and reduces the strain in the neck caused by the weight of the head.

The arm begins to lower en bas as soon as the body bend is initiated. The back is straight, lengthened outward until it reaches the 90% angle. Hips stay directly over feet.

The body initiates the backbend with a strong lift upward "out" of the hips.

The pelvis remains directly over the feet. The shoulders remain in line with each other.

## Common errors in cambrés

**INCORRECT** **INCORRECT** **INCORRECT** **INCORRECT**

Pushing the hips back as the body bends forward.

Leaving the arm behind as the body bends over.

Arching the back to initiate the bend.

Rounding the back before reaching the 90° bent-forward position.

The back initiates the upward recovery, lengthening outward as the arm passes through 1st position on its way to 5th en haut.

To recover, the upper body lengthens outward as it comes upright. Halfway up, the arm begins to open to the side. The little finger "draws" an imaginary diagonal line through space toward the 2nd position, arriving there without need for readjustment of the elbow.

| INCORRECT | INCORRECT | INCORRECT | INCORRECT |

Sinking into the hips and pushing the pelvis forward as the backbend begins.

Dropping the head below the arm.

Leaving the arm behind as the body recovers, and twisting the upper body outward away from the barre.

Coming upright with the elbow dropped in 2nd position.

# Cambrés en fondu in open poses

## Cambré to the side

Lengthen the waistline and hold the pelvis over the supporting leg. Keep the shoulder of the arm in 5th pressed down, maintaining the space between the upper arm and the ear. On the recovery, keep lengthening the body and overhead arm outward as the torso comes upright.

## Half-cambré en avant in arabesque à terre

NOTE: The buttocks are **always** lower than the shoulders.

The Pennsylvania Ballet's corps de ballet cambrés forward in a croisé pose en fondu in *Schumann Symphony No. 4.* Photo: Steven Caras.

## Cambré en avant with a full lunge

As the foot slides back, keep the weight well forward over the supporting thigh. The arm extends with a breath, then lowers from 2nd to 5th en bas, with the eyes following the hand.

## Cambré en avant in pointe tendue devant

This cambré has the feeling of a formal bow. The back stays straight as the body inclines forward to a 45° angle.

Effacé devant with hand extended, palm up, toward the foot.

"Hunching" the back and burying the head.

**THE RECOVERY**

Full cambré position with the arm in 1st, close to the supporting leg. Note the straight line from the head to the back foot.

The upper body, **not the buttocks,** initiates the recovery.

The illusion created is that of lifting something up from the floor with the arm as it comes up through 1st to 5th en haut.

# Cambré en rond

This port de bras develops flexibility in the upper torso. All the movement is isolated above the waist; take care to keep the hips centered directly over the feet at all times.

## EN DEDANS

   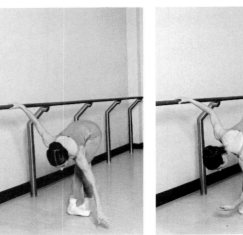

Beginning with the arm in 2nd, allongé the hand and reach outward.

Inclining the body slightly away from the barre, bend forward with a straight back, lowering the arm en bas.

Drop the head to the knees and circle the body in toward the barre, maintaining the arm curved in 5th.

## EN DEHORS

   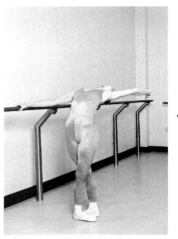

Reach across the body, turning the shoulders slightly toward the barre.

Open the arm forward through 1st, inclining the body slightly forward from the waist.

Continue opening the arm, reaching sideways with the palm up, leaning slightly away from the barre.

Lifting the arm in reverse from 2nd to 5th, continue reaching back into a full backbend.

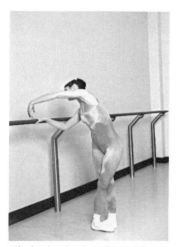

Lift the body, bending sideways toward the barre.

Reach back to the diagonal.

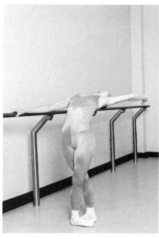

Continue reaching back into a complete backbend with the arm in 5th.

Circle the body outward while coming upright, and recover with the arm in 2nd (not shown).

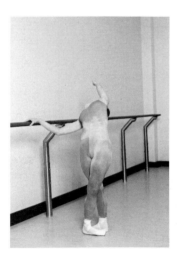

Twist toward the barre, reaching for the back diago-

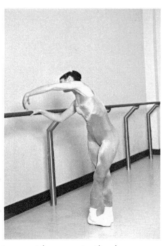

Lean sideways to the barre, with the arm passing over the head in 5th.

Bend forward from the hips, taking the head to the knees with the arm en bas.

Recover, reaching outward, and finish upright (not shown) with the arm à la seconde.

# Grand port de bras en rond

## Preparatory port de bras for pirouettes

### PREPARATION FOR PIROUETTES EN DEDANS

Begin in pointe tendue croisée devant.

On the upbeat, with a breath, lift the fingers and look up to the top hand.

Lunge forward, maintaining a straight line in the back from head to back foot. Top arm lowers to meet side arm in 1st.

Bend upstage sideways, opening the upstage arm to 2nd and lifting the other to 5th.

### PREPARATION FOR PIROUETTES EN DEHORS

Begin in pointe tendue croisée devant.

On the upbeat, with a breath, lift the fingers and look up to the top hand.

Lunge forward, maintaining a straight line in the back from head to back foot. Top arm lowers to meet side arm in 1st.

Bend upstage sideways, opening the upstage arm to 2nd and lifting the other to 5th.

## Soviet syllabus 6th port de bras

From the croisée pose, on the upbeat, look up to the top hand. Slide the pointed foot back into a lunge, maintaining the arms in 3rd. As the body arrives at the deepest part of the lunge, the top arm (with eyes following the hand) lowers to meet the side arm, which lowers en bas and lifts to 1st.

**Without bending the back knee**, transfer the weight swiftly upstage onto a straight back leg. Reach "past" the extended foot, traveling as far back as possible.

Circle the overhead arm diagonally upstage, to the back in 5th, to 2nd as the body comes upright, and finally across the body to the preparatory pose 3rd low. The lunge in 4th position is maintained throughout.

Exchange the arms over the top of the head as the body moves around through the backbend and recovers upright with the arms in high 3rd.

Lower the top arm directly down to 1st position as the back knee bends into 4th position demi-plié.

Reaching upstage and around into a backbend, exchange the arms through the 3rd position big poses. (They **do not** meet in the 5th position.)

From the final pose, conclude the port de bras by transferring weight forward (not shown) through 4th demi-plié to pointe tendue croisée derrière.

# Running and Walking in the Classical Ballet Style

Mastering the classical ballet-style runs and walks is fundamental in the training of a dancer. They are used to enter and leave the stage and thus create all-important first and last impressions. They are also frequently employed in the choreography to move the dancer about the stage.

The standard ballet walk, with the toe leading, should be mastered in the first year of training. (For the beginner, walking properly provides important practice in transferring the center of weight from one leg to the other.) **Practicing running and walking should never be neglected and should be included in one form or another in every ballet class.** Students must learn to perform these movements with natural-looking elegance and aplomb, and, in the case of running, with smooth abandon.

The port de bras during a walk or run may be moving or static, but never stiff or rigid. The weight must be transferred from one leg to the other evenly, with equal time spent on each step. The dancer must never drop the head and look at the floor. The upper body must be well lifted "off" the legs.

**Four basic rules for walking in the classical ballet style:**

1. Barely lift the feet from the floor.
2. Do not "sit" in demi-plié.
3. Do not jump.
4. Never trail the feet behind. Lean back slightly as you go forward, keeping the feet in front of you.

## Standard ballet walk

Extend the foot, pointed and slightly turned-out devant. Using a small plié, step forward past the foot into pointe tendue derrière, pushing the supporting heel forward.

## Standard ballet run in demi-plié

Staying in demi-plié and keeping the head at the same level (i.e., without bobbing up and down), run forward, fully stretching the legs front and back and transferring the weight by means of a small développé from back to front.

Performing with the New York City Ballet, Mikhail Baryshnikov
runs across the stage. Photo: Steven Caras.

Bring the back leg forward with a tiny développé (with the toe close to the
ground). Extend the leg devant, using a small plié, and step forward to the pointe
tendue derrière.

## *Walk on the high demi-pointe* *(for women only)*

This walk is performed in a smooth, stately manner. The legs should be tautly pulled-up.

## *Light run, the feet flicking up to the back* *(for women only)*

This run seems to skim the top of the floor. The transfer of weight from one leg to the other feels almost like a tiny grand jeté en avant. The arms are usually thrown open widely to the side and pressed back slightly. The chest is lifted and the head is thrown slightly back with an upward gaze.

In the U.S.S.R., a corps de ballet in *Les Sylphides* runs in formation. Photo: Juri Barikin.

# 2 ✍ The Ideal Body Structure and Proportions for Classical Ballet Dancers

Many criteria help to determine whether an aspiring student can realistically be considered competitive in the field of professional ballet. In auditions, company and school directors evaluate a dancer's potential in several categories, including coordination, musicality, movement quality, expressiveness, and ability to assimilate corrections and learn combinations of movements quickly. **Most important,** however, is the evaluation of (1) a dancer's natural physical capacity for classical technique with regard to "turn-out," extension, and ballon, and (2) a dancer's feet, height, weight, and body proportions. The charts on the following pages are intended to lend insight into the mystery of "what professionals look for in a ballet audition," thus helping teachers, parents, and students to better judge the chances for success.

It is important to remember that large classical ballet companies look for dancers who will blend easily into the already-established "look" of their corps de ballet—that is, dancers with approximately the same height, build, and body type. The "look" varies considerably from company to company, and a dancer who is turned away at one audition may do quite well at another. Some smaller companies, which do not mount large productions requiring a corps de ballet, may be more interested in a dancer's individuality, soloist potential, and technical versatility.

All aspiring ballet dancers, however, must meet certain basic requirements; it is **never** acceptable to be overweight, awkward, extremely "turned-in" or inflexible, or to possess certain exaggerated physical characteristics that do not conform to the traditional classical look. Classical ballet is a visual art form, and what audiences see on the stage must be pleasing to the eye. A plain, even unattractive face can be made to seem attractive with clever makeup. Plastic surgery can make oversized bosoms smaller, weak jawlines more definite, and nonexistent arches more shapely. There are numerous examples of such alterations on the ballet stage today. Some things, however, can never be changed. A 6' ballerina will be 6'8" en pointe, impossible to partner, and unsuitable in appearance for the standard female classical repertoire. Very short men encounter difficulties in partnering and rarely win "danseur noble" roles, regardless of their technical ability, simply because they do not "look" the part. Even very short women often find themselves limited to demi-caractère or childlike roles.

As a teacher, however, I have often witnessed unexpected changes in students: bulky bodies become slim and flexible, short teen-agers grow, earthbound dancers develop acceptable ballon, and rather bland personalities become expressive performers. Many things can be successfully developed and improved in the classroom (particularly feet, extension, ballon, and expressiveness), but it is important for a teacher to recognize those physical "givens" that cannot be affected by **any** degree of hard work and to encourage students with limitations to be realistic about their chances for competitive professional careers. Dancers can experience considerable heartbreak when they fail to win professional jobs because of their appearance or because their bodies have been weakened by injuries caused by years of being forced to do movements for which they were totally unsuited.

I have always encouraged students who really want to dance to work hard and to think positively. There are many places other than top professional companies in which one can experience the joy of dancing. Opportunities to perform with civic and regional companies abound, and their criteria are much more flexible than those of major professional companies. One cannot expect to make a living working in these companies, but one can at least enjoy the performing experience.

Finally, it is important to remember that there are always certain extraordinary dancers whose exceptional movement quality, technical virtuosity, and charismatic presence as performers have caused audiences to overlook certain aspects of their physiques which, in classical dancers of only average talent, would be considered extremely distracting. As ballet lovers, we can be grateful that we have not been deprived of the pleasure of these artists' performances simply because they were too tall or too short or had legs less than ideally "turned-out." However, I have adjudicated many professional auditions, and it would be misleading to say that these exceptions to the rule often do well in audition situations. The adjudicator's eye is first drawn to, and usually stays with, the dancers with good classical physiques. Often, auditioning dancers are simply asked to stand in a line, and first eliminations are made based solely upon the look of their bodies. Those coming closest in appearance to the physiques described on the following pages may be asked to stay and show what they can do. Even then, if a dancer is very nervous, it may be impossible to appraise his or her artistic potential accurately. Stories abound of famous dancers who were initially overlooked or rejected at auditions.

Young dancers who feel, along with their teachers, that they meet professional physical standards should persevere. They may go to several auditions before their talent is noticed. Many factors can cause such an oversight: an overcrowded room in which the judges cannot see all the dancers equally well; judges who are tired; judges who have already found what they were looking for. Some people are better classroom-audition dancers than others; some need a stage to really bloom. Frequently a director rejects a dancer for a job and later sees the dancer in performance and regrets the decision. The dancer may get a second chance with this director; thus dancers often move from smaller into larger, more important companies, positions, and even roles.

The two professional dancers on the following pages, Valerie Madonia and Ross Yearsley, have excellent physiques in the classical ballet tradition. They know that doors automatically opened for them (with regard to winning auditions, scholarships, and professional jobs) because of their physiques. However, they also acknowledge that a good body is only a springboard to a professional career. The ability to survive physically and psychologically the long years of training and self-discipline, combined with the inherited assets of intelligence, dramatic presence, musicality, coordination, and expressiveness, are equally important in becoming a successful ballet artist.

# The Ideal Female Dancer's Body

Height,
5 feet 2 inches—
5 feet 8 inches

Weight, 85–115
pounds

Long neck in
proportion to
rest of body

Small bust

Narrow hips

Small posterior

Slim thighs that
appear to be about
the same width as
the calves

Thin ankles and
long feet

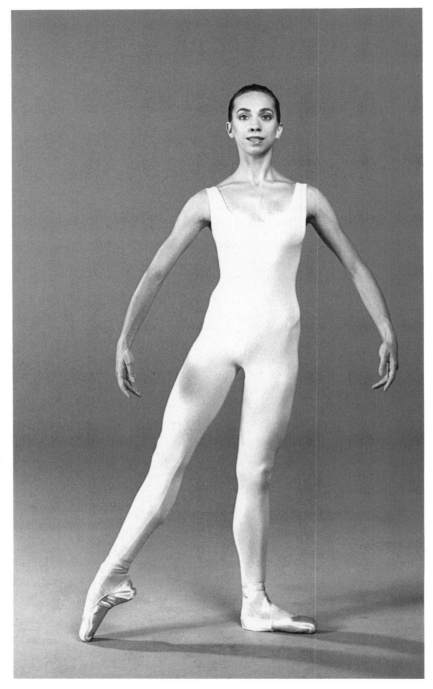

Small head

Slightly sloping
shoulders that are
wider than hips

Straight back and
slim waistline, with
torso neither too
long nor too short
in proportion to
rest of body

Long arms and
hands

Long, straight legs
with slight hyper-
extension and
minimal visible
muscular bulk

Well-arched foot
with all toes
approximately
the same length

# *Other important physical criteria for the female dancer*

A female with excellent physical potential for classical ballet will display all the assets below **without any training whatsoever.** Execution of these positions by a flexible child is easy and harmless. (NOTE: It is not necessary to plié in a position as turned-out as the one demonstrated here in order to ascertain the length and flexibility of the Achilles tendon.)

 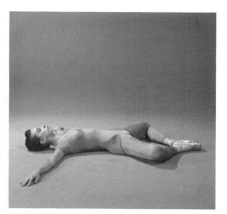

Natural "turn-out" (ample rotation in the hip joint). Note that the back is flat on the floor in the side view.

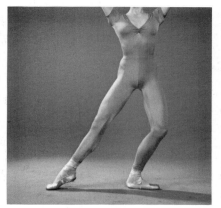 

Long Achilles tendon for deep demi-plié.

Flexible lower back for arabesques and backbends.

 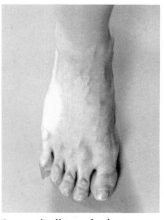

Well-stretched hamstrings for high extension.

Squared-off toes for better distribution of the weight en pointe.

# The Ideal Male Dancer's Body

Height,
5 feet 9 inches–
6 feet 2 inches

Weight, 135–
165 pounds

Straight back and
slim waistline

Narrow hips

Small posterior

Thigh muscles
slightly larger than
the calves

Straight legs

Average head with
long neck in pro-
portion to rest of
body

Wide shoulders,
without overly
developed trapezius
muscles

Torso neither long
nor short in
proportion to
rest of body

Long arms and
hands

Leg muscles not
overly bulky

Long, moderately
arched feet

The same criteria that apply to women with regard to turn-out and length of Achilles tendon (see pp. 66–67) also apply to men. However, it is not as important for men as it is for women to have great flexibility in the hamstrings and lower back. Men are rarely required to perform the extremely high extensions of the leg that are considered essential to a female dancer's technique. For most male dancers, stretching the legs to the point of extreme flexibility is considered counterproductive because it can hinder the development of the strong leg muscles necessary for grand allegro technique, the most important virtuoso aspect of male dancing. Considerable upper-body, arm, and lower-back strength are also essential for men. Auxiliary exercises (such as push-ups) outside the classroom are necessary to develop the extra strength needed for partnering, or pas de deux, work. Weight lifting in excess is **not** recommended as it can produce overdeveloped, bulky-looking muscles with limited flexibility.

Since men are not required to dance en pointe, the extreme hyper-mobility of the ankle joint essential for female dancers is not as important a prerequisite for them. Indeed, an overly arched foot is sometimes considered undesirable for male dancers, because it may appear somewhat feminine.

# Common Variations in Body Types

## Legs

The two common leg configurations pictured here may be corrected by exercising certain muscles and making adjustments in proper alignment and weight distribution. A knowledgeable ballet instructor or a dance therapist should be consulted for the appropriate exercises to help overcome such structural problems.

Hyper-extended legs.     Corrected.     "Bowed" legs.     Corrected.

## Proportions of the torso

In regard to classical line, neither of these body types is aesthetically preferable; but it is not uncommon for excellent professional dancers to have such proportions. Neither type is considered a hindrance to the development of technical strength.

Long-waisted.     Short-waisted. Note scoliosis, also common in varying degrees in many dancers.

# Common Variations in Types of Feet

Beautifully arched feet are not only crucial to a dancer's line, but are also essential for relevé and/or pointe work. In order to achieve a vertical position of the foot en pointe, as well as to rise to a three-quarter position en demi-pointe, the combination of the ankle and the instep must be hyper-mobile. This hyper-mobility is produced by three joints working together: the ankle, the subtalar joint beneath the ankle, and the midtarsal joint (Hamilton, *The Best Body for Ballet,* p. 83). Hyper-mobility is something with which an individual is naturally endowed, and it is highly valued in the classical ballet world. "Good feet" are always noticed in a ballet audition! It should be noted that little can be done to increase looseness in tight, relatively inflexible insteps; the study of classical ballet is therefore not recommended for persons with such feet.

A simple test for evaluating the suitability of a person's feet for classical ballet is pictured below. Sit on the floor with the legs stretched out straight in front of the body. Keeping the knees taut, point the foot, pressing the big toe down toward the floor. If the ball of the foot can reach a point closer to the floor than the ankle bone, the foot is suitably flexible for ballet. The left and the right foot should be evaluated separately.

ACCEPTABLE

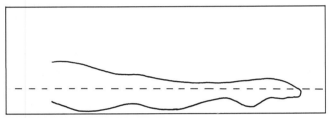

UNACCEPTABLE

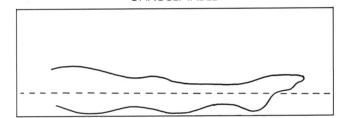

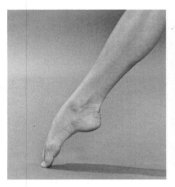

Good foot.

Overly arched foot with high instep is beautiful, but can be weak en pointe and prone to "rolling."

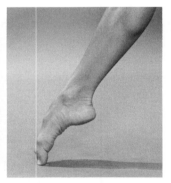

Straight foot lacks desired arch, but is acceptable if used well.

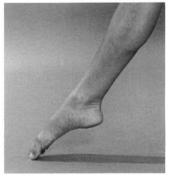

Unacceptable foot; ankle is unable to stretch fully.

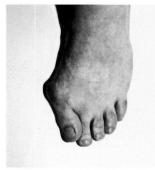

Bunion (enlarged joint of big toe) will make both demi-pointe and pointe work painful.

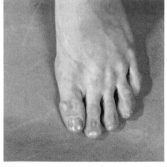

Having small toes longer than big toe will cause discomfort in a pointe shoe.

# 3 ✒ The Ballet Class: Notes for Teachers

## The Rationale behind the Ritual

The technique of classical ballet is learned and perfected in a highly structured daily regimen of classroom work. It takes approximately eight years of attending classes, usually begun at the age of nine or ten, to produce a dancer of professional-level competency. In order to maintain their techniques, ballet professionals—regardless of their degree of accomplishment— continue to study on a daily basis, throughout their entire dancing lives. Most of them readily agree that they are striving for a level of perfection that is virtually unattainable; and most admit to being addicted to the challenge presented by each class, to the feeling of being in control of their bodies to an extreme degree, and to the "high" they experience in motion, especially when airborne. In class they return to the basics: exercises composed of movements from the traditional vocabulary of classical ballet. It is here in this concentrated, hour-and-a-half session (based upon traditions more than three hundred years old) that technique is maintained, strengthened, and constantly refined.

To insure complete physical versatility, all movements performed on one leg must also be practiced on the other, all turns to the right must also be executed to the left, and steps traveling forward must also be learned traveling backward. Natural physical weaknesses must be exposed and corrected. In class, away from the judgmental eyes of critics and audiences, it is "safe" for dancers to confront their flaws, to struggle with movements not yet perfected, to show effort—even to fall down. Endless repetition is essential to success. Dancers know that the daily try-and-try-again rituals of the classroom will sooner or later produce results; that frustration will eventually turn to pride with the achievement of each step toward the goal of technical and artistic excellence.

## The Role of the Teacher

The teacher's tasks in the ballet classroom are (1) to conduct the class so that it is both physically beneficial and instructive, (2) to provide objective and constructive criticism regarding technique and artistry, (3) to encourage self-discovery and nurture the development of each student's unique artistic qualities, and (4) to create a positive and inspiring atmosphere for learning.

To accomplish these tasks, a teacher must prepare as diligently and methodically as a teacher of any academic subject. It is not enough for the aspiring teacher simply to have been an accomplished dancer, although that is generally considered one of the prerequisites for success. Additional expertise is necessary.

Fortunately, several books on teaching ballet are now available, the most complete of which are translations from Soviet texts; also available are a number of videotapes of well-known teachers conducting classes (see reading list following bibliography). Aspiring teachers should attend teaching courses in all the various syllabi; periodic seminars in the Bournonville and Soviet techniques, two of the most useful, are now offered in many places. Finally, those new to teaching must avail themselves of every opportunity to observe experienced, reputable, professional teachers at work. Most cities have a local ballet company. These companies are often receptive to inquiries from serious would-be teachers and will occasionally permit them to observe company class. Just as dancers can learn a great deal from watching other dancers, teachers can do so by watching other teachers. For all teachers, regardless of their degree of experience, the process of searching for new sources of inspiration and knowledge should be never-ending.

*Demonstrating*
*Exercises*
*Effectively*

A teacher must communicate several things when setting a new exercise:

1. The meter of the exercise (4/4, 3/4, 6/8, etc.).
2. The tempo, or speed, at which the exercise is to be performed, including the amount of time allotted in the music for the preparation, or "lead-in."
3. The direction in which the steps are to be performed (i.e., front, side, back, or in any of the other classical poses or directions of the body).
4. The direction, if any, in which the exercise travels.
5. The actual movements, or steps, of which the exercise is composed, including all port de bras and head movements.
6. The number of repetitions to be performed.
7. The opening and closing poses at the beginning and end of the exercise.
8. The dynamics (i.e., smooth, sharp, bright, legato, etc.) of each movement.

Most teachers demonstrate exercises using a combination of words and physical movements. Many also sing, hum, or chant the rhythm while they demonstrate. This practice is helpful because most students learn and remember an exercise much more easily if they are shown the rhythm and content simultaneously. Before beginning to teach a new exercise, a teacher should first indicate to the accompanist the meter and dynamic of the type of music desired for the exercise; this will allow the musician time (while the students are learning the movements) to choose the most appropriate musical accompaniment.

Because most teachers are retired professional dancers and are often no longer able to demonstrate all movements with absolute technical finesse, some degree of "marking" when demonstrating is acceptable. Most teachers rely on a combination of words, arm gestures (a kind of dance "sign" language), and limited leg and body movements. These must, however, be precise. After observing the teacher, there should be no doubt in the students' minds about exactly what is required. Beginner-level students, obviously, need to see steps more clearly and completely than do upper-level students, who, being more familiar with the ballet movement vocabulary, are able to visualize the teacher's instructions with minimal demonstration.

In order to discourage the natural tendency of students to imitate the subtle movement mannerisms of their teacher, I recommend that teachers limit their demonstrating as much as possible. However, a certain amount of actual demonstration is essential; dancers learn choreographed movement best by observing it, and the ability to be visually perceptive must be developed in the classroom. When demonstrating, a teacher should clearly show the coordination of all the body parts involved in each movement (i.e., head, arms, body, legs). The students must learn to absorb all the details at the same time and not, for instance, to focus simply on the feet. This is a difficult task, but teachers who demonstrate in a complete rather than a piecemeal manner are helping their students to learn to memorize movements as a whole.

Certain practices should be avoided in demonstrating exercises. An exercise should never be verbalized in a monotone without a sense of rhythm or correct dynamics. Trying to learn a movement sequence taught in this manner is akin to trying to learn a poem one word at a time. Vagueness about the music (i.e., exactly what happens on each count and what the meter of the exercise is) will lead to confusion for both accompanist and students. Also, a teacher should never be imprecise about where the feet close (e.g., front or back in 5th position) within the combination, what the port de bras is, how many repetitions are to be performed, or how the exercise is to be finished. The teacher should be absolutely sure of the structure of an exercise before beginning to demonstrate it; showing an exercise several times in slightly different ways, each with new additions and deletions, will confuse the students. Finally, an exercise should always be shown at least once, and preferably always, in the tempo in which it is to be performed.

Perhaps the most important element to be communicated when demonstrating an exercise is the dynamic, or quality of the movements. Watching the teacher, students learn how to shade or accent a movement, how to interpret it musically, how to breathe life into it. Dancing, like speaking, is ineffective if it is monotonous. To be interesting, it must have nuance, high points, low points, and emotional overtones. It is the teacher's responsibility to point out to students the variety of dynamics within each combination of movements. This can easily be done without doing the exercises "full-out." Vocal sounds and verbal analogies can help if the teacher's ability to move is limited.

## Finding the Right Words in Class

It is essential that teachers verbalize instructions and corrections clearly. To lead students toward technical accuracy as well as artistic effectiveness, teachers must be specific, avoiding such vague and often misinterpreted admonitions as "Stay up!" or "Be less awkward!" Precise instructions (such as, "Keep the hands level with the base of the ribcage," or "Close the second side of the body faster") are easily understood by students and therefore considerably more effective.

In addition, a teacher should employ a wide range of imaginative verbal analogies to which different age groups of students can relate (for example: "Your bourrées must look like sunlight sparkling on the surface of a lake," or "Please try not to position your front arm in arabesque as if you were looking down the barrel of a rifle!"). Such comments are effective in helping a dancer find the correct movement quality for a step and often introduce tension-relieving humor into the classroom atmosphere. Most teachers agree that tension is a dancer's greatest enemy. Not only does it inhibit both technical progress and movement flow; it also often leads to injury. Furthermore, a tense dancer is not an attractive sight. Teachers should constantly seek creative ways to reduce classroom tension.

## French ballet terms

Many reputable teachers differ on occasion in their use of some of the French ballet terms. This is the result of three hundred years of development in a technique that has expanded to include scores of movements inconceivable to early ballet dancers; these changes have developed simultaneously in several different countries, each of which has its own interpretations of the French language. Regardless of the terminology chosen, however, a teacher should be absolutely consistent on a daily basis. Always referring to a step by the same name in class is a practice that will facilitate speedy, accurate communication with students.

Most English-speaking teachers alternate between using the correct French term for a movement and its English translation. This is completely acceptable as long as both are frequently used, so that the students are familiar with both. In some cases, it can be extremely useful for a student struggling to find the correct dynamic for a step to be made aware of the actual translation or derivation of its French name (ballotté, for instance, comes from ballotter, "to toss," and jeté from jeter, "to throw"). Keeping in mind that dancers will undoubtedly study with many different teachers during their careers, a teacher may point out that a certain step may be referred to elsewhere by another name; for example, in the English school, a royale is called a changement battu.

## Musicality

Being musically knowledgeable is a necessity for a ballet teacher. A fundamental knowledge of music aids the teaching process in many ways; four of the most basic are: (1) in communicating with an accompanist in "musical" as opposed to "dance" terms, which usually seem rather vague to a musician; (2) in the traditional practice of alternating slower exercises with faster ones to avoid overworking students' legs (e.g., ronds de jambe par terre, followed by frappés, then développés); (3) in combining movements performed at a variety of tempi within the same exercise (e.g., two tendus in two counts each, followed by four in one count each), which helps students to develop rhythmical accuracy; and (4) in choosing the most effective and complementary kind of music and tempi for each exercise.

The right choice of musical accompaniment encourages dancers to breathe correctly. Students with such self-defeating, tension-building habits as holding their breath can often improve their technical proficiency by relating their breathing to a specific pattern dictated by the music. An example of this would be instructing a student to breathe out on the final note of the preparation for a pirouette and to breathe in sharply on the following upbeat as he or she executes the relevé for the turn. This practice may enable the student to achieve the coordination necessary to spin easily.

The importance of varying the musical accompaniment from class to class cannot be overstressed. It forces the students to listen, to develop their ear for music. A good teacher will ask students to be aware of the specific quality (adagio, allegro vivace, happy, sad) of each piece of music and to reflect this quality in their movements.

While it is common for students who are concentrating hard on the mechanics of a movement to become insensitive to the music, teachers should not indulge this tendency. When setting a combination of movements to music, one must keep in mind the degree of difficulty the exercise will present to the dancers. A complex exercise performed to complex music may be more than a student can handle. In lower-level classes, where students have minimal muscular control and are still struggling with the basics of correct stance, turn-out, and total body coordination, musical simplicity is essential. This is also true when a new step is being introduced in any class for the first time.

To enable students to think simultaneously about executing the step correctly and performing it to the music, the melody and rhythm must be clearly recognizable, with the tempo set at a speed that is realistic, given the students' ability. The music must be slow enough to allow the dancers time to prepare mentally before executing each movement and time to recover upon completion before proceeding to the next one. For a beginner, holding a position for more than one beat often allows time to "feel" the muscles, and in so doing strengthens them. Following is an example of how the level of difficulty of an assemblé exercise might be increased rhythmically as a student becomes more accomplished. The music for this exercise is a polka in ¾ time, with each count equaling 2 beats.

## Beginner

    1–2  Demi-plié in 5th position, taking the full 2 counts to descend
    +3     Assemblé dessus, finishing in 5th position plié
    4      Straighten the knees in 5th position
           (Repeat 4 times, alternating legs)

## Intermediate

           (Demi-plié in 5th position on the last count of the preparation)
    +1     Assemblé dessus, finishing in 5th position plié (landing on the count)
    +      Straighten the knees in 5th position
    2      Demi-plié in 5th position
           (Repeat 8 times, alternating legs)

The above exercise also works well in a 3/4 rhythm, using the same counts.

## Advanced

           (Demi-plié in 5th position on the last count of the preparation)

| +1 | Assemblé dessus (landing on the count) |
| +2 | Assemblé dessus |
| +3 | Assemblé dessus |
| + | Straighten the knees in 5th position |
| 4 | Plié in 5th position |
| | (Repeat 4 times) |

In all exercises, a clear musical lead-in, or "preparation," is essential. This preparation, usually two or four musical counts, indicates the rhythm and tempo of the exercise to the dancers and allows them time to prepare mentally and physically before their bodies begin to move. In short, the preparation serves to stimulate the "thought" from which all movement must originate and is responsible for "leading" the dancer into movement.

It is also important that an exercise conclude musically in an easily identifiable way—that is, the dancers can tell that the end of the music is coming and can prepare mentally to finish with control (which is sometimes difficult, as after a fast series of spinning turns). A strong musical ending also demands from the dancers a confident and securely executed final pose or exit, which will be absolutely essential later in front of an audience.

Teachers are often frustrated by their students' lack of musicality. Unfortunately, few dancers are naturally, instinctively musical (that is, without thinking about it they are always "on" the music). Students may be encouraged to learn to dance musically in the following ways.

1. If students are dancing "off" the music, stop the exercise and make them aware of the problem. Insist that they discipline themselves to dance "on" the music.
2. If, in repeating the movements and attempting to stay "on" the music, they are unable to do so, help them by simplifying the exercise either technically or musically (slower tempo, more time between the steps, etc.).
3. Have the students stand still with their eyes closed and listen to the music while envisioning themselves performing the exercise.
4. On occasion, quiz students informally during class ("What ballet is that music from?" "Is that a waltz or a mazurka?" "Is this exercise in 3/4 or 4/4 time?").
5. When it is possible to do so, perform the same exercise in different meters and discuss the effect of the change in music upon the movement (e.g., "Why did the ballottés feel easier to do in 6/8 time than in 4/4 time?").
6. On occasion, use music with an irregular number of beats per measure. Exercises performed in 5/4 or 7/8 time provide students with a rhythmic challenge, preparing them for the time when, as professionals, they will have to dance in ballets with complex contemporary scores.
7. In upper-level classes, to test both music and coordination skills, occasionally have students perform exercises in which the feet and the arms execute opposing, or cross, rhythms. An example would be a jumping exercise set to a bouncy polonaise (3/4), with the feet executing a repeating pattern of three movements while the arms move "against" them in a repeating pattern of four movements.
8. Whenever possible, avoid shouting over the music. While it is certainly true that the teacher's voice can be a strong motivating factor in inspiring students to work to their fullest capacity, it is also true that if students are always listening to the teacher's voice, they will not be listening to the music. It is much more effective to correct a student verbally **after** the exercise has been completed than to shout over the music during the exercise. The music may prevent the student from hearing the correction accurately or, indeed, from hearing it at all. It is also sometimes difficult for students to correct what they are doing in mid-exercise. A verbal command given at the wrong moment can throw a dancer's timing off and actually cause an accident.

9. Ask a student who is having trouble performing an exercise musically to repeat the exercise without musical accompaniment while singing the melody and/or counting out loud. Encourage the student to note and verbalize the beats between each count and the movements that must be performed on each of them if the transitions from step to step are to be musical.

10. In class, use uplifting, enjoyable music with strong preparations and endings. Avoid monotonous, rambling improvisations that seem to have no emotional motivation or musical shape. Remember that in a class with inspiring music, the exercises will seem less difficult. The music will carry the dancers through sequences demanding a great deal of stamina. The entire class will seem less like drudgery and more like fun.

*The Content of the Class: Developing Effective Exercises*

It would be impossible to utilize the entire range of movements in the classical vocabulary in any single hour-and-a-half class. Drawing from the almost infinite variety of ballet movements, and guided by the needs of the students, the teacher choreographs a new set of exercises for each class—always keeping in mind the following basic rules that must be observed for safe and effective instruction.

1. Each exercise must contain enough repetition to be beneficial in developing correct muscular habits.
2. Each exercise must reflect an intelligent use of the music.
3. Each exercise must make sense choreographically, avoiding awkward transitions or groupings of steps that do not belong together traditionally.
4. In some way, each exercise must relate to the overall theme of the class. (Choosing the theme of a class is discussed later in this chapter.)
5. Each exercise must be neither too long nor too short. If an exercise is too long, an excessive amount of classroom time is spent in learning it, leaving too little time for practicing and perfecting it. If the class is working in alternating groups, those students not dancing will spend too much time standing around on the sidelines, where their muscles can get "cold" very quickly.

   In addition, an exercise that is too long can tire students to the point at which they lose muscular control. Dancing without being totally in control is not beneficial to technical development and can be dangerous. Teachers should keep in mind the stamina level of their students when setting the length of exercises; lower-level students will obviously have less endurance than those in upper-level or professional classes.

   It is also important to remember that overworking any particular set of muscles can result in the unbalanced development of the physique and the acquisition of unsightly muscular bulk. Indeed, the stress produced by overzealous repetition of a particular movement can lead to permanent physical damage. To be accomplished safely, the development of the extreme flexibility and strength required of a ballet dancer must progress slowly. This is why it takes a minimum of six to eight years of daily training to achieve professional-level competency.

   An exercise that is too short does not challenge students aerobically and does not warm up muscles properly. Also, it does not train the student to learn a number of steps quickly and to remember them correctly in sequence. The ability to do this will later be very important to the dancer when, working professionally, he or she must quickly assimilate long, complex combinations of movements.

6. Exercises should not be overly complex in construction. Trying to crowd too much choreographic material into an exercise is detrimental to the learning process. A dancer needs time to think about doing each movement absolutely correctly in class, and this is difficult if the exercise is too "busy."
7. The exercise should be at the correct level of difficulty for the class, neither too advanced nor too easy. If an exercise is too advanced, students will not get the full muscular benefit of all the movements because they will tend

to fake, or "mark," through the parts that are too hard for them to do correctly. If the exercise is too easy, the students will not be challenged, and their strength and technical ability will not improve.

8. Each exercise must occur in its correct place in the traditional sequence of ballet classroom exercises. In each of the three parts of a class (barre, centre, allegro), the order of the exercises should begin with rather slow, small movements and gradually progress to faster, bigger ones (see following section, "Class Structure"). Even in advanced classes, complex, physically taxing movements should never be performed before a careful warm-up period. Failure to adhere to this practice of progressing from slow to fast, simple to complex, will result in unnecessary discomfort for the dancers and will impose dangerous stress on their bodies that could lead to injury.

## Class Structure: Order of the Exercises

The following list indicates the traditional order of the exercises in an advanced ballet class, according to the Soviet system; it is the one I recommend. (Please note that beginner and intermediate classes include considerably fewer exercises in each class than the number listed here. However, the sequential order of the exercises in each section of class almost never varies.)

### Barre work

1. Pliés
2. Battements tendus
3. Battements dégagés
4. Ronds de jambe par terre
5. Battements fondus
6. Ronds de jambe en l'air
7. Battements frappés
8. Battements développés (and related adagio movements)
9. Petits battements
10. Grands battements
11. Optional: Stretches
12. Optional: Fast dégagés or relevés facing the barre

With certain limitations, the barre order listed above can be rearranged. Slow, preliminary warm-up tendus in 1st position are often done before pliés, and stretches can be inserted (1) before the développés, (2) in combination with the développés, or (3) just before the grands battements. In advanced classes, fondus, ronds de jambe en l'air, frappés, and petits battements can be combined with each other and re-ordered in a number of effective ways: fondus with ronds de jambe en l'air, for instance, or frappés with petits battements. However, développés and grands battements, being the most physically demanding of the exercises, should always be executed at the end of the barre work period, when the body is well on its way to being completely warmed up. (For the same reason, the grand adagio and grand battement are executed at the end of the centre work and the grand allegro at the end of the jumping exercises.) Perhaps the most commonly neglected step at the barre is battement fondu, an important exercise that relates to all jumps landing on one leg. It should never be omitted from the barre work.

### Centre work (in the middle of the room)

1. Port de bras and small adagio movements that emphasize transfer of weight (temps lié, for instance) and provide a gradual transition from the stability and security of the barre work to the centre exercises
2. Centre barre exercises such as tendus, dégagés, fondus, etc., in combination with pirouettes
3. Grand adagio and grandes pirouettes
4. Grands battements

### Allegro work (jumping)

1. Petit allegro (small jumps and batterie)
2. Medium allegro (slower, heavier jumps that provide the link between petit and grand allegro, and include movements such as sissonnes and cabrioles)

3. Grand allegro (large jumps such as grands jetés)—to include, or be followed by, coda sequences such as turns en diagonale or fouettés for women, movements en manège, and grandes pirouettes sautillées or tours en l'air for men
4. Small, fast jumps to "warm down"

*Révérence (final port de bras, cambrés, and bows)*

## Relationship of Barre Exercises to Centre and Allegro Movements

It is important to remember that, in addition to warming up the body, all barre exercises relate directly to movements that occur later in class, in the centre and allegro work. A good teacher will make sure that students understand this relationship and know what they are working toward. Whenever possible, it is advisable to execute exactly the same movement at the barre that will be studied later in the class in the centre. Thus, in a class that will feature grandes pirouettes in attitude derrière, the barre could include half-turns in attitude derrière, perhaps as part of the développé (adagio) exercise; or if the grand allegro is to include grand fouetté sauté, the grand battement exercise might include grand battement fouetté relevé. The following list links basic barre exercises with some of their centre or allegro counterparts:

Pliés—The beginning and ending of all jumping movements

Tendus; dégagés—Assemblés

Dégagés pointés—Cabrioles

Petits développés; pas de cheval—Ballottés

Ronds de jambe par terre—Pas de basque

Fondus—All jumps landing on one leg (in particular, ballonnés)

Passés relevés—Pirouettes in retiré position

Ronds de jambe en l'air—Ronds de jambe en l'air sauté; gargouillades

Frappés—All small, quick jumps (in particular, those initiated by a sharp outward thrust of the leg, such as petits jetés). The speed at which the frappé leg stretches outward and the ensuing hold at a point in space is analogous to the speed at which the legs are thrust away from the floor in any jump and to the strong contraction of the muscles at the top of the jump which "freezes" the pose en l'air. This "freeze" action makes the dancer appear suspended in air as if in defiance of gravity. Frappés executed in a sluggish manner will lead to a lethargic petit allegro without brilliance or speed.

Développés; relevés lents—Similar center adagio movements

Développés ballottés—Ballottés at 90°

Grands fouettés relevés—Similar centre adagio movements; grandes pirouettes that finish with fouettés to another pose

Petits battements—Batterie, by emphasizing: (1) patterns for exchanging the legs relating to simple beats; (2) fast, strongly accented rhythms; (3) the correct placement of the foot sur le cou-de-pied (fully pointed, not wrapped), which is analogous to the final pose of small, beaten steps landing on one foot (entrechat trois, cinq, etc.); (4) maintenance of turned-out thighs and sideways motion of the legs during batterie.

Grands battements—All grand allegro steps; all grandes pirouettes. It is important to note that, because of the correlation between this exercise and the fast grand battement initiating all big jumps, grand battement should never be performed as a slow exercise in an advanced class. The leg should lift to its full height on the upbeat and close on the downbeat, just as it does when performing grand jeté (and it should do so at a speed comparable to that of the battement for a big jump).

Grands battements développés—All big jumps involving a développé action of the leg(s), such as grande sissonne développée ouverte, temps de flèche, grand jeté développé en avant ("split" jeté)

Grands battements fouettés—Grands jetés entrelacés ("tours" jetés); grands fouettés sautés

Grands battements tombés—The landing from all big jumps that finish on one leg (in particular, grand jeté)

Relevés—Allegro and pointe work

Piqué turns en dehors—Sauts de basque

## The Study of Allegro

It is important to note that all basic jumps (temps levés, assemblés, jetés, ballonnés, cabrioles, etc.) should initially be studied at the barre, although this is not done during the routine barre work in the first part of class. Before introducing a new jumping movement in the allegro section of class, a teacher should ask the students to return to the barre. Holding onto and facing the barre, they will feel more secure when attempting a new movement in the air. They will also be able to use the barre to keep themselves off the floor long enough to concentrate on feeling the correct position of their legs in the air. After practicing the jump at the barre for a number of classes, the students may then come to the centre to attempt the step without support. Finally, it is important to keep in mind that the only way to develop a strong allegro technique is through the concentrated repetition of jumping exercises. Therefore, the time allotted for allegro work in a class should never be sacrificed to other areas of study.

## The Set vs. the Varied Barre

Opinions vary among teachers on the pros and cons of a set barre (the same routine daily) versus one that is newly choreographed every day.

A set barre saves time. The students memorize it, and class time need not be spent in teaching and learning the exercises. In addition, the students can truly perfect such a barre. However, the disadvantages are obvious. No one set of exercises can encompass every movement that ought to be studied at the barre, and students do not receive the intellectual challenge of having to learn new exercises on the spur of the moment.

Most teachers reach some sort of compromise. Some choreograph a new barre at the beginning of each week and have the students repeat it for the rest of the week. Some do a varied barre each day but often repeat a few particularly challenging exercises for a day or two. Some always vary certain exercises while doing others each day in exactly the same form.

## The Allotment of Class Time

The traditional length of a ballet class is one-and-a-half hours. In a beginner class, a greater proportion of this time is spent at the barre than in the centre. In an advanced class, the time is ideally divided as follows: the first thirty-five minutes for barre work, followed by thirty-five minutes of centre work, concluding with twenty minutes of allegro exercises. In order to keep to this schedule, teachers should plan their classes carefully beforehand and should not be reluctant to refer to their notes in class. A teacher has a great deal to think about in a class: correcting mistakes, adjusting tempi, guiding the accompanist in the correct choice of music, organizing the placement of the students, and keeping the class on schedule. By using notes prepared ahead of time, teachers enjoy the freedom of not having to think about what exercise comes next. They are thus able to concentrate completely on watching and helping the students. Carefully preparing exercises ahead of time and bringing notes into the studio are definite recommendations for any teacher just starting out, particularly if prone to stage fright when facing a group.

*Keeping the class moving.* One of the arts of teaching ballet is being able to choose what to say or not to say in each class in order to keep the dancers moving for the maximum amount of time. It is impossible to administer every correction needed by every student during any one class. However, each student should be acknowledged in some way, if only with the smallest reminder.

In speaking to the class or to an individual, it is important to avoid lengthy demonstrations or discussions. Dancers get stiff standing around while the teacher rambles on, and, in beginner classes especially, their minds begin to wander. In advanced classes precious dancing time is lost, and the hour-and-a-half session is over before all the planned material has been covered. In such situations the last part of the class tends to suffer most. Loss of the time planned for jumping (ideally at least twenty minutes in every advanced class) will prove extremely counterproductive to the development of a strong technique.

## The Importance of Relevé Work

It is beneficial to include extensive relevé work at the barre and in the centre practice in upper-intermediate and advanced classes. Although this practice is often shunned in the West because it is incorrectly assumed to build large calf muscles or to be "too hard" for the dancers to accomplish, it is strongly advocated by the Soviet school.

There is almost no way a dancer can be incorrectly placed and still maintain vertical stability en relevé. Therefore, exercises such as fondus, ronds de jambe en l'air, and développés, when performed in the centre en relevé, often force a dancer to confront rather than avoid important aspects of placement and alignment. Although dancers may initially find executing such exercises on the demi-pointe frustrating, they will eventually appreciate the new strength achieved as they develop the control to stay on relevé. This control has obvious benefits for the study of all pirouettes. I have found no evidence to suggest that extensive relevé work in upper-level classes causes the development of unsightly muscle bulk. Indeed, I have found exactly the reverse to be true. If the exercises are well constructed with sufficient emphasis on the use of both demi-plié and relevé, students' legs become more "pulled-up," even slimmer in appearance.

## Developing a Theme for Each Class

There should be a beautiful logic to a ballet class. In striving for this, I find it best to begin the preparation for my classes from the jumping (allegro) exercise and work backwards, trying to relate almost everything in the class to the final, most difficult jump to be studied that day. (This method of preparation, of course, applies only to upper-level classes that include grand allegro.) Asaf Messerer, the revered ballet master of the Bolshoi Ballet, has said:

> The teacher is obliged to come to class with a distinct knowledge of his problem for the day; he must know what he wants to achieve through the study of certain ballet exercises. . . . Each class must have its special purpose, theme, problem or leitmotif. . . . Of course, one can always give a class in which there is a bit of everything, but such a class is like a lecture where one talks of "everything and nothing." In a ballet class, logic must prevail as it does in the lectures of university professors. . . . From beginning to end a ballet class must be conducted in correct proportions, succession, and progression of the selected exercise. (*Classes in Classical Ballet*, p. 23)

This method of class construction, in which the entire class is built around the study of one particular movement coordination, produces notable results. The more often a movement coordination is repeated in all its various forms (from à terre, to relevé, to en tournant, to en l'air) within the same class, the better the student will learn it. Repetition is the key to developing muscle memory as well as an intellectual understanding of one's own technique; both are necessary for consistent performance.

In addition to focusing almost everything in the class on the coordination necessary for the "jump of the day," I also usually choose for emphasis one of the nine directional poses of the body or one of the four arabesques. In this way, students receive consistent reinforcement of two concepts throughout the class session—one dealing with a particular movement coordination and one with the study of a particular shape.

An additional benefit of this method of class construction is that once the initial explanations of the "movements for the day" are made by the teacher, only short verbal reminders are necessary throughout the rest of the class. The end result is less talking and more dancing, and the class can move along at a desirable brisk pace.

*Pointe Work*    In the West, where men and women commonly train together, the study of pointe technique, because it is for women only, usually occurs at a time other than the regular hour-and-a-half ballet class. However, it is often recommended in advanced classes that women put on their pointe shoes for the allegro portion of the class. Their feet thus become more accustomed to these initially uncomfortable shoes, as well as stronger (because of the greater effort required to point a pointe shoe in the air, as opposed to the softer, more pliable ballet slipper). In addition, the turns that are often included at the end of the grand allegro combination can be practiced en pointe in the same virtuoso fashion in which they would be performed at the end of a solo variation on stage. See chapter 14, beginning on page 349, for more detail on pointe work.

No student should ever be encouraged to dance en pointe unless she can practice in her pointe shoes, supervised in class, a minimum of three times a week, preferably every day. Pointe work is not for once-a-week amateurs. Only with continued practice will a dancer form the necessary calluses on her toes and gain sufficient strength in her legs, feet, and ankles to dance en pointe safely. Professional dancers, if not rehearsing or performing regularly en pointe, guard against allowing their feet to soften by putting on their pointe shoes for at least a few minutes of relevés every day. In this way they avoid the pain of tender, blistered toes. Contrary to popular belief, pointe work is not usually painful for the trained dancer, whose feet are remarkably tough and strong.

Although men, by tradition, do not dance en pointe, it is occasionally beneficial for a male student with poor feet (i.e., not arched enough) to practice at the barre in pointe shoes. In this way, he can often increase the stretch of his instep and thus improve the look of his foot.

*Utilizing Material from Various Syllabi*    Each of the best-known international schools (i.e., methods, syllabi) of ballet has a particular strength lacking in the others. The Danes have a musically unique, intricately linked set of medium-tempo allegro exercises that are especially useful for men's classes. Balanchine's petit allegro moves faster and covers more space than that of any other school. The training in the U.S.S.R. produces the strongest, most exciting grand allegro technique in the world, as well as the most beautifully coordinated upper body movements. The English and the French are masters in the area of intricate petit allegro movements and batterie.

In short, each school has a specific area in which its students notably excel. Analyzing and using in class the particular exercises that produce such excellence has been my practice for many years, and one that I highly recommend. Teachers should seek opportunities to increase their knowledge of the balletic vocabularies of the various schools. Many systems offer periodic teacher-training or refresher courses that are both educational and stimulating and can provide a teacher with a wealth of new classroom material.

*New Approaches*    Although the manner in which ballet classes are taught is steeped in tradition, teachers should always be open to useful new classroom techniques. After twenty years of teaching, I have discovered three rather unconventional but highly effective practices that I strongly recommend.

The first is the use of a video camera to record students' progress. About every six weeks, I videotape my classes. On the following day, the students and I watch the video together, commenting upon what we observe. For many students, seeing themselves is quite a shock; often, they are finally able to comprehend and accept a correction that I have been trying to communicate to them verbally for weeks. It is a well-known fact that some students learn better visually while others respond better to auditory stimuli. For those who are more visually oriented, the use of video can become an important learning tool. For all students, however, this practice has many benefits. It trains them to be observant and analytical about both the technical and the artistic aspects of their dancing. Above all, it helps them to become objective and realistic about their personal strengths and weaknesses in the classroom.

Another untraditional practice I have found useful is to eliminate the studio mirrors in beginner-level classes. I have found that students actually commit the correct positions of the body to "muscle memory" faster if they are forced to learn them by "feel" rather than by constant visual imitation (i.e., copying the teacher in the mirror). In upper-level and professional classes, however, the mirror is a crucially important tool; dancers use it constantly to assess and readjust their line.

Finally, a recent study of the manner in which dancers learn combinations of steps (Puretz, "Psychomotor Research," pp. 280–81) has revealed that most students transfer enchaînements better from one side to the other when they are initially taught on the student's non-preferred (usually left) side. For many years in ballet classes, combinations of steps were commonly taught on the right side first (i.e., traveling to the right, with the first movement on the right foot). This was generally the easier and more comfortable side for students (most people being right-handed).

Since new exercises are usually taught slowly and methodically, students will obviously have a longer time to learn the combination on whichever side is taught first. Because the non-preferred side always presents dancers with greater difficulty, it is logical to assume that they would benefit from having extra time to assimilate an enchaînement on this side. In addition, because they must make a greater conscious effort to learn the sequence on the side that feels less "natural" to them, the information is more rigorously memorized. It therefore seems easier to transfer quickly to the preferred side when the time comes. However, since every class will inevitably contain one or more left-handed students, the best practice is probably to alternate between teaching exercises to the right first on some days and to the left on others.

Teachers should note that the field of dance science has expanded rapidly in recent years. Many new books and studies have been published. Some of the best are included in the recommended reading list at the end of the bibliography in this book.

## The Successful Student

In the end, of course, regardless of all the knowledge and expertise a teacher may exhibit in the classroom, students are really responsible for "teaching" themselves. Through exercises and guidance, the teacher provides the correct atmosphere in which the student grows and learns, but it is the student's intelligence, stamina, and dedication that eventually determine whether or not he or she will become a dancer. Mikhail Baryshnikov has said of his own teacher, the great Alexander Pushkin,

> He taught in such a way that the dancer began to know himself more completely, and that, I believe, is the first key to serious work, to becoming an artist—to know oneself, one's gifts, one's limitations, as fully as possible. Pushkin had this ability to guide the dancer down the right path toward being realistic about his gifts, and then to inspire him to work, and work hard, at making the most artistically of those gifts. He also taught me that no one else can assume this responsibility—an invaluable lesson. He didn't force you, he gave his wisdom freely, and you did with it what you could and would. (*Baryshnikov at Work*, p. 8)

# Part II

## The Movements
## of Classical Ballet

The photographs and accompanying captions in Part II illustrate and define the entire range of movements in the vocabulary of classical ballet. The dancers who posed for the pictures were instructed to break down each ballet step into its component parts. Each part was photographed separately. The pictures were then assembled to form a complete movement. In some sequences, especially those picturing large, complicated jumps (such as grand pas de basque sauté or revoltade), it would probably not be humanly possible to perform each component part as perfectly as it is pictured here. It is important, however, for dancers to **attempt** to execute each of these component positions, for if the transitional positions (i.e., those which occur between the beginning and ending poses) are blurred, the correct shape of the step will most certainly be lost. I often tell my students that ballet is like calligraphy in air. In the same way that forming letters carelessly results in unaesthetic script, so does forming ballet steps inaccurately result in unattractive dancing. In addition, when any aspect of a step is incomplete, the step loses some of its specific identity, or that which makes it uniquely different from any other step.

Most classical ballet steps are completed in a fraction of a second, a time too short for the eye to absorb all the detail contained therein. Instead, the onlooker is left with an impression. What kind of impression is dependent not only upon the dramatic and/or musical nuances employed by the dancer, but also upon the technical accuracy with which the step is performed. A jump, for instance, in which the dancer assumes and temporarily holds a clean position in the air will **appear** higher than one of the same altitude in which the dancer does not achieve a clean position. Part II of this book is designed to help dancers and teachers understand all the component parts of any given ballet step, which, performed together properly, result not only in technical accuracy but also in theatrical effectiveness. As noted in the introduction, the information contained herein is intended for use in conjunction with, never instead of, actual classroom instruction.

The French terminology used in this volume is that which I use in my classes and which I have found to be most widely understood by American dancers. In those few cases where a movement is commonly referred to by more than one name, both have been noted. Whenever the translation of the French term (e.g., ballotté means "tossed") seems helpful in gaining a better understanding of the correct movement quality of a step, the translation is included. It should be noted, however, that the translation of many ballet terms is irrelevant to the manner in which the steps are performed and is therefore of interest only from the point of view of historical derivation. Readers may refer to dictionaries of ballet terms for further information on this topic.

Many French and English terms are used interchangeably by teachers in the classroom. In writing the captions, I have followed this practice. For those who are still learning the terminology, a French-English pronunciation guide appears at the end of this book (beginning on p. 371), followed by a glossary defining many common dance terms and figures of speech. When looking at the pictures, readers should also note the information contained in the captions underneath them. Because of space limitations, it was not always possible—particularly for steps that involve a large number of individual movements—to show every one of the sequential positions through which the dancer must move. However, the captions always note any omission in the photographs and describe the complete mechanics of all steps pictured. Thus, the captions are often important for purposes of clarification.

Each of the steps pictured may, of course, be performed in a large variety of different ways simply by changing body direction, leg direction, and/or port de bras. Again because of limited space, only one example of each individual step is presented here. The positions of the arms, legs, and body in each picture were arbitrarily chosen by the author based upon one or more of the following reasons: (1) the manner in which the step is demonstrated is the one most commonly executed by dancers; (2) if several derivative variations of a step (such as the various forms of battement tendu) are shown, each is demonstrated in a different direction (i.e., with the working leg moving to the front, side, or back) in order to indicate that all can be executed using any one of the possible leg directions; (3) the direction pictured is the one that most clearly reveals the exact mechanics of the step.

Whenever possible, traveling movements were pictured moving in all directions (forward, sideward, and backward), and turning movements were pictured both en dehors and en dedans. Movements en tournant were pictured only with single rotations, but in cases where these movements are commonly performed with multiple turns, this has been noted in the captions.

Occasionally it seemed important to clarify the unique rhythmical nature of a step. Musical beats and counts were added underneath the photographs in such cases.

Dancers do a great variety of stretching exercises in order to increase their flexibility. Such exercises were not included in this book because they are not part of the traditional vocabulary of ballet movements. (Ladies and gentlemen of the seventeenth and eighteenth centuries who developed the technique of classical ballet did not think it either necessary or appropriate to cultivate the ability to lift their legs above waist height!) Students are urged to consult their teachers or a dance therapist for information concerning the correct manner in which to stretch. Stretching incorrectly or stretching too forcefully before being adequately warmed up can easily result in injury. In class, stretching exercises are perhaps most beneficial when performed toward the end of the barre work; teachers often insert them in the adagio exercise or just after grand battement at the end of the barre. Most dancers find it necessary, however, to develop personalized stretching routines for use outside the classroom as well.

When composing exercises for the classroom, teachers should use the movements illustrated in this book as springboards for their imaginations. Each step pictured can be performed with many variations of port de bras and direction. All movements at the barre can also be executed in the centre; the element of turning can be added to almost all of them, as well as to all small jumps. The possibilities are almost infinite, and teachers who make full use of them will find that the variety added to the routine of their daily classes will have a marked and beneficial effect on the strength and versatility of their students.

# 4 ∾ Exercises at the Barre

Every ballet class begins with a set of standard exercises at the barre. They are the foundation upon which classical technique is built and are used by dancers to warm up their bodies. **Each of the barre exercises bears an important, direct relationship to movements that are practiced later in the centre portion of class;** students should be aware of these relationships (see p. 78).

The function of the barre itself is to help the dancer achieve stability in the turned-out position. With the help of the barre, the dancer can improve flexibility, strength, line, and ability to execute movements perfectly turned-out. Instructions on how to hold onto and stand at the barre appear on p. 7.

The ten standard exercises at the barre are performed in every ballet class in the same traditional sequence. In order to develop physical versatility and balanced strength, all exercises at the barre are performed first on one leg, then on the other (i.e., on both sides). The correct order of the exercises, as well as information on devising a logical and effective barre, appear on p. 77.

The basic forms and variations of all the standard barre exercises are pictured on the following pages. Each exercise demonstrated is usually pictured with the dancer using only one direction of the legs. It should be noted, however, that all battements should be practiced in **all** directions. In upper-level classes the element of turning may be added to almost all of the barre exercises. All turning movements and ronds de jambe at the barre should be performed **both** en dehors and en dedans. In addition, the teacher, in order to vary the exercises at the barre from day to day, can add different elements of body direction, port de bras, and relevé work to the basic forms.

Barre exercises for beginning students must be straightforward and simple in construction with a minimum of upper-body movements. For advanced students who are able to assimilate more complicated coordinations involving the total body, the exercises can be more elaborate. In upper-level classes certain exercises at the barre can be combined (see p. 78). Fondus, for instance, are often combined with ronds de jambe en l'air. This is a useful, time-saving device in advanced classes, where there is much material to be covered in the centre portion of every class.

The rhythm of barre movements should match that of similar movements to be performed later in the centre. For example, assemblés are usually in the air on the upbeat and down on the count; therefore, the dégagés at the barre should be executed out on the upbeat and in on the count. The correct patterns of coordination among the arms, head, and legs should be reinforced by having students execute them at the barre exactly as they will be performed later in the centre during moving steps. This is particularly important when practicing preparatory movements at the barre for pirouettes, or when practicing preparatory movements for jumps, such as jetés, in which the arms not only aid in the correct execution of the jump, but also give the movement grace and design in midair.

Finally, it is important to note that **all exercises at the barre should be practiced in the middle of the room**. This is referred to as centre barre work. It occurs directly after the barre and usually includes, in any one class, not more than three separate types of barre exercises. It is customary to include the study of the direction of the body, as well as pirouettes, in the centre barre work.

# Plié

Demi-pliés and grand pliés are, by tradition, the first exercises performed at the barre in each class. They are executed in 1st, 2nd, 4th, and 5th positions, often in combination with port de bras, cambrés, rises, and balances on the demi-pointe.

Correct development and use of plié are essential to a dancer's technique. Pliés act as the springboard for all jumps and are instrumental in providing the force for turns. Most important, they provide the cushion for landing from jumps and are necessary to produce smooth, pliable transitions between movements.

When executing pliés, constantly lift the weight of the body up off the legs. The knee joints must be relaxed, and the movement up and down must be continuous, without jerks. Take special care to maintain turn-out whenever the knees are bent in plié; in this position the knee is most vulnerable to injury. Following are several illustrations of correct and incorrect execution of pliés.

INCORRECT

Demi-plié in 1st. Heels are pressed into floor. Note that there is no readjustment of the torso when the knees bend. **Correct stance, including erect back, is maintained in all pliés.** Weight is always equally distributed over both feet.

The pelvis has been incorrectly tucked under in an effort to achieve a greater degree of turn-out.

Grand plié in 1st. The heels are released from the floor as little as possible. **Never** force the relevé.

INCORRECT    INCORRECT

Demi-plié in 2nd position.

Grand plié in 2nd—**the only grand plié in which the heels are not released from the floor.**

In 2nd: Pelvis has been lowered too far below level of knees, at the base of the grand plié.

"Sitting" back at the base of the grand plié. The weight of the body is no longer over the feet.

Grand plié in 2nd, demonstrated by a dancer with the ideal degree of natural turn-out.

Grand plié in 2nd, demonstrated by a dancer with an acceptable degree of natural turn-out.

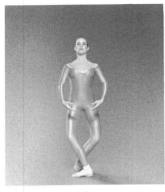

Demi-plié in 4th position.

Grand plié in 4th position.

Grand plié in 4th with the weight correctly centered between both legs.

The weight of the body is not centered. In all pliés the weight should be equally distributed over both feet.

Demi-plié in 4th with the back knee "rolled" in. Maximum turn-out should have been maintained.

Demi-plié in 5th position.

Grand plié in 5th position.

"Sickling" the back heel out. The heels should be held together at the base of the plié.

# The coordination of port de bras with grand plié

In the following two examples, note that the eyes follow the hand throughout the movement.

## Half port de bras with grand plié at the barre

As the knees begin to bend in demi-plié, the arm lowers from 2nd position.

At the base of the grand plié, the arm curves in front of the knee in 5th en bas.

As the dancer returns to demi-plié, the arm lifts to 1st position.

As the knees straighten, the arm opens to 2nd.

## Reverse full port de bras with grand plié at the barre

As the knees begin to bend, the arm lifts from 2nd position.

At the base of the grand plié, the arm curves into 5th position en haut.

As the dancer returns to demi-plié, the arm lowers to 1st position.

As the knees straighten, the arm may open directly à la seconde from 1st, or may lower to 5th en bas and lift outward to 2nd position.

In Tbilisi, U.S.S.R., first-year students practice grand plié in 1st position in the centre.
Photo: G. Warren.

# Battement Tendu

In this book the terms "battement tendu" or just "tendu" refer to the completed tendu movement, both outward and inward. The term "pointe tendue" refers to the outward movement that is held in the open position with the foot stretched, toe to the floor, or to the open position by itself. (For more detail on the correct execution of battement tendu, see p. 16.)

*Various Forms of Tendus*

1. Tendu with demi-plié in either the open or the closed position
2. Tendu with flexing of the ankle in the open position
3. Tendu double with and without plié in the open position
4. Tendu with "turn-in/turn-out" rotation of working leg in the open position
5. Tendu with temps lié
6. Tendu en tournant
7. Tendu pour batterie

SHOWN À LA SECONDE

From 5th, keeping knee straight, slide toe outward to the fully pointed position à la seconde.
Slide foot inward to close in 5th.

## Tendu with temps lié

SHOWN EN AVANT

From 5th position, pointe tendue devant. Demi-plié in 4th position. From plié, transfer the weight forward, straightening up onto the front leg into pointe tendue derrière.

SHOWN DE CÔTÉ TRAVELING AWAY FROM BARRE

From 5th position, pointe tendue to the side. Demi-plié in 2nd position. From plié, transfer the weight to the side, straightening up onto the outside leg and pointing the inside leg à la seconde.

# Tendu double

## Soviet tendu double (without plié)

In this exercise, the weight of the body is maintained over the supporting side throughout the movement, with the working hip dropping, of necessity, as the heel is lowered. Both thighs must be strongly pulled up, with a sensation of lengthening the working leg as the heel lowers. This version of tendu double is primarily useful for warming up the metatarsal. There may be one, two, or three fast heel drops with each tendu double.

The working leg opens sideways on the upbeat, the heel is dropped on the beat, and the foot is quickly re-pointed on the following upbeat, giving the ankle action a fast, rebound quality.

## English tendu double (without plié)

In the English version, the tempo is slower and more even than in the Soviet tendu double, allowing time for the weight transfer. The hips (unlike those in the Soviet version above) remain level throughout. The weight is fully transferred from one leg to both legs and back to one leg. This exercise is often executed with a demi-plié in the open position (2nd or 4th).

Pointe tendue 2nd.

Lower through the foot into 2nd, transferring the weight onto both feet.

Re-point the working foot à la seconde.

## Tendu pour batterie *(Soviet syllabus)*

This exercise is useful in strengthening the inner thigh for beaten jumps. It may be executed with more than two beats (as pictured here) before re-opening the leg to the pointe tendue. It may also be performed opening the pointe tendue either devant or derrière. During the exercise, the working leg moves continuously (without stopping in 5th position) through the series of beats.

SHOWN À LA SECONDE

From pointe tendue à la seconde—

Strongly flex ankle.

Close behind in 5th without putting weight on back foot.

## Tendu en tournant

Tendu en tournant is useful as a preparatory exercise for the study of turns on one leg. It is executed at the barre as well as in the centre, in all directions (devant, derrière, à la seconde), using all the poses of the body. It may be performed with various degrees of rotation from one-eighth to full turns and is executed both en dehors and en dedans. The turn itself happens **as the working leg moves outward from the initial closed position**. It is incorrect to assume the new direction as the leg closes.

### With one-eighth turn

SHOWN À LA SECONDE
EN DEHORS

Begin the movement by **turning in 5th position**, pivoting on the ball of the supporting foot and opening the leg to the pointe tendue **simultaneously** with the conclusion of the turn. The movement finishes in the new direction with the leg closing to 5th.

### With three-eighths turn

SHOWN À LA SECONDE
EN DEDANS

Open sideways a little.    Close in front without put-    Re-point to the side.
                           ting weight on front foot.

In the Vaganova school in Leningrad, U.S.S.R., students practice battement tendu à la seconde in the centre.
Photo: Paul B. Goode.

# Battement Dégagé

*(battement tendu jeté in Soviet syllabus, battement glissé in English school)*

**SHOWN À LA SECONDE**

From 5th—

Brush the leg outward through the pointe tendue position.

Release the toes from the floor.

## Dégagé pointé (or piqué)

**SHOWN DEVANT**

*Prepare—*      *and* ♪      *one* ♪      *and-ah* ♫

From 5th, dégagé devant and quickly lower and lift the leg in the open position, bouncing the toes off the floor with a sharp, rebound quality.

NOTE: This step is an important preparatory movement for cabriole and may be done with more than one pointé in the open position before closing. It is also performed to the side and back.

## Dégagé pointé (or piqué) with demi-rond

**SHOWN EN DEHORS**

From 5th—

Dégagé devant.

Lower to the pointe tendue.

Rebound, lifting the leg in a small arc to 2nd.

NOTE: This movement is also performed en dedans and may be executed with more than one pointé in any of the positions to the front, side, or back.

Return to 5th, passing through the pointe tendue.

Battement dégagé is the basic preparatory exercise for all petit allegro steps. The leg brushes through the pointe tendue, lifts off the floor, and returns (passing again through the pointe tendue) to the initial closed position. The height to which the leg is thrown depends on the tempo of the exercise, varying from 45° (slower) to 25° (faster).

Equally important to the correct execution of the step are a strong, energetic closing of the leg and a dynamic outward brush. The inner-thigh strength employed in the closing directly relates to the strength with which the legs must be joined en l'air in assemblés, as well as in all movements using batterie.

All forms of battement tendu (see pp. 90–93) may also be performed with battement dégagé.

Lower to pointe tendue à la seconde.

Rebound, lifting the leg in a small arc to the back. Lower to pointe tendue derrière.

# Dégagé en cloche

## (battement tendu jeté passé in Soviet syllabus)

This movement is most commonly executed in a series, with the leg swinging continuously from front to back to front again without stopping at any point. It may begin from either the front or the back.

From 5th, brush the leg devant. Return, brushing the leg through 1st to the back.

# Pas de cheval

This movement may be executed in all directions.

SHOWN DEVANT

From 5th, lift the foot to cou-de-pied devant.

Keeping the knee well turned-out, lift the foot up and forward in a small arc.

Lower to the pointe tendue devant.

Finish closing 5th.

# Dégagé with petit passé

This movement may be executed in all directions and with a change of foot on the petit passé (i.e., dégagé with one foot, passé with the other). The passés may be either dessous or dessus. As it is demonstrated below, the exercise is an excellent preparation for the study of temps de cuisse (see p. 282).

SHOWN À LA SECONDE WITH PASSÉ DESSUS

From 5th, dégagé à la seconde. Close in back and passé dessus at ankle height.

John Turjoman and Patrick Bissell bow in pointe tendue croisée devant in American Ballet Theatre's production of *Romeo and Juliet*. Photo: Mira.

# Rond de Jambe par Terre

EN DEHORS

The exact pattern in reverse would apply for rond de jambe en dedans: the leg opens to the back, circles to the side, then circles to the front, and returns to 1st.

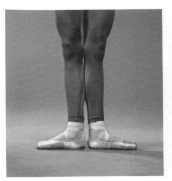

From 1st—

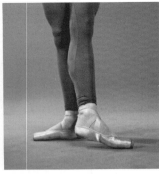

Slide the working leg forward through a small 4th position, keeping the heels in line.

Stretch the foot, bringing the toes in line with the supporting heel.

The musical accent in rond de jambe par terre is as follows: the working leg passes through the 1st position **on the count** (i.e., the accent) and executes the outward circle on the upbeat.

A demi-rond is half of a rond de jambe. There are four possible directions for demi-ronds: front to the side (en dehors), side to the back (en dehors), back to the side (en dedans), and side to the front (en dedans). They may be executed à terre, at 45°, and at 90° or above.

Grand rond de jambe (either en dehors or en dedans) is a full half-circle of the leg, front to back or vice-versa, performed at 90° or above. It may be done slowly as an adagio movement (beginning with a développé or relevé lent) or, for advanced dancers only, quickly (beginning with a grand battement). For instructions on the correct execution of grand rond de jambe at 90°, see pp. 22–23.

## Small double rond à quart with toes only

This step is a small, fast double rond in which the toes inscribe one or more tiny circles in the front or back pointe tendue position before continuing around to complete the full rond de jambe. It is used (in advanced classes only) to strengthen the quick reflex action in the metatarsal, which is utilized in petit allegro.

SHOWN EN DEHORS

From 1st—

Pointe tendue devant.

Release the toes, making a small outward circle on the floor.

Rond de jambe en dehors, opening the leg to the side, then to the back.

When in back, the toe should be in line with the hip.

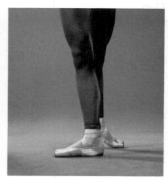

From the fully stretched position derrière, drop the heel to a small 4th position (heels in line).

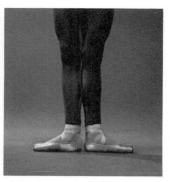

Slide the working leg to 1st position.

## Various Forms of Rond de Jambe par Terre

1. Demi- and full rond de jambe en plié
2. Small rond à quart (double or triple with toes only)
3. Demi- and full rond de jambe at 45° and en relevé at 45°
4. Double and triple rond de jambe par terre

Complete the circle inward, re-pointing the toes.

Rond de jambe the leg outward through 2nd to the back.

Close to 1st.

# Double rond de jambe par terre

*Prepare—* ♪          *one* ♪ ⟶

Begin in pointe tendue back (or side).

Rond de jambe en dehors, passing through 1st position on the count.

NOTE: Both double and triple ronds de jambe par terre are executed in one count.

# Rond de jambe en plié

SHOWN EN DEDANS

From 1st (may also begin from demi-plié)—

Plié on the supporting leg, extending the working leg (with straight knee) derrière.

Rond the leg to the side and continue bringing it to pointe tendue devant.

Complete the rond, either staying in plié (shown) or straightening the supporting leg.

# Rond de jambe en demi-pointe

SHOWN EN DEHORS AT 45°

From 1st—

Dégagé devant, rising onto demi-pointe.

Circle the leg to the side and then back, maintaining the height of the leg at 45°.

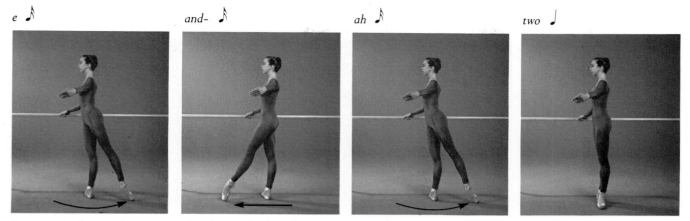

$e$ ♪        $and$- ♪        $ah$ ♪        $two$ ♩

Execute two fast ronds on succeeding beats, finishing by passing through 1st on the next count.

# Movements To Combine with Rond de Jambe par Terre Exercises at the Barre

In intermediate and advanced classes, rond de jambe exercises at the barre have traditionally been structured to include a variety of specialized, complementary movements. Listed here are some of the most common and useful; several of them are pictured on the following pages.

1. Passé par terre
2. Temps lié through 4th position plié
3. Grand rond de jambe jeté
4. Grand battement passé développé
5. Relevé lent to 90°
6. Half and full pirouette and grande pirouette by half-turn
7. Slow fouetté at 90°
8. Battement soutenu at 45° and 90° with and without relevé
9. Soutenu en tournant to the pointe tendue en plié
10. Cambré (upper body bend on one or both legs)

## Passé par terre

In rond de jambe exercises, passé par terre may be executed at the end of a series of ronds or in a series by itself. It may also be executed à terre, at 45°, or at 90°; and also with rises to demi-pointe on the front and back extensions.

SHOWN AT 45°
ON THE WHOLE FOOT

In a smooth, legato manner, brush the leg through 1st to 45° devant or derrière.

## Soutenu en tournant to the pointe tendue

This entire sequence is performed in one smooth motion, pausing only in the final pointe tendue. It may also be executed in reverse, with the soutenu turn en dedans finished in pointe tendue derrière; and with the turn en demi-pointe.

SHOWN EN DEHORS, FINISHED IN POINTE TENDUE DEVANT

From 1st—

Stretch the leg forward and plié, opening the leg through 2nd to the back (rond de jambe en dehors).

## Grand battement passé développé

This step is executed as one smooth, continuous movement that stops only upon the completion of the final développé. It reverses exactly and is often completed in plié. It may begin and/or end on relevé, and may also be executed with the final développé à la seconde instead of front or back.

SHOWN FRONT TO BACK

From 1st—

Grand battement devant.

## Battement soutenu relevé

SHOWN AT 90° DEVANT, DERRIÈRE, À LA SECONDE

From 1st—

Brush the leg forward smoothly (through the pointe tendue) and plié as the leg lifts devant.

Lower the leg, drawing it in to 5th en demi-pointe.

NOTE: This step may also be performed with soutenu en tournant simultaneously with the closing of the leg.

Relevé, drawing the foot in to close behind in 5th, and execute a soutenu turn en dehors, changing the back foot to the front.

At the conclusion of the turn, release the front leg, extending it to the pointe tendue devant while simultaneously lowering the supporting heel into plié.

At the top of the extension, bend the leg, lowering the arm toward en bas position.

Arrive in the passé position with the arm lifting to 1st.

Développé the leg derrière, opening the arm à la seconde with the head following the hand.

Plié on the outside leg, lifting the inside leg derrière.

Soutenu relevé.

Lift the outside leg to 2nd in plié.

Straighten, lowering the leg to pointe tendue (or soutenu relevé to 5th).

# Grand rond de jambe jeté *(Soviet syllabus)*

In this difficult movement (for advanced dancers only), the leg is brushed through 1st and thrown swiftly and energetically from the front (or back) in a high arc through 2nd. Take care not to twist the torso toward the working leg as it inscribes the arc. The shoulders should remain level, with the arm held securely in 2nd, throughout the movement.

Trajectory of the leg en dehors.

Trajectory of the leg en dedans.

## Side view

**EN DEHORS**

From 1st—

Brush to a low, "open" (in line with 1st) attitude devant.

Straighten the knee at 30° forward **en diagonale** (as if to effacé).

**EN DEDANS**

This movement pattern is identical to that of en dehors except that the leg brushes back first, then arcs to the front.

SHOWN EN DEHORS

From 1st, brush to a low, "open" (in line with 1st position) attitude devant.

Straighten the knee at 30° forward **en diagonale** to the effacé.

From the low effacé position, raise the leg in an arc to its highest point in 2nd.

Continue the arc down through the low effacé derrière position to finish pointe tendue back (toe in line with hip).

Without pausing, lift the leg to the highest possible pointe à la seconde.

Pushing the leg in back of the shoulder, lower it to an open (effacé) position derrière at 30°.

Continue pushing the leg back and place it pointe tendue derrière.

To finish, pass the leg through 1st position to pointe tendue devant.

Note the rotation of the heel forward as the leg lowers from 2nd to pointe tendue devant.

# Battement Fondu

Battement fondu is an important preparatory exercise for the study of all jumps on one leg. It may be performed à terre (to the pointe tendue), at 45°, or at 90°. When it is executed at 90°, the working leg may come to the extended position by means of a passé développé or may lift directly from the cou-de-pied through attitude to the extension. There are many forms of fondu exercises; in all of them the bending and stretching of both legs must always be smoothly coordinated. (See p. 18 for an explanation of the correct placement of the foot in fondu sur le cou-de-pied.) Although fondus are easily combined with a variety of other exercises, I strongly recommend, because of the importance of this step, that a separate fondu exercise be included in every barre.

## Fondu at 45°   $\frac{2}{4}$ ♪| ♫♩ ♫♫ |

SHOWN À LA SECONDE

*Prepare—*        *one* ♪.        *and* ♪        *two* ♫

From 5th, open the arm slightly to the side with a breath and return it en bas.

Fondu sur le cou-de-pied devant, lifting the arm to 1st.

As the foot begins to open, the plié deepens. Strictly maintain turn-out in both legs.

Both legs stretch simultaneously as the arm opens to 2nd.

When battement fondu is performed in a series, the working leg returns between each extension to the position fondu sur le cou-de-pied in the following manner: The working thigh remains immobile at its full height as the legs begin to bend. As the plié on the supporting leg deepens, the working knee returns to the side of the body, with the thigh lowering slightly as the foot assumes the cou-de-pied position. Maintain turn-out in both legs throughout.

## *Fondu double* (*Soviet syllabus*)   $\frac{2}{4}$ ♪| ♫♩ ♫♫ |

*Prepare—* ♪        *one* ♪. ⟶ *and-*

SHOWN DEVANT AT 45°

⟶

The working leg moves **continuously** throughout **both** of the "fondu/straighten" movements of the supporting leg.

Like rond de jambe par terre, fondu combines well with a variety of different movements, which are commonly incorporated into the fondu exercise in intermediate and advanced classes. Listed below are some of the most useful; several of them are pictured on the following pages.

*Various Forms of Battement Fondu*

1. Basic fondu (à terre, at 45°, at 90°)
2. Fondu relevé
3. Fondu double
4. Fondu with demi- and grand rond de jambe
5. Fondu tombé and tombé en tournant
6. Fondu with half-turns
7. Fondu with fouettés
8. Fondu with pirouettes from open positions
9. Fondu with soutenu and soutenu en tournant

At the Vaganova school in Leningrad, U.S.S.R., students fondu at the barre with their legs extended to the front. Photo: Paul B. Goode.

*ah* ♪          *two* ♫

# Fondu with tombé

SHOWN EN AVANT AT 45°

Fondu relevé devant. The straightening of the supporting knee and subsequent release of the heel from the floor are performed as one smooth movement.

On the upbeat, allongé the arm with a breath, lifting the extended leg 2 inches.

Fall forward past the extended toe, lowering the arm en bas. Take care to prevent the torso from twisting toward the barre at this moment.

# Fondu with fouetté

## Without plié

SHOWN EN DEDANS AT 45°

Fondu relevé devant.

Fouetté en dedans (toward the barre), arms joining momentarily in 1st. Take care not to allow the working leg to drop at any time.

## With plié

SHOWN EN DEHORS AT 45°

Execute a fondu relevé derrière.

Plié, lifting the foot slightly and maintaining the weight well forward.

Fouetté en dehors (away from the barre), momentarily releasing both hands from the barre in 2nd. Take care not to allow the level of the working leg to drop at any time.

NOTE: Fondu with fouetté may also be executed using the inside leg as the working leg.

Finish in fondu sur le cou-de-pied derrière, with both legs strongly turned-out and the arm in 1st.

The same rules of execution apply to fondu tombé en arrière: From the extended position derrière en relevé, fall back past the toe to finish in fondu cou-de-pied devant. The arm passes through en bas and lifts to 1st.

## Fondu with half-turns

During this exercise, the leg at 45° must not be allowed to open sideways from the front or back position. Force for the turn is provided instead by a strong plié-relevé action and a simultaneous thrust of the supporting heel en dehors or en dedans in the direction of the turn. Fondu with half-turn may also be executed using the inside leg as the working leg.

EN DEHORS, SHOWN DEVANT AT 45°

Execute a fondu relevé devant.

Plié, lifting the foot slightly.

Relevé with half-turn away from the barre, maintaining the leg directly in front of the body at 45° and momentarily releasing both hands from the barre in 2nd.

EN DEDANS, SHOWN DERRIÈRE AT 45°

Execute a fondu relevé derrière.

Plié, lifting the foot slightly and maintaining the weight well forward.

Relevé with a half-turn toward the barre, maintaining 45° arabesque, closing outside arm quickly to meet barre arm in 1st position (both hands momentarily off the barre), before opening the arms strongly to 2nd at the finish of the turn.

# Fondu with tombé en tournant

In this exercise (after the initial battement fondu), the tombé, swivel turn, and relevé développé blend together as one smooth, **continuous** movement.

   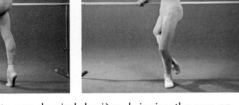

Fondu relevé devant.

Tombé en avant to cou-de-pied derrière, bringing the arm en bas and up to 1st.

Fondu relevé derrière.

Tombé en arrière to fondu sur le cou-de-pied devant. Instead of inclining the head (as shown above), the dancer may turn the head and look over the outside shoulder, in anticipation of the direction of the turn.

Swivel toward the barre, deepening the plié. The lifted foot passes from back to front at the side of the ankle. The arms join in 1st.

Finish the half-turn in cou-de-pied devant, returning the inside hand to the barre.

Relevé développé devant at 45°—

**or** à la seconde.

Swivel away from the barre, deepening the plié, arms joined in 1st, lifted foot passing the side of the ankle.

Finish the half-turn in cou-de-pied derrière, returning the inside hand to the barre.

Relevé développé derrière at 45°—

**or** à la seconde.

# Battement Soutenu

Battement soutenu is executed à terre, at 45°, at 90°, and to relevé (on the final drawing of the legs together). It may also be performed en tournant with either half or full soutenu turns during which the feet exchange places in 5th.

## Soutenu à terre

SHOWN DEVANT

Begin in 5th. Keeping weight on back leg, slide front leg out straight, releasing heel from the floor as the fondu begins. Complete the movement in pointe tendue in deep demi-plié.

Straighten the supporting leg, drawing the working leg (knee straight) back into 5th position.

## Soutenu en tournant

DEVANT EN DEDANS, AT 90°

From 5th—

Plié, sliding the foot devant.

Lift the foot through pointe tendue devant to 90°.

DERRIÈRE EN DEHORS, AT 90°

From 5th, plié, sliding the foot derrière and lifting it through pointe tendue to 90° arabesque.

NOTE: Battement soutenu en tournant may also be executed à la seconde both en dehors and en dedans.

# Soutenu développé relevé

SHOWN AT 45° À LA SECONDE

When executed in 1 count, the leg action pictured above is a smooth, continuous movement from 5th to 5th, with a slight pause only in the final closed position. If done in 2 counts, count 1 is the finish of the développé, and count 2 is the soutenu movement to 5th.

NOTE: Battement soutenu développé à terre (i.e., finishing in pointe tendue) is the preparation for sissonne tombée (p. 232). As shown above, and at 90°, it is the preparation for sissonne développé (pp. 279–80). It may also be executed without relevé in 5th. It is performed in all directions, and en tournant.

The working leg closes in front from the open position. Turn toward the barre with most of the weight on the front foot, adjusting the other foot closely around it in 5th position. The turn, which changes the feet, **appears** to be taking place on two feet, but it is only at the end of the turn that the weight is placed back equally on both feet.

Close the leg in back, drawing up to relevé, and turn "away" from the barre, changing the feet, with the arms in 1st during the turn. Execute the turn with most of the weight on the front foot, adjusting the other foot closely around it in 5th position.

# Rond de Jambe en L'Air

The accent in rond de jambe en l'air is always strongly out on the count. For an explanation and side view of this movement, see p. 34.

see p. 34.

Rond de jambe en l'air at the barre is the basic preparatory exercise for rond de jambe en l'air sauté. It is important to remember that once the height (30°, 45°, or 90°) of the working leg has been established in the starting position à la seconde, **it is maintained without adjustment** of the thigh (up or down) during the entire sequence of circling movement(s), including the final extension à la seconde. The only exception to this is the very high rond de jambe en l'air done

## Action of the leg in double rond de jambe en l'air

SHOWN EN DEHORS

Make two elongated egg-shaped circles under the thigh, with the working toe passing the **side** of the supporting knee each time.

# Battement Frappé

Frappé is a sharp movement and must always be performed in a dynamic manner. The fast speed with which the leg brushes outward is **directly related** to the speed with which the legs must push off from the floor when ascending into a jump. Performing frappé in a sluggish, legato manner is therefore counterproductive to the development of a quick petit allegro technique. The accent in frappé is always out on the count, and more time is spent **in** the final, outstretched pose of each frappé than is spent getting there.

## Battement frappé with a brush

SHOWN À LA SECONDE

Flexed position sur le cou-de-pied devant.

Keeping the thigh immobile, open the lower leg sideways, brushing the toes quickly and lightly across the floor.

by female dancers, which begins at 90° and finishes with a lift to 120°. It is considered an adagio movement and appears in the classical repertoire in Odette's variation in Act II of *Swan Lake*. As a variation, double (or triple) rond de jambe en l'air may also be completed with an extension devant (after rond en dehors) or derrière (after rond en dedans.)

*Various Forms of Rond de Jambe en L'Air*

1. Single, double, and triple rond de jambe en l'air at 30°, 45°, and 90°
2. Rond de jambe en l'air relevé
3. Rond de jambe en l'air plié (on either the rond or the final extension)
4. Rond de jambe en l'air with high développé on final extension (for women only)

*Various Forms of Battement Frappé*

1. Basic battement frappé (two versions)
2. Frappé to the pointe tendue
3. Frappé en relevé
4. Frappé with plié on the opening
5. Double and triple frappé

Fully stretch the toes, finishing the extension sharply at 30°. (The level of the thigh has not changed.)

Bend the leg, returning the foot sharply to the flexed cou-de-pied position **without touching the floor.**

# Battement frappé without a brush *(Soviet syllabus)*

SHOWN À LA SECONDE

From the wrapped cou-de-pied position, the leg extends sharply to 30° without brushing or changing the shape of the foot.

Both types of basic frappés pictured (with and without brushing) are valuable. The brushed frappé (pp. 114–15) done from a flexed position sur le cou-de-pied is beneficial to the development of the quick reflex action of the ankle and foot necessary in jumping. The frappé without a brush (in which the foot is fully pointed throughout the movement) is particularly strengthening for the plantar muscles underneath the foot. These muscles are important for control in landing "through the foot" from jumps.

The controversy among teachers about which type of frappé is preferable originates from the fact that the relaxed, flexed-foot position (used in the frappé that brushes) is not applicable to any acceptable classical position of the foot. Many teachers fear that practicing frappé with the ankle flexed will lead to the unsightly habit of flexing and pointing on the inward-outward thrusts of the working leg in jumps such as petits jetés or ballonnés.

I believe that the benefits of practicing both types of frappés far outweigh any potential drawbacks. I recommend teaching students the frappé **without a brush** first, because the fully pointed, wrapped position of the foot sur le cou-de-pied emphasizes the complete turn-out of the upper thigh. Only after students have completely mastered this frappé should the brushed frappé be introduced.

# Double frappé relevé to the pointe tendue plié

DEVANT AND DERRIÈRE

From pointe tendue à la seconde—

Relevé without plié, sharply bringing the foot to cou-de-pied derrière.

Open the foot slightly to the side and beat it in to cou-de-pied devant (wrapped).

Développé plié to pointe tendue devant.

It returns in the same manner.

In class, Galina Shlyapina practices double frappé en relevé. Photo: J. Tomas Lopez.

Relevé, sharply returning the foot to the wrapped cou-de-pied devant.

Open the foot slightly to the side and beat it in to cou-de-pied derrière.

Développé plié to pointe tendue derrière.

NOTE: Double frappé relevé may also be executed to pointe tendue **without** plié. Both forms (with and without plié) may be executed with single or triple frappé.

# Flic-Flac and Temps Relevé

Flic-flac and temps relevé are auxiliary movements used in combination with other barre exercises (battement fondu, frappé, and rond de jambe en l'air being the most common). They are first studied independently in the manner shown below. For the advanced forms of flic-flac and temps relevé en tournant, see pp. 154–57.

## Flic-flac

Flic-flac is an energetic, lashing movement. In its final, advanced form it is performed quickly in one count with the accent out on the final extension. Note the use of overcrossed positions sur le cou-de-pied front and back. Flic-flac may also open devant (after en dehors) or derrière (after en dedans). Flic-flac en dedans is executed in the exact reverse of the pattern pictured below, with the working leg brushing first front, then back.

SHOWN EN DEHORS TO RELEVÉ, OPENING À LA SECONDE

From à la seconde—

Bend the knee, brushing toes along the floor inward to finish in a fully pointed, slightly overcrossed cou-de-pied derrière.

## Temps relevé (Soviet syllabus)

The accent in temps relevé is always strongly **down on the count** in the initial fondu sur le cou-de-pied, with the leg moving quickly à la seconde immediately thereafter. It is first studied without a relevé on the opening of the leg. Temps relevé en dedans begins in fondu sur le cou-de-pied derrière, with the leg opening through the effacé derrière position to 2nd.

SHOWN EN DEHORS TO RELEVÉ

From 5th—

Fondu sur le cou-de-pied devant on the count, lifting the arm to 1st.

Open the lower leg **diagonally** forward (effacé). The arm follows the working leg.

Open the lower leg slightly to the side.

Relax the toes and brush them inward along the floor to finish in a fully pointed, slightly overcrossed cou-de-pied devant.

Vigorously open the leg à la seconde, lifting the supporting heel.

Continue opening the leg, deepening the plié.

At the last moment straighten both legs into relevé à la seconde. The arm arrives in 2nd simultaneously with the leg.

**TRAJECTORY OF THE WORKING LEG IN TEMPS RELEVÉ EN DEHORS**

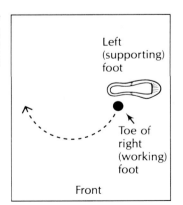

From cou-de-pied the foot barely opens forward before moving outward through efacé to 2nd. It never passes through the full devant position.

# Passé and Retiré

## Passé at 90°

From 5th—

Lift the front leg through fully pointed cou-de-pied devant, sliding it up the supporting leg until the toe touches just beneath the knee (retiré devant).

Lift the toe in an arc above the level of the knee at the side of the leg.

Passé: A **movement** of the working leg, either bent or straight, past the supporting leg from one position to another (for example, from 5th position in front to 5th behind, or from an extended pose à la seconde through passé to an extended pose in arabesque, or from pointe tendue devant through 1st to pointe tendue derrière).

Retiré: The **action** of drawing the working leg, with knee bent, up alongside the supporting leg and returning it down to the position (1st or 5th) from which it began; or, the **position** with the working leg bent, foot touching the supporting leg.

## Petit retiré

SHOWN WITH PLIÉ RELEVÉ, DEVANT AND DERRIÈRE

From plié in 5th—

Relevé to cou-de-pied devant with the toe placed just above the ankle.

Close in 5th plié.

Relevé, lifting the inside foot to cou-de-pied derrière.

Place the toe in back of the knee to retiré derrière and continue sliding it down the back of the leg.

From the cou-de-pied derrière position, close the foot in back in 5th.

## *Passé par terre en tournant at 90°*

### EN DEHORS, SHOWN FROM ÉCARTÉ DERRIÈRE TO 4TH ARABESQUE

From extension écarté derrière en relevé, quickly lower the leg to 1st, dropping the supporting heel and turning backward away from the barre, while maintaining the weight on the ball of the supporting foot. The toes of the working leg must be energetically pulled back in 1st. From 2nd the arms close strongly to 1st for the turn.

Finish the half-turn with grand battement to 4th arabesque, lifting the supporting heel without plié.

### EN DEDANS, SHOWN FROM ÉCARTÉ DEVANT TO CROISÉ DEVANT

From extension écarté devant en relevé, quickly lower the leg to 1st, dropping the supporting heel and turning toward the barre, while maintaining the weight on the ball of the supporting foot. The heel of the supporting foot must be thrust strongly forward into the turn.

Finish the half-turn with grand battement to croisé devant, lifting the supporting heel without plié.

NOTE: This is a very fast movement. From relevé, the supporting heel drops quickly as the working leg lowers to 1st—then rebounds up **without plié** as the working leg battements to the new position. Take care to maintain the integrity of the turn-out in 1st throughout the turn.

# Développé and Relevé Lent *(Soviet syllabus)*

Développé and relevé lent are generally considered to be adagio movements. They are always performed in a smooth, unbroken manner; the working leg should never stop moving until the full height of the extension has been achieved. In the Soviet syllabus relevé lent is introduced before développé; it is the first exercise in which students lift the leg to the 90° level.

Development of the high extension pictured here is the result of a combination of factors including natural physical capability for extension, a great deal of stretching, and many years of study. High extensions are considered more desirable for female than for male dancers. For men the degree of stretching necessary to produce such extension can be counterproductive to the development of the strength necessary for a strong allegro (jumping) technique.

Développé and relevé lent may be executed with either the inside leg or the outside leg at the barre, and in all directions and poses. For a detailed explanation of the cou-de-pied position through which the leg lifts in the execution of développé, see p. 18.

The port de bras that accompanies extensions of the leg is up to the discretion of the teacher and may take many forms. In all cases, however, the arm movement must be well coordinated with that of the leg and must reflect the adagio quality of this type of exercise.

*Various Forms of Développé and Relevé Lent*

1. Développé/relevé lent with plié and with relevé
2. Développé/relevé lent with demi- and grand rond de jambe
3. Développé/relevé lent balancé
4. Développé/relevé lent tombé
5. Développé ballotté
6. Développé d'ici-dela

## Relevé lent

SHOWN À LA SECONDE

Relevé lent is a slow, continuous lifting of the leg, with a straight knee from 5th or pointe tendue to the full height of the extension.

During a rehearsal break in Moscow, Galina Shlyapina warms up at the barre with développé à la seconde.
Photo: Juri Barikin.

# Développé

  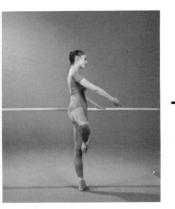

From 5th, bend the knee, lifting the leg through cou-de-pied devant (fully pointed, not wrapped) to retiré devant. The arm lifts to 1st. **Do not pause in retiré**.

À LA SECONDE

  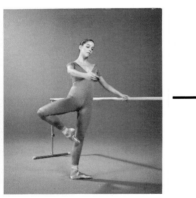

From 5th, bend the knee, lifting the leg through cou-de-pied devant (fully pointed, not wrapped) to retiré devant. The arm lifts to 1st. **Do not pause in retiré.**

DERRIÈRE

  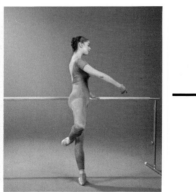

From 5th behind, bend the knee, lifting the leg through cou-de-pied derrière to retiré derrière. The arm lifts to 1st. **Do not pause in retiré**.

Continue lifting the leg through high attitude devant and extend it to its full height **without dropping the level of the knee**. The arm arrives in 5th simultaneously with the finish of the développé.

Lift the toe to the side, above the knee, raising the thigh to its full height; then extend the lower leg **without dropping the level of the knee.** The arm opens to 2nd, finishing with the final extension.

Raise the knee, pressing it in back of the shoulder and lifting it through high attitude derrière. Continue lifting the leg into the final extension while increasing the tilt of the body forward to accommodate the height of the leg. The arm simultaneously opens from 1st position into 2nd arabesque.

# *Développé ballotté* (Soviet syllabus)

Retiré devant, lifting the arm to 1st.

Développé devant with plié, simultaneously arching the upper body back, maintaining correct placement of the pelvis in plié développé. The arm opens to 2nd.

Passé, returning the body upright. The arm lowers en bas and lifts to 1st.

Plié développé derrière with penché, opening the arm to 2nd.

## *Common errors in développé ballotté*

**INCORRECT**        **INCORRECT**        **INCORRECT**

The dancer is not arching the upper back fully. The shoulders are twisted open, away from the barre, instead of remaining squarely placed, facing the front.

The supporting knee in plié is rolled in, and the elbows are too far in back of the torso.

The pelvis has been tucked under, which rounds the lower back and prevents the upper torso from arching back.

# *Développé balancé*

**SHOWN DEVANT**

one ♩         two ♪         and ♪         three ♩

Développé devant to the full height. **Quickly** drop (4 inches) and re-lift the leg to its initial height. **Hold** the extension briefly before continuing with the next movement.

NOTE: This is a strength-building but stressful exercise and should not be practiced every day. It is performed in all directions.

# Développé grand rond de jambe

**EN DEHORS**

Développé devant.

Open the arm outward from 5th to 2nd as the leg circles à la seconde.

Push leg behind hip (without turning heel under) as far as possible. The arm lowers en bas and lifts to 1st.

Continue the demi-rond to arabesque, extending the arm forward to 2nd arabesque.

**EN DEDANS**

Développé derrière. Dip the body slightly forward, eyes lowering to the hand in 1st, and rotate the heel under, bringing the leg à la seconde as the arm opens sideways. **Take care not to lean toward the barre while executing this movement**.

Continue the rond en dedans to the front, lifting arm directly from 2nd up to 5th.

# Développé d'ici-delà  $\frac{4}{4}$ ♩ ♫ ♩ ♩ |

This difficult, advanced exercise is performed in quarter-circles (as pictured here) both en dedans and en dehors, with the initial développé either devant, derrière, or à la seconde. It may also be executed in half-circles, swinging the leg from the front en dehors to arabesque and returning it en dedans to the front (or in reverse, beginning from the back). Développé d'ici-delà is always a moderately fast movement.

*one* ♩   *two* ♪   *and* ♪   *three* ♩

Développé devant.

Quickly demi-rond the leg to 2nd and **immediately** return it (demi-rond) to the front. Hold the leg in the final pose briefly before continuing with the next movement.

# *Movements To Combine*
# *with Développé and Relevé Lent*

1. Half-turn at 90°
2. Grand fouetté relevé en tournant
3. Tombé at 90°
4. Bends of the body with the leg at 90°

NOTE: Since dancers vary considerably in their ability to achieve height in extension, the words "at 90°" are used in this text to imply 90° or higher, depending on the dancer.

## *Half-turn at 90°*

**DEVANT, TURNING EN DEHORS**

| | | | |
|---|---|---|---|
| Développé devant. | Plié at 90°. | Relevé with half-turn away from the barre, maintaining the leg at 90° in front of the body throughout. | The arm lifts directly from 2nd to 5th at the end of the turn. |

**DERRIÈRE, TURNING EN DEDANS**

| | | | |
|---|---|---|---|
| Développé derrière. | Plié at 90°. | Relevé with half-turn toward the barre, briefly joining the hands in 1st position in mid-turn. Maintain the weight well forward during the turn. | Do not allow the leg to drop. Re-open the arm to the side upon completion of the turn. |

# *Grand fouetté relevé en tournant*

This movement may be performed entirely on the whole foot, or on the demi-pointe without plié relevé.

EN DEHORS

From arabesque, plié at full height with arm in 2nd.

Relevé, turning away from barre and rotating leg in hip joint to 2nd without allowing it to drop. Both arms are off the barre in 2nd.

Continue turning, pulling hip of lifted leg back, and finish at 90° devant. Raise outside arm from 2nd to 5th as the movement is completed.

EN DEDANS

From plié at 90° devant with the arm in 2nd—

Relevé, pressing supporting heel well forward, turning toward barre while rotating leg to 2nd, and lifting outside arm to 5th.

Continue to turn with the arms joining momentarily in 5th as the body faces the barre in 2nd.

Turn the body one-quarter into arabesque (without dropping level of leg), with outside arm lowering to arabesque as inside hand returns to barre.

# Tombé at 90°

SHOWN À LA SECONDE (WITH A PIQUÉ RECOVERY)

From à la seconde on the demi-pointe, lift the foot slightly (with a preparatory intake of breath) and tombé out past the foot to finish in plié à la seconde at 90°. Without hesitation, at the moment the outside toe touches the floor, execute a swift grand battement with the in-side leg, to facilitate the immediate transfer of weight onto the new supporting leg.

Piqué back to the barre with a grand battement, returning to the starting pose in 2nd on demi-pointe.

NOTE: This movement may also be done to a pose with the foot pointed à terre instead of lifted to 90°. Tombé at 90° is also commonly performed en avant, from front extension with tombé to arabesque, and in reverse, from arabesque to extension devant.

# Bends of the body with the leg at 90° or above

Arabesque penchée.        Cambré in extension devant.

Other variations of bends in extension include: side bend to the barre with the leg lifted à la seconde, forward bend over the leg devant, and back bend with the leg in arabesque (although the last is anatomically difficult to achieve when the leg is higher than 90°).

# Petit Battement

## *Petit battement sur le cou-de-pied* (Soviet syllabus)

From "wrapped" cou-de-pied devant—

Open foot sideways 2 to 3 inches.

Replace foot sur le cou-de-pied derrière.

Repeat in series.

At no time during this exercise does the level of the thigh move up or down. The knee stays immobile, with the lower leg swinging in and out as if hinged at the knee. The level of the foot placed in back in cou-de-pied must be the same as the level of the foot in the wrapped cou-de-pied devant.

An alternate form of petit battement uses the fully pointed cou-de-pied devant position instead of the wrapped position shown here. In a third form, the Cecchetti method, the foot (with the toes flexed) moves in and out of the cou-de-pied position with the ball of the foot resting lightly on the floor.

In class, Galina Shlyapina practices petit battement battu derrière. Photo: J. Tomas Lopez.

# Petit battement battu (or serré)

This step consists of several small, fast, continuous beats of the little toe (devant) or heel (derrière) against the supporting foot (en demi-pointe). The lower leg rebounds to a tiny 4th position at the end of each beat. Take care not to move the thigh.

Battement battu is performed by Odette, the Swan Queen, at the end of the pas de deux in *Swan Lake*, Act II. The beats in the Ivanov choreography are executed by opening the leg to the side (écarté), a somewhat easier method than the opening to 4th pictured below. The waltz variation in Fokine's *Les Sylphides*, however, uses the devant form below.

DEVANT

From the fully pointed position cou-de-pied devant, open the foot 2 inches to the front, then beat it sharply back against the ankle. Repeat this action quickly several times.

DERRIÈRE

From cou-de-pied derrière, open the foot 2 inches to the back, then beat the heel sharply back against the ankle. Repeat this action quickly several times.

# Grand Battement

Grand battement is the major preparatory exercise for all grand allegro jumps. Executed at 90° or higher, it is a swift, energetic movement and must **never** be performed in a labored, sluggish, or legato manner. Though learned slowly, it is ultimately executed quite fast, in one count, with the leg being lifted on the upbeat and closed on the count (i.e., accent "in"). This timing directly relates to the timing of the takeoff and landing of all large jumps such as grand jetés. (The leg is thrown into the air on the upbeat; the landing occurs on the following count.) Grand battement is performed in all directions and poses.

*Various Forms of Grand Battement*

1. Grand battement balançoire
2. Grand battement fouetté
3. Grand battement tombé
4. Grand battement pointé
5. Grand battement with demi- and grand rond de jambe
6. Grand battement développé
7. Grand battement passé développé
8. Grand battement relevé

**SHOWN DEVANT**

   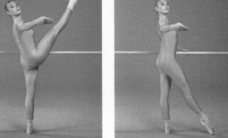 

From 5th, brush the leg forward through pointe tendue and lift it quickly to its full height. Maintain correct placement of the back, with the shoulders down. There should be no visible sign of effort in the upper body.

Lower the leg quickly, in a controlled manner, through the pointe tendue. Close to 5th.

Susan Jaffe, partnered by Clark Tippet, executes a grand battement derrière in the Black Swan pas de deux from American Ballet Theatre's production of *Swan Lake*. Photo: Mira.

# Grand battement balançoire *(or en cloche)*

This step is executed in a swinging manner, without stops in any position.

From pointe tendue der-
rière—

Brush leg through 1st into grand battement devant, leaning
back. Keep shoulders level as leg goes to full height.

# Grand battement développé

This step involves a soft, quick unfolding of the leg to the full height on the upbeat, with the subsequent closing on the count. There are no stops at any point
until the movement is completed in the final 5th position. It may be executed
in all poses and directions.

SHOWN À LA SECONDE

From 5th, in one continuous motion, lift the leg through retiré to high attitude.

# Grand battement passé développé

This step is executed as one swift, continuous movement, without pause until
the final développé is completed. It is also done in the exact reverse of the sequence pictured here.

From 5th, execute a grand battement devant to the full height, then quickly retract the lower
leg through a high attitude position.

Lower the leg, brushing it back through 1st while bringing the body upright.

Execute a grand battement derrière with penché forward, keeping the shoulders level.

Continue in a series.

Without pausing, continue to extend the leg to its full height.

Lower the leg through pointe tendue and close in 5th position.

Continue the movement, drawing the leg through passé into développé derrière. Close to 5th. Note the coordination of the arm with the leg: from 2nd, it lowers en bas and lifts to 1st as the leg comes to passé, then reopens à la seconde, and finally closes en bas when the leg closes to 5th.

# Grand battement fouetté relevé

This movement is executed as **one continuous action without pause** until the completion of the fouetté. Performed en dedans, it is an important preparatory exercise for grand jeté entrelacé and grand fouetté sauté en dedans to arabesque.

During grand battement fouetté the dancer must have a sense of elongating and lifting the raised leg throughout the movement. Once the position of the toe in the air is established on the initial battement, **it does not move** (down or sideways) except to lift as it goes through à la seconde into the final pose. The slight torso inclination at the top of the initial battement helps the dancer to anticipate the correct placement of the body weight in the final pose at the end of the fouetté.

EN DEDANS

Brush through 1st plié **without leaning forward**, then relevé battement devant. The arm comes en bas and lifts to 1st.

EN DEHORS

Brush back through 1st plié, then relevé battement derrière. The arm lowers en bas and lifts to 1st.

## Common errors in grand battement fouetté relevé

INCORRECT SERIES
(EN DEDANS)

After brushing through 1st, the body inclines toward the battement devant leg. As a result, the leg drops (instead of lifts) into the fouetté, and the weight is not sufficiently forward in the final arabesque pose.

Lean back slightly at top of battement.

Fouetté through 2nd, turning toward the barre to finish in arabesque. The leg should lift throughout the entire movement.

Penché slightly forward at the full height of the battement derrière.

Fouetté through 2nd, turning away from the barre, and finish in the devant pose with the arm coming directly from 2nd up to 5th position.

**INCORRECT SERIES (EN DEHORS)**

After brushing from front to back through 1st, the weight is not adjusted forward in the battement arabesque, causing the leg to drop during the fouetté and the body to fall forward at the end of the movement.

# Grand battement pointé

*Tango*
$$\frac{2}{4} \quad \text{♪♪} \; | \; \text{♩ ♪♪} \; |$$

During the execution of grand battement pointé, the weight must be strongly maintained over the supporting side or the working leg will appear (and feel) heavy, as if unable to lift quickly and easily. The toes, strongly pointed, must never relax as they touch the floor for the pointé. The leg must appear to move up and down lightly and easily throughout the sequence.

This movement may be executed in all directions and poses and with several continuous pointés and battements in one direction before closing. It may also be executed with grand battement développé on the initial battement.

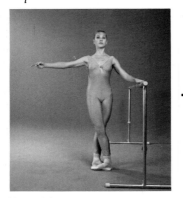

From 5th—

## Grand battement pointé with demi-rond

*Waltz*
$$\frac{3}{4} \quad \text{♩ ♩ ♩} \; | \; \text{♩ ♩ ♩} \; | \; \text{♩ ♩ ♩} \; |$$

This advanced exercise is also performed in the reverse with the demi-ronds executed en dedans.

**SHOWN EN DEHORS**

*and* ♩    *one* ♩ >    *and-* ♩    *ah* ♩

From 5th, execute a grand battement devant.

Lower the leg lightly to pointe tendue and execute another grand battement, lifting the leg with demi-rond in an arc to the highest point à la seconde.

## Grand battement with demi-rond at 90°

*Polka*
$$\frac{2}{4} \quad \text{♪♪ ♩} \; | \; \text{♪♪ ♩} \; |$$

**SHOWN EN DEHORS FROM FRONT TO SIDE IN TWO COUNTS**

*Prepare——*    *one* ♪    *and* ♪    *two* ♩

Execute a grand battement 90° devant and immediately demi-rond the leg à la seconde. Close to 5th, passing through pointe tendue. (May also be done with the initial battement à la seconde, followed by demi-rond en dehors to arabesque.)

*and-ah* ♫    *one* ♩    *and-* ♪    *ah-two* ♫

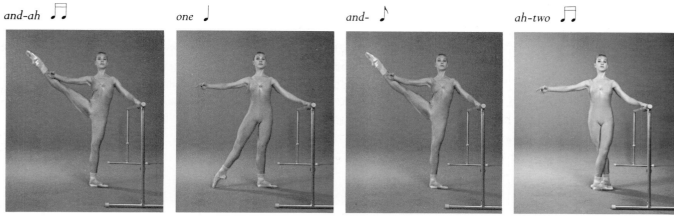

Execute a grand battement à la seconde.

Lower to pointé tendue in 2nd (no weight on the toes).

Immediately re-lift the leg to the full height in 2nd; then lower and close to 5th, passing through the pointe tendue.

*two* ♩>    *and-* ♩    *ah* ♩    *three* ♩>

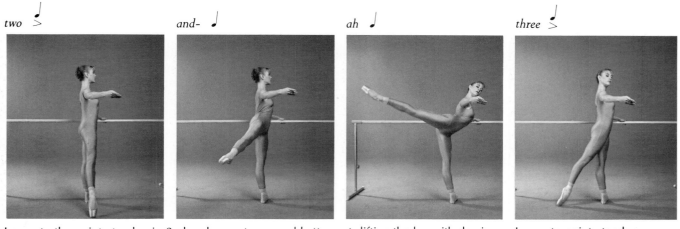

Lower to the pointe tendue in 2nd and execute a grand battement, lifting the leg with demi-rond in an arc to its highest point in arabesque.

Lower to pointe tendue or close to 5th position.

*Tango*

**SHOWN EN DEDANS FROM BACK TO SIDE IN ONE COUNT**

*Prepare—*    *and-* ♪    *ah* ♪    *one* ♩

On the upbeat, execute a grand battement 90° derrière and immediately demi-rond the leg en dedans to 2nd, lowering through the pointe tendue to close in 5th on the count. The tempo of the music must be slow enough to accommodate all the movements that occur on the upbeat. (May also be done with initial battement à la seconde, followed by demi-rond en dedans to the front.)

# Grand battement tombé

Grand battement tombé is the major preparatory exercise for landing from big jumps. It is important to cover as much distance as possible in this step and to effect an **immediate** transfer of weight from one leg to the other at the moment of tombé. It is also important not to twist the shoulders open at the completion of the movement. Both sides of the torso must remain upright (with shoulders parallel to the floor) throughout the tombé.

**EN AVANT**

From 5th—

Execute a grand battement relevé devant with full port de bras (en bas, up to 1st to 5th). (Shown en pointe, but may be done en demi-pointe.)

Fall forward **past the toe**. The arm opens en dehors into full port de bras.

Finish in plié, lifting back leg **immediately** to 90° at the moment the weight falls onto the front leg. The arm simultaneously completes full port de bras to the arabesque line.

**EN ARRIÈRE**

From 5th, execute a grand battement relevé derrière and fall backward past the toe, to finish in plié 90° devant. The arm lowers from 2nd en bas and lifts to 5th.

**INCORRECT SERIES**

From the battement relevé, the leg is dropped **before** the dancer pushes the body forward off balance. The undesirable result is that the distance traveled forward is shortened.

# 5 ~ Turns at the Barre

Practicing turns at the barre is important for several reasons:

1. In order to be able to execute them, the dancer must maintain correct alignment with a strongly "pulled-up" torso; pirouettes at the barre cannot be "faked." In addition, most pirouettes at the barre are finished "up," forcing the dancer to maintain placement over the supporting leg en demi-pointe at the end of the turn. This is excellent practice for performing this same difficult task—i.e., finishing "up" instead of falling out of turns—later in the centre.

2. Turns at the barre reinforce the correct coordination of arms, head, torso, and legs, necessary for turns in the centre. They are especially useful in training a dancer to execute the essential press forward of the supporting heel and inner thigh that motivates a turn and enables it to be performed turned-out.

3. A student who falls forward, back, into, or away from the barre while turning becomes instantly aware of the direction in which he or she has incorrectly thrust the body. The barre, in other words, acts as a gauge. It helps the student to ascertain what correction must be made on the next try in order to remain vertical and execute the turn smoothly.

4. The more a student executes turning movements, the less mysterious and fearful these movements will seem. Many students have difficulty turning, often because of a mental block. If, early in their training, turns of one form or another are integrated into their barre work, most students will never develop this block.

5. Inserting into the barre work the same turns that will later be studied in the centre contributes a sense of continuity to a class. If, for instance, arabesque pirouettes en dedans are to be part of the adagio in the centre, then half-turns en dedans in arabesque can be included in the barre développé exercise. Or, if saut de basque is to be part of an allegro combination, then piqué turns en dehors at the barre will reinforce the correct coordination needed for that jump.

The first turns to be learned at the barre are half-turns on two feet. These turns (détournés and soutenus) are useful for changing sides between repetitions of an exercise. However, they should first be studied as separate exercises.

Next, in preparation for pirouettes (turns on one leg en demi-pointe), students should practice relevés to the retiré position, utilizing the correct preparatory positions and arm coordinations for turning. Once these are mastered, they can begin the practice of half-turns at the barre with relevé to retiré.

When the correct patterns of coordination and sufficient strength in the pirouette position have been attained, students may begin centre practice of quarter-turns, half-turns, and finally full turns. I recommend that full turns be attempted first in the centre **before** they are included in the barre work. This is because students should not have to worry about colliding with the barre when they are making their first unsteady attempts at the tricky coordination necessary for a single turn. Once the dancer has acquired the correct "feel" for turning, single (and later double) pirouettes may be added to the barre work.

Many turning movements on the whole foot, with the supporting leg either straight or in plié, can be useful at the barre. Several of these are pictured elsewhere in the book and include such exercises as temps lié en tournant through demi-plié in 4th position, tendu and/or dégagé en tournant (see p. 92), fondu-tombé en tournant (see p. 110), and passé par terre en tournant (see p. 121).

# Turns on Two Legs

All turns at the barre may be performed either en pointe or en demi-pointe. Détournés are performed quickly and energetically, with a slight spring onto the relevé. Both détourné and soutenu en tournant are commonly used to change sides at the barre in mid-exercise. During these turns the feet **always** exchange places.

## Détourné with half-turn

EN DEDANS

  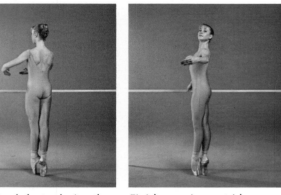

From plié in 5th with the arm in 2nd—

Relevé on two feet, turning toward the back foot, closing the arms to 1st, and transferring the weight onto the front foot. Readjust the back foot around the front foot during the turn.

Finish opening outside arm to 2nd, as inside hand returns to the barre, and replace weight equally on both feet.

NOTE: This turn is en dedans because it is executed while turning **toward** the inside (supporting) leg at the barre.

EN DEHORS

  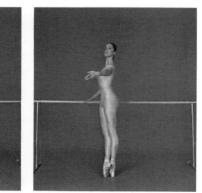

From plié in 5th with the arm in 2nd—

Relevé on two feet, turning toward the back foot, closing the arms to 1st, and transferring the weight onto the front foot. Readjust the back foot around the front foot during the turn.

Finish opening outside arm to 2nd, as inside hand returns to the barre, and replace weight equally on both feet. The feet are in the opposite relationship from the way they began.

NOTE: This turn is en dehors because it is executed while turning **away** from the inside (supporting) leg at the barre.

# Détourné with full turn

This turn appears to be occurring on two feet. Most of the weight, however, is on the front foot during the turn. Only at the end of the turn is the weight placed back equally on both feet. It may also be executed in reverse, starting with the outside foot placed in 5th behind and turning outward away from the barre.

SHOWN EN DEDANS

  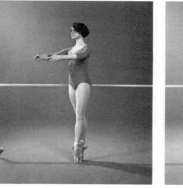 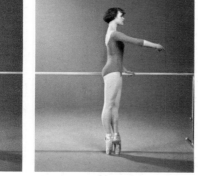

Plié in 5th.

Relevé, turning toward the barre on the front foot and readjusting back foot around in 5th.

Feet finish in 5th, in the opposite relationship from the way they began.

# Soutenu

## Soutenu en tournant to 5th position

SHOWN WITH HALF-TURN
EN DEDANS

From pointe tendue à la seconde with the supporting leg in plié—

Relevé on the inside leg, drawing the outside leg to 5th in front, and turn toward the barre with the weight on the front foot, readjusting the other foot around it in 5th.

Finish in 5th with the feet opposite from the way they began.

NOTE: Soutenu en tournant may also be executed from pointe tendue devant or derrière, as well as from 2nd as pictured here.

## Soutenu en tournant finished in open position

### WITH WHOLE TURN EN DEHORS FINISHED DEVANT

From pointe tendue à la seconde—

Relevé on the inside leg, drawing the outside leg to 5th behind, and turn away from the barre on the front foot, readjusting the other foot around it in 5th. The arms close as the leg closes.

Finish in plié, extending the leg directly to pointe tendue without passing through 5th position demi-plié.

### WITH HALF-TURN EN DEDANS STAYING ON DEMI-POINTE (SHOWN FROM À LA SECONDE TO À LA SECONDE)

From 90° à la seconde en demi-pointe—

Close in front, turning toward the barre, exchanging feet in the turn. Arms pass through 1st.

Finish releasing the front leg into battement à la seconde without lowering from demi-pointe. Arms open sharply to the side with the leg.

NOTE: This is a very fast movement. The soutenu turn is performed on the upbeat and the subsequent opening of the leg to the side on the following count. It is a useful transition for changing sides during rond de jambe en l'air exercises.

In class, Galina Shlyapina executes a petit développé à la seconde in preparation for a soutenu en tournant en dedans. Photo: J. Tomas Lopez.

# Turns on One Leg

## Piqué turns in retiré

Piqué turns at the barre may be performed with half, single, one-and-a-half, or two rotations. Two examples are pictured here.

### Piqué turn en dehors by half-turn

Plié with the leg extended forward at 45°.

Step forward past the pointed foot directly onto the demi-pointe, turning toward the barre and bringing the back leg immediately to the retiré position. The pointed foot passes the side of the knee as the body faces the barre and finishes retiré devant. The arms pass through 1st.

### Full piqué turn en dedans

Plié with the leg extended back at 45°.

Turning the body outward, away from the barre, face the lifted leg and step forward directly onto the demi-pointe. Bring the other leg immediately to retiré behind the knee, turning toward the barre. The second side of the body closes strongly as the arms join in 1st for the turn. Press the supporting heel forward throughout the turn.

# Piqué turns finished in open poses

These controlled turns may be inserted into adagio combinations. The dancer momentarily steps away from the barre, then turns back, prepares, and executes a piqué turn to return to the barre. Piqué turns to open poses may also be executed traveling forward and backward alongside the barre. There are many possible variations: turns may be half, three-quarter, or full turns and may finish in any position. Two examples are pictured here.

## Full piqué turn en dehors

**SHOWN EN POINTE FINISHED IN 4TH ARABESQUE**

  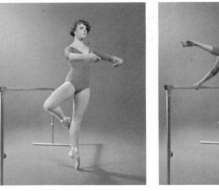

Face the barre diagonally in plié in pointe tendue croiseé devant, with arms in the preparatory low 3rd pose for turns.

Piqué toward the barre, stepping directly onto pointe (or demi-pointe) and turning backward toward the lifted leg in retiré (away from the supporting leg), with the retiré foot **behind** the knee and the arms in 1st.

Finish extending the retiré leg to 4th arabesque, returning the inside hand to the barre.

## Piqué en tournant by half-turn en dedans

**SHOWN EN POINTE FINISHED IN CROISÉ DEVANT**

Face the barre diagonally in plié, with the inside leg in pointe tendue devant and the arms in the preparatory pose for turns.

Piqué back to the barre, stepping directly onto pointe (or demi-pointe) and turning toward the barre with the arms in 1st. The lifted toe passes the side of the knee and comes to the front.

Finish extending the passé leg to croisé 90° devant, with the outside arm in 5th and the head turned to look over the inside shoulder.

# Pirouette

## Pirouette from 2nd position

### EN DEHORS

Prepare in 2nd position plié with the outside arm in 1st, the inside hand on the barre (or off the barre in 2nd). Relevé on the inside leg, turning away from the barre. The foot is placed retiré front.

Continue turning with the arms held in 1st. Upon completion of the desired number of rotations, return the inside hand to the barre.

### EN DEDANS

Prepare in 2nd position plié with the outside arm in 2nd, the inside hand on the barre. Exert a slight downward pressure on the barre to help motivate the beginning of the turn. Relevé on the inside leg, closing the arms to 1st and turning toward the barre.

Continue turning with the foot in retiré front. Upon completing the turn, return the inside hand to the barre.

NOTE: In an alternate preparatory pose for en dedans turns, the inside hand is off the barre in 1st position and the outside arm is in 2nd. This exactly duplicates the preparatory pose used for these turns in the centre.

## Half-pirouette en dehors from 5th (lifting inside leg)

From 5th plié with the outside arm in 2nd, relevé on the front (outside) foot, closing the arms to 1st and turning toward the barre. Execute a sharp passé with the back leg.

The toe passes the side of the supporting knee when the body faces the barre. Finish with the toe in front of the knee. The inside hand returns to the barre on completion of turn.

# Full pirouette from 5th (lifting outside leg)

## EN DEHORS

Prepare in plié, with outside foot in front in 5th position. Inside hand is on the barre (or lifted in 2nd); outside arm is in 1st.

Relevé on the inside leg, bringing the outside leg to retiré devant, turning away from the barre, and closing the arms to 1st.

Return the inside hand to the barre upon completion of the turn.

## EN DEDANS

  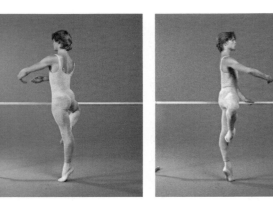

Prepare in plié, with outside foot in back in 5th position. Inside arm is in 1st (or on the barre); outside arm is in 2nd.

Relevé on the inside leg, bringing the outside leg to either the front (as shown) or the back of the knee, turning toward the barre, and closing the arms to 1st.

Return the inside hand to the barre upon completion of the turn.

# Half-pirouette en dedans from 5th (lifting inside leg)

Prepare in plié, with the outside leg in 5th position in back. The outside arm is in 2nd (or 1st).

With the inside hand exerting a slight downward pressure on the barre to motivate the turn, relevé on the back leg, turning away from the barre and closing the arms to 1st. Execute a sharp passé with the front leg, taking it to the back, past the side of the knee, to finish in retiré derrière. Upon completion of the turn, return the inside hand to the barre.

# Pirouette from 4th to an open pose

### EN DEHORS TO ATTITUDE DERRIÈRE

Prepare in 4th position plié, with the outside arm in 1st. Relevé on the front (inside) leg, turning away from the barre, bringing the back leg to retiré devant, and closing the arms to 1st. Just before completing the turn, pass the lifted leg to the back, past the side of the knee, into attitude derrière.

The body weight must adjust forward for the finish in attitude. Lift the outside arm to 5th simultaneously with the finish of the turn in attitude. Return the inside hand to the barre.

### EN DEDANS TO ATTITUDE DEVANT

Begin from the preparatory 4th position lunge, with the outside arm in 2nd and the inside arm either in 1st or on the barre. Relevé on the inside (front) leg, turning toward the barre, bringing the back toe **immediately** to the front of the knee, and closing the arms to 1st.

The outside leg lifts to attitude devant and the outside arm to 5th, simultaneously **with** (not after) the finish of the turn.

NOTE: Turns from the 4th position may also finish in the "closed" pirouette (retiré) position.

# *Pirouette from an open position with plié-relevé*

## EN DEHORS FROM 45° DEVANT

Plié at 45° devant, with the outside arm à la seconde.

Sharply relevé, pulling knee **directly** back to retiré devant and turning outside, away from the barre, with the arms in 1st.

## EN DEDANS FROM 45° DERRIÈRE

Plié at 45° derrière with the outside arm à la seconde.

Sharply relevé, pulling foot **directly** to back of knee into retiré derrière and turning toward the barre with the arms in 1st. Actively press the supporting heel forward throughout the turn.

NOTE: These turns are commonly used in battement fondu exercises and are often performed from 2nd position at 45° in combination with rond de jambe en l'air.

## Pirouette from an open position without plié-relevé

These turns may be inserted into advanced fondu and rond de jambe en l'air exercises at the barre. Force is provided by the coordinated closing of the arm and leg, the supporting heel, and a slight downward pressure of the hand on the barre as the turn begins.

These turns may also be executed from open positions devant and derrière, turning both en dedans and en dehors.

SHOWN EN DEDANS FROM 2ND TO 2ND AT 45°

From 2nd position at 45° en demi-pointe, sharply draw the foot back into retiré devant, closing the arms to 1st and turning toward the barre. Upon completion of the turn, re-open the outside arm and leg à la seconde, staying on the demi-pointe.

In Tbilisi, U.S.S.R., a young student balances at the barre in the correct position for pirouettes. Photo: G. Warren.

## Grande pirouette by half-turn

These turns may be done either from 90° or from a preparatory plié in 4th position, in all devant or derrière poses, both en dehors and en dedans. Turns à la seconde are executed with only a quarter-turn. Two similar exercises are battement fondu with half-turns at 45° (p. 109) and battement développé with half-turns at 90° (p. 128).

SHOWN IN ATTITUDE DERRIÈRE EN DEDANS

From attitude derrière at 90° en demi-pointe (or on the whole foot)—

Plié, opening the arm à la seconde and lifting the back leg slightly.

Relevé, turning toward barre and closing arms to 1st. Maintain weight well forward. Do not drop back leg.

Complete half-turn, opening outside arm to 2nd and returning inside hand to the barre.

## Fouetté rond de jambe en tournant

In this turn, take care to maintain the weight of the body directly over the supporting leg at the moment of the demi-rond. This is particularly difficult to accomplish in fouetté rond de jambe en tournant en dedans, in which the natural tendency is to push the weight backward and toward the barre as the leg comes à la seconde.

EN DEHORS

From retiré devant on the whole foot (or demi-pointe) with the arm in 1st—

Plié développé devant just below the 90° level.

Demi-rond en dehors, deepening the plié and simultaneously opening arm to 2nd.

EN DEDANS

From retiré derrière on the whole foot (or demi-pointe) with the arm in 1st—

Plié développé derrière just below the 90° level.

Demi-rond en dedans, deepening the plié and simultaneously opening arm to 2nd.

Shown below is an alternate preparation for grandes pirouettes by half-turns, identical to the position from which the dancer performs grandes pirouettes in the centre (i.e., without the barre).

From the preparatory 4th position lunge for pirouettes en dedans, execute a grand battement relevé to attitude derrière, turning toward the barre with the arms in 1st. Finish the turn by replacing the inside hand on the barre and lifting the outside hand to 5th.

Relevé retiré devant, closing the arms to 1st and turning away from the barre. At the conclusion of the turn, replace the inside hand on the barre (not shown).

Relevé retiré devant, closing the arms to 1st and turning toward the barre. At the conclusion of the turn, replace the inside hand on the barre (not shown).

# Flic-flac en tournant

This step rises sharply from the whole foot **without** a preceding demi-plié, the force for the turn being provided by the arms, the flic-flac foot action, and the supporting heel. It may be executed without a turn (p. 118), with half-turn, or with full turn as shown.

Flic-flac en tournant should initially be studied from pointe tendue à la seconde and finished after a half-turn with the working foot in cou-de-pied. Whole turns are first studied from pointe tendue à la seconde and finished with the working leg opening to the side at 30°.

After this rather advanced movement is mastered, it can begin and end in any open pose from any height. Two examples of the many possibilities are pictured here. To facilitate clean execution of all the component parts of flic-flac, the step is initially studied in two musical counts. The final version, however, is performed quickly and fluidly in one count, with the flic-flac movements occurring on the upbeat and the final opening of the leg on the count. Proper coordination of the arms, as pictured here, is essential to the smooth execution of flic-flac en tournant.

## Full turn en dedans

SHOWN FROM 2ND
À TERRE,
FINISHED DERRIÈRE AT 45°

  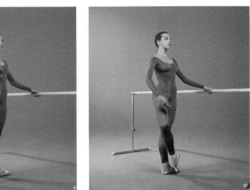

Begin on the whole foot in pointe tendue à la seconde, arms in 2nd.

Brushing the ball of the foot inward along the floor, flic to an overcrossed cou-de-pied devant, sharply lowering the arms en bas.

## Full turn en dehors

SHOWN FROM ÉCARTÉ
DERRIÈRE, FINISHED
IN ATTITUDE DEVANT AT 90°

Begin en demi-pointe in écarté derrière.

Lower the supporting heel and flic to an overcrossed cou-de-pied derrière, turning away from the supporting leg (outward from the barre). The arm opens through 2nd to 5th en bas.

In class in Tbilisi, U.S.S.R., company dancers complete flic-flac en dedans en tournant in attitude derrière. Photo: G. Warren.

Rising to the demi-pointe and turning toward the barre, open the foot slightly to the side and lift the arm to 1st.

Flac to cou-de-pied derrière, continuing to turn toward the supporting leg en demi-pointe. The arms are in 1st.

Complete the whole turn, opening the leg to 45° derrière on the demi-pointe and simultaneously opening the arm to 2nd.

Lift the supporting heel, opening the foot slightly to the side, and flac to cou-de-pied devant as the turn continues with the arms in 1st.

Finish the turn en demi-pointe, lifting the leg to attitude devant and the arm to 5th.

# Temps relevé en tournant *(Soviet syllabus)*

This step is unique to the Soviet syllabus. It is most often used in combination with rond de jambe en l'air, and is first studied without a turn (see p. 118). The turn is always very fast, with a whipping quality, and may be completed with the lifted leg either open or retiré. It differs from fouetté rond de jambe en tournant (pp. 152, 194) in that it eliminates the fully stretched devant (or derrière) position entirely. The leg moves quickly from a small attitude position devant (or derrière) through a stretched position effacé, arcs to 2nd, and immediately closes into retiré for the turn.

EN DEHORS

On the count, fondu sur le cou-de-pied devant, with the arm passing through 5th en bas to 1st.

Deepening the plié, take the leg to an open attitude devant and stretch it diagonally forward (effacé). The arm begins to open with the leg.

EN DEDANS

On the count, fondu sur le cou-de-pied derrière, with the arm passing through 5th en bas to 1st.

Deepening the plié, take the leg to an open attitude derrière and stretch it diagonally backward (effacé). The arm begins to open with the leg.

Relevé on the upbeat, opening the leg à la seconde, then closing into a fast pirouette en dehors (in the manner of fouetté rond de jambe en tournant).

Finish on the count en demi-pointe, with a fast développé à la seconde.

Relevé on the upbeat, bringing the leg à la seconde and closing into a fast pirouette en dedans (in the manner of fouetté rond de jambe en tournant).

Finish on the count en demi-pointe with a fast développé à la seconde.

In Tbilisi, U.S.S.R., a young student completes temps lié en avant in 5th position croisé. Photo: G. Warren.

# 6 ⁓ Traditional Transfer-of-Weight Movements

Temps lié and pas de basque are traditional dance movements that are particularly beneficial when included in the initial port de bras (small adagio) exercise in the centre. Both are exercises for the study of transfer of weight and help students to make the transition from supported (barre) work to unsupported (centre) work. With their very specific traveling patterns and somewhat complex coordinations of head, arms, and legs, these exercises teach grace and coordination, as well as stability, in the transfer of body weight from one leg to the other.

Temps lié is one of the oldest traditional groupings of steps in the classical ballet vocabulary. Each of its traveling sequences moves along the floor at right angles to the one that preceded it. This floor pattern is very specific: The dancer first moves forward, then travels to the side toward the front foot, and finishes by closing the extended foot in 5th position in front. In reverse, the movement travels back, then sideways toward the back foot, and closes in 5th position in back. Regardless of the many complications that may be added to the basic form of temps lié (e.g., temps lié with pirouettes, temps lié at 90°, or temps lié to the demi-pointe), the traditional floor pattern never changes. It should be memorized by all students.

Several of the many different forms of temps lié and pas de basque are pictured here. A jumping form, petit pas de basque sauté, is also included, but should be performed in the allegro portion of class and not as part of the first centre port de bras exercise. Two other forms of jumping pas de basque appear in chapter 11, "Allegro" (pp. 262 and 292). Both are executed as complete steps rather than as linking movements or transfer-of- weight exercises. It should be noted that abbreviated forms of pas de basque and temps lié are commonly used as linking steps in both pirouette and allegro combinations.

In class, Galina Shlyapina begins temps lié at 90° à la seconde with a développé plié à la seconde. Photo: J. Tomas Lopez.

159

# Temps Lié

*(in 4 counts, without plié during the transfer of weight)*

$$\frac{4}{4} \; \flat \; | \; \downarrow \; \sqcap \; \sqcap \; \downarrow \; |$$

## En avant

Prepare—          and ♪          one ♩          two ♪

From 5th croisé—

On the upbeat, execute a small preparatory "breath" port de bras.

Close the arms en bas with demi-plié.

Pointe tendue croisée devant in plié, lifting the arms to 1st. Incline the head upstage.

## Continued de côté

and ♪          five ♩          six ♪

Rise, lifting the eyes to the top hand and turning the body en face.

Demi-plié in 5th, lowering the top arm to 1st.

Stretch the front leg à la seconde, opening the arm from 1st to 2nd.

## The reverse

From 5th plié croisé—

Pointe tendue croisée derrière.

Step back to croisé devant.

Close in 5th devant.

Temps lié is one of the oldest traditional ballet steps. It is primarily useful as a basic transfer-of-weight execise. The courtly manner in which it is performed is extremely beneficial to the development of a student's coordination and sense of elegance and presence.

The floor pattern for temps lié is traditional and never varies: Step forward toward the front foot and close the back leg behind in 5th; step sideways toward the front foot and close the other leg in front in 5th. In reverse: Step backward toward the back foot and close the front foot in 5th; step sideways toward the back foot and close the other foot in back in 5th.

*and* ♪

Deepen plié, sliding the toe forward.

*three* ♪

Step directly onto a straight leg into pointe tendue croisée derrière.

*and* ♪

Close to 5th.

*four* ♩

Close to 5th.

*and* ♪

Increase the plié, sliding the toe outward to the side.

*seven* ♩

Take a wide step sideways onto the extended leg. Note the use of épaulement, with the palms turned to the floor in 2nd.

*eight* ♩

Close in front in 5th croisé, lowering the arms en bas.

Turn en face.

Extend back leg to the side.

Step to the side.

Close behind in 5th croisé.

Temps lié is first studied in the slow four-count form shown on pp. 160–61. As the student masters the movement, the two-count, and later the one-count, versions may be introduced.

## Temps lié en avant with plié   $\frac{4}{4}$
(in 2 counts)

and
one
and
two

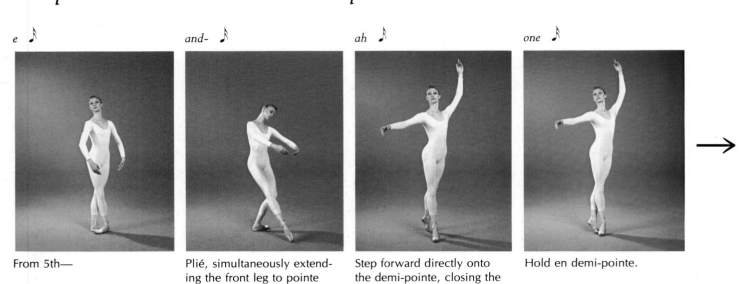

From 5th—

Plié, simultaneously sliding the foot to pointe tendue croisée devant and lifting the arms to 1st.

Transfer the weight forward through demi-plié in 4th position to the pose pointe tendue croisée derrière.

NOTE: En arrière follows the same pattern as the reverse sequence pictured on pp. 160-61.

## Temps lié en avant to the demi-pointe (in 1 count)   $\frac{2}{4}$

e
and-
ah
one

From 5th—

Plié, simultaneously extending the front leg to pointe tendue croisée devant and lifting the arms to 1st.

Step forward directly onto the demi-pointe, closing the back leg **immediately** to 5th (without dragging it along the floor).

Hold en demi-pointe.

NOTE: En arrière follows the same pattern as the reverse sequence pictured on pp. 160–61.

## CONTINUED DE CÔTÉ

*and* ♪

On the upbeat, turn en face, closing the back leg to 5th with a small rise. At the same time, the eyes lift to the hand en haut and follow it down as it lowers into 1st position.

*three* ♪

Extend the front leg to pointe tendue à la seconde in plié, opening the arms in 2nd.

*and-* ♪

Transfer the weight sideways through demi-plié in 2nd position.

*ah* ♪

Straighten into pointe tendue à la seconde and close the extended leg in front (on count 4) into 5th position croisé, lowering the arms en bas (not shown).

## CONTINUED DE CÔTÉ

*e* ♪

As the body turns en face, the eyes lift to the hand en haut and follow it down as it lowers into 1st position.

*and-* ♪

Extend the front leg à la seconde, staying in plié and opening the arms to the side.

*ah* ♪

Step to the side onto demi-pointe, quickly closing the foot in front to 5th.

*two* ♩

From this position, lower the heels and close the arms to 5th en bas in croisé (not shown).

# Temps lié at 90° en demi-pointe

This movement may also be executed on the whole foot and en pointe.

EN AVANT

*Prepare*— ♪       *one* ♩       *two* ♩       *three* ♩

From 5th croisé— | Execute the fondu and retiré devant simultaneously. | Développé 90° croisé devant. | Piqué en avant to attitude croisée derrière. Lower the heel gently on count 4 (not shown), maintaining the 90° pose.

EN ARRIÈRE

*Preparation*— ♪       *one* ♩       *two* ♩       *three* ♩

From 5th croisé, fondu retiré and développé croisé derrière in plié.

Piqué directly back into attitude croisée devant and lower heel gently.

NOTE: In the Soviet syllabus version of temps lié en arrière at 90°, the front leg, instead of lifting directly to the attitude, executes a développé croisé devant, passing through retiré devant on the piqué.

Turn en face, closing the back leg through a small rise in 5th. Eyes lift to the hand en haut.

Lower the side arm through 5th en bas and lift it to 1st to meet the top arm (as it lowers from 5th). Simultaneously execute fondu retiré devant.

Développé à la seconde at 90° and piqué to the side directly onto the demi-pointe, immediately lifting the other leg to 90°. Lower the supporting heel gently, maintaining the 90° extension. On count 8 (not shown), close the leg in front to 5th croisé, bringing the arms en bas.

*and* ♪                  *five* ♩                  *six* ♩                  *seven* ♩

Turn en face, closing the front leg in 5th en demi-pointe. Eyes lift to the hand en haut.

Lower the side arm through 5th en bas and lift it to 1st to meet the top arm (as it lowers from 5th). Simultaneously execute fondu retiré derrière.

Développé à la seconde at 90° and piqué to the side directly onto the demi-pointe, immediately lifting the other leg to 90°. Lower the supporting heel gently, maintaining the 90° extension. On count 8 (not shown) close the leg in back to 5th croisé, bringing the arms en bas.

# Pas de Basque à Terre

It is important to remember that pas de basque is a **traveling** step. To be effective, it must be executed in a very broad, almost lush manner, covering as much distance as possible. In its advanced form (in one count) it should be performed as one continuous, sweeping movement without pausing in any of the positions.

In the Soviet syllabus, pas de basque is executed as a jumping movement, in the following manner: After completing the rond de jambe and transfer of weight to the side as pictured here, slide the foot through 1st (either to the front or to the back) and execute an assemblé par terre (either en avant or en arrière), finishing in 5th position plié. However, I often include this movement in class as pictured here (without a final assemblé) in a variety of tempi in centre combinations.

EN AVANT (IN THE SIMPLE FORM, IN 4 COUNTS)

one          two          e          and

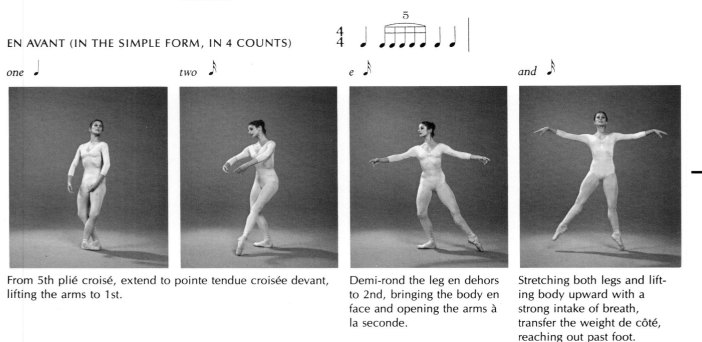

From 5th plié croisé, extend to pointe tendue croisée devant, lifting the arms to 1st.

Demi-rond the leg en dehors to 2nd, bringing the body en face and opening the arms à la seconde.

Stretching both legs and lifting body upward with a strong intake of breath, transfer the weight de côté, reaching out past foot.

NOTE: Seven head positions are used in pas de basque en avant.

EN ARRIÈRE (IN THE INTERMEDIATE FORM, IN 2 COUNTS)

and          one          e          ah

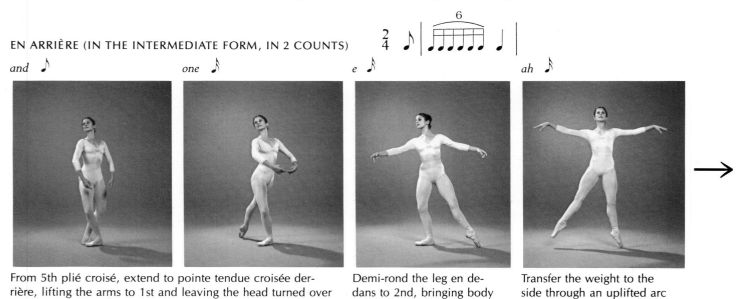

From 5th plié croisé, extend to pointe tendue croisée derrière, lifting the arms to 1st and leaving the head turned over the downstage shoulder.

Demi-rond the leg en dedans to 2nd, bringing body en face and opening arms à la seconde.

Transfer the weight to the side through an uplifted arc in 2nd.

NOTE: In pas de basque en arrière, only six positions of the head are used.

*e* ♪

Finish the transfer in fondue pointe tendue à la seconde. The head has changed to the new supporting side.

*ah* ♪

Lower the arms through 5th en bas, closing the leg and passing it through 1st on the diagonal.

*three* ♩

*four* ♩

Extend the leg croisé devant, lifting the arms to 1st. Deepen the plié and slide the toe as far forward as possible before transferring the weight en avant through 4th position demi-plié (not shown) to the croisé derrière pose.

*and* ♪

Finish the transfer in fondue pointe tendue à la seconde. The head has changed to the new supporting side.

*e* ♪

Lower the arms through 5th en bas, closing the leg and passing it through 1st on the diagonal. The head remains turned over the downstage shoulder.

*ah* ♪

*two* ♩

Extend the leg croisé derrière, lifting the arms to 1st. Deepen the plié and slide the toe as far backward as possible before transferring the weight en arrière through 4th position demi-plié (not shown) to the croisé devant pose.

Both versions of pas de basque pictured here are executed in one musical count with all movement before the final pose occurring on the upbeat in one smooth, continuous motion. The final position is executed on the count.

Other forms of pas de basque jumped and en pointe appear on pp. 172, 262, 292, 360.

## *"Stepped" pas de basque* (to open pose with demi-rond at 45°)

SHOWN EN AVANT

From 5th plié, extend the leg croisé devant, lifting it into a demi-rond en dehors at 45° in plié and opening the arms à la seconde.

Simultaneously, rotate the body en face, leaning slightly away from the working leg as it continues to demi-rond to the side.

## *Petit pas de basque sauté*

SHOWN EN AVANT

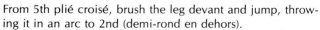

From 5th plié croisé, brush the leg devant and jump, throwing it in an arc to 2nd (demi-rond en dehors).

Simultaneously turn the body en face, leaning slightly away from the arcing leg as the arms open à la seconde.

Step onto the working leg, transferring the weight **widely** to the side. The arms lower en bas.

Bend the other leg through passé at ankle height to a low développé croisé devant, and piqué en avant to attitude croisée derrière. The arms lift through 1st and open to 3rd high on the piqué.

 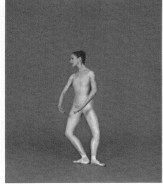 

Transfer the weight sideways in the air and land on the leading leg. Immediately slide the other leg forward through 1st position to 4th in plié.

The arms lower en bas and lift to 1st. From 4th position the movement may be completed by straightening and closing the back leg or by executing an assemblé par terre en avant.

# 7 ✍ The Method for Turning Centre Barre and Petit Allegro Steps

Centre barre movements performed en tournant are not only challenging but also valuable as preparatory exercises for all pirouettes. Indeed, I recommend that tendu en tournant be the first form of turns on one leg studied by lower-level intermediate students. Such exercises are beneficial because they emphasize the important practice of rotating the inner thigh and supporting heel forward when initiating a turn. They are also useful in reinforcing the correct manner for coordinating the arms and head with the body when turning.

All centre barre movements performed en tournant require considerable control and stability on the part of the dancer. They are particularly strengthening for the muscles of the torso. Students learn how to "stay over the supporting side" and how not to be thrown off-balance by either the force of the turn or the movements of the working leg.

The following centre barre exercises are performed en tournant with eighth, quarter, half, and full turns: tendus, dégagés, ronds de jambe par terre and en l'air, fondus, frappés, demis and grands ronds de jambe, développés, and grands battements. Some of these, such as tendus and ronds de jambe par terre, are always executed turning on the whole foot. Others, such as frappés, may (in advanced classes) be performed staying en demi-pointe while turning.

Petit allegro movements, such as temps levés, assemblés, petits jetés, ballonnés, and brisés, are also often performed en tournant. Landing with control from a jump that includes a rotation in the air is particularly challenging. Such jumps are difficult for students, but they provide important preparation for the much more difficult grand allegro movements en tournant (for example, grands jetés entrelacés, tours en l'air, revoltades) that are required of advanced dancers.

The pictures on the following pages illustrate the correct method for executing centre barre and petit allegro movements en tournant. Because space is limited, only a few of these types of exercises can be pictured. Teachers should use their imaginations and, following the rules laid down here, utilize the full scope of possibilities in this category of classroom exercises.

# Centre Barre Exercises en Tournant

## Battement tendu en tournant

Tendu en tournant may be executed with quarter, half, and full turns in all directions and poses. It is incorrect to change direction when closing the foot to 5th.

### DEVANT BY QUARTER-TURN EN DEHORS

Turn **in 5th position**, sliding the foot to the pointe tendue at the last moment upon changing direction. Close to 5th in the new direction (not shown). The weight is on the ball of the back foot in 5th during the turn, with the heel barely released from the floor.

### DERRIÈRE BY HALF-TURN EN DEDANS

Turn **in 5th position**, sliding the foot to the pointe tendue at the last moment upon changing direction. Close to 5th in the new direction. The weight is on the ball of the front foot in 5th during the turn, with the heel barely released from the floor.

## Battement tendu with fouetté

### SHOWN EN DEDANS WITH HALF-TURN

From pointe tendue devant, plié on the supporting leg, lowering the top arm into the preparatory 3rd position for turns. Close the arms to 1st, executing a fouetté en dedans à terre through écarté to 3rd arabesque. The supporting heel must actively press forward throughout the movement. Close to 5th in the new direction.

# Rond de jambe par terre en tournant

In this exercise the body turns **at the same time** that the working leg inscribes the outward half-circle on the floor. The leg passes through 1st with the body in place, facing the new direction. These ronds de jambe may be performed with quarter, half, and full turns, both en dehors and en dedans.

SHOWN EN DEHORS
BY QUARTER-TURN

From 5th, rond de jambe en dehors, turning the body en dehors.

# Pas de basque en tournant

These may be executed with quarter, half, three-quarter, and full turns, both en dehors and en dedans.

SHOWN EN AVANT BY HALF-TURN

From 5th plié, rond de jambe the working leg en dehors, simultaneously executing a half-turn en dehors.

# Battement divisé en quarts *(Soviet syllabus)*

This is an excellent exercise for balance, control, and stability. It is usually performed in a series of four sets, each completing a quarter-turn, but may also be done with half-turns. It is also performed en dedans.

SHOWN EN DEHORS

From 5th, passé développé devant, lifting the arms to 1st.

Complete the rond de jambe **fully** to the pointe tendue derrière. (There is a tendency to cut corners here. The leg must finish behind the hip and not out to the side in back.) Having arrived in the new direction, pass the foot through 1st to the front (not shown).

Transfer the weight sideways. Slide the foot through 1st and step en avant in croisé in the new direction.

Plié at 90° and relevé, opening the leg and arms à la seconde while simultaneously executing a quarter-turn en dehors. Lower the supporting heel without plié, bending the working leg to retiré at the side of the knee and closing the arms en bas.

# Passé relevé en tournant

This is a slow, controlled movement, rather like a tour lent en demi-pointe. The supporting heel must be strongly pressed forward throughout. Passé relevé en tournant may be executed both en dehors and en dedans and with quarter, half, and full turns.

SHOWN WITH THREE-
QUARTER TURN
EN DEDANS TO 3RD
ARABESQUE À TERRE

From plié pointe tendue devant, relevé, turning toward the back foot and lifting the front leg directly to the passé position with the toe in front of the knee. The arms simultaneously close to 1st.

# Flic-flac en tournant

SHOWN EN DEHORS TO CROISÉ DEVANT

From 2nd en face, flic to cou-de-pied derrière, executing a relevé with quarter-turn en dehors. Open the leg slightly to the side, continuing to turn. The arms lower en bas on the initial flic, then lift to 1st.

NOTE: It is essential that the supporting heel be strongly pressed forward throughout this movement.

# Promenade *(tour lent in Soviet syllabus)*

SHOWN EN DEDANS
À LA SECONDE

Promenades are slow turns executed on the whole foot with the other foot raised in retiré, attitude, or fully extended at 90° (or above). They are most commonly used in grand adagio exercises in centre work. Performed in attitude or with full extension at 90°, they are considered the basic preparatory exercises for grandes pirouettes. They are executed in all poses, turning both en dehors and en dedans.

Keeping the leg at 90°, execute approximately eight tiny, equal pivots of the supporting heel forward.

Continue turning on the demi-pointe; the lifted toe slips around the side of the knee to the back. Finish with plié développé to 3rd arabesque à terre.

Flac to cou-de-pied devant, continuing to turn en dehors. Finish **on the demi-pointe** with développé to croisé devant 45°. From this point the movement is usually completed with a coupé over or a tombé en avant.

Turn en dedans in what appears to be one slow, continuous rotation.

Keep the weight firmly on the supporting side to prevent wavering during the movement. Throughout the rotation, shoulders are directly over the top of the hips, arms stay aligned with each other in 2nd, and supporting knee is straight.

# Petit Allegro Steps en Tournant

## Petit jeté en tournant

SHOWN BY HALF-TURN DERRIÈRE (DESSUS)

From 5th plié croisé, brush the back leg à la seconde, jumping and **simultaneously** turning en l'air toward the front leg. Complete a half-turn, landing in fondu sur le cou-de-pied derrière.

NOTE: These jetés en tournant are also executed devant (dessous). In both directions (dessus and dessous), the body may turn either toward the brushing foot or toward the "push-off" foot (as shown). They may be performed with quarter-turns as well.

## Brisé en tournant

SHOWN EN AVANT WITH QUARTER-TURN

From 5th plié effacé, brush the back leg, jumping and turning in the new direction. Execute a brisé en avant, traveling downstage. Close the front leg to 5th upon completion of the movement (not shown).

NOTE: These jumps are also executed en arrière, with the dancer traveling backward and turning toward the leg being thrown to the back.

# 8 ~ The Traditional Turns of Classical Ballet

There are three categories of traditional ballet turns executed en relevé: (1) those in which the weight is quickly changed from one leg to the other during the turn (e.g., chaînés, glissades en tournant), (2) those in which a single pose on one leg is sustained for the duration of the turn (e.g., pirouettes in retiré, grandes pirouettes, piqué turns), and (3) those on one leg in which the pose of the body changes during the turn (e.g., fouettés ronds de jambe en tournant, grandes pirouettes finished with fouetté). Several examples of the most common forms of turns in all three of these categories are pictured on the following pages. All are shown with a single rotation, as they are first learned, but all may also be performed with multiple rotations.

Women practice all turns en pointe, as well as en demi-pointe; examples of both are interspersed throughout this chapter. Additional turns en pointe are demonstrated in chapter 14, "Pointe Work." Traditionally, men perform a greater number of turns from a single relevé preparation than do women. The ability to do this is emphasized in their training, and some virtuoso male dancers have been known to execute more than ten rotations without stopping. For a woman, the performance of three or more rotations en pointe is considered a commendable technical feat.

It should also be stressed that form and control while turning are ultimately more important than the number of rotations performed. The beautiful effect of spinning depends on the dancer's ability to maintain the shape of his or her pose en relevé, without any distortion or show of effort whatsoever. Two perfectly executed rotations finished with ease and control are always preferable to four frantically performed ones finished with a crash landing. As with all other movements in classical ballet, the challenge of turning is to make it look effortless.

I recommend that students be introduced to turning movements gradually almost from the beginning of their training at the barre. Commentary on this method appears on p. 141. The correct progression for the study of pirouettes in retiré, as well as for grandes pirouettes, is as follows:

1. At the barre: the acquisition of stability on one leg on the whole foot in the correct pirouette position.
2. At the barre: the same as no. 1, but on demi-pointe.
3. In the centre: the practice of nos. 1 and 2 and then tour lent (promenade) in the pose.
4. At the barre: the practice of half-turns in the pose
5. In the centre: the practice of quarter- and half-turns, which are completed by tour lent (promenade) before lowering the lifted leg.
6. In the centre: full (single) turns in the pose.
7. In the centre: double, then multiple, turns in the pose.

NOTE: When single and double turns in retiré have been mastered in the centre, they may then be included in the barre work.

Turns such as fouettés ronds de jambe en tournant or grandes pirouettes finished with fouetté are advanced movements and should not be attempted by students until they can easily perform multiple pirouettes and grandes pirouettes. The basic coordinations and component parts of these difficult turns are first studied slowly at the barre and then in the centre on the whole foot. In this way, students have time to analyze exactly what must happen technically during the fast transitions of position that occur when these turns are executed up to tempo in their final form.

The recommended order for the study of classical ballet turns from the easiest (no. 1) to the most difficult (no. 13) is listed below:

1. Bourrée turns in 5th position
2. Détournés
3. Soutenus en tournant
4. Glissades en tournant (piqués soutenus en tournant)
5. Pirouettes from 2nd and 5th positions in retiré
6. Pirouettes from 4th position in retiré
7. Piqués en tournant in retiré
8. Chaînés
9. Grandes pirouettes, in the following order: attitude derrière (en dedans, then en dehors), arabesque (en dedans), à la seconde (en dedans, then en dehors), attitude devant (en dedans, then en dehors), devant (en dedans, then en dehors), arabesque (en dehors)
10. Piqué turns at 90°
11. Fouettés ronds de jambe en tournant
12. Grandes pirouettes sautillées
13. Grandes pirouettes finished with fouetté or with pirouettes in retiré

Teachers should note that it is counterproductive to introduce any turn to a class before the students have gained complete stability in the pose of that turn en demi-pointe without turning. The only thing students learn from falling over is to be fearful. Requiring them to attempt movements for which their bodies have not been adequately prepared and strengthened is not only dangerous but also a waste of time. Anxiety about turning, which is common among many dancers, is often the result of unnecessary negative experiences early in their training.

In addition to possessing the strength to sustain a particular pose en relevé, several other important elements are necessary to execute turns successfully: (1) the ability to "spot," (2) the ability to utilize breathing correctly, (3) the ability to correctly coordinate the arms, (4) the ability to maintain turn-out while turning, (5) the mastery of efficient preparations, and (6) the ability to control the end of a turn.

"Spotting," or the ability to whip the head around quickly with each rotation of the body, re-focusing the eyes on each turn to prevent dizziness, is an essential skill. Some students take to it naturally. Others, particularly those with excessive tension in their necks, weak vision, or inner ear problems, can have substantial difficulty mastering it. A student should never be allowed to acquire the habit of turning without spotting. Not only can it be dangerous, but such a student will never feel comfortable turning (especially at a fast tempo), nor will he or she ever be able to master multiple turns. And once this bad habit becomes firmly ingrained, it is almost impossible to break. Instruction on the correct manner of using the head when turning appears on p. 38.

A dancer practicing turns will often find it helpful to exert conscious control over his or her breathing. Before a turn, as the preparatory plié is deepened, the dancer should breathe out. Then, executing the relevé into the turn, the dancer should breathe in sharply and hold the breath throughout the duration of the turn. The process of breathing out in the preparation for the turn often relaxes a student, making it easier to feel the correct placement of the body in the preparatory position. The intake of breath often helps to sustain the dancer en relevé throughout the turn. It also reinforces the pulled-up feeling of the muscles in the turning pose.

The correct coordination of the arms in turns is essential for producing the momentum that keeps a turn going. Well-placed, efficiently used arms also contribute to the desirable look of ease while turning. Instruction on the correct use of the arms in turns appears on pp. 36–37.

Turn-out must be maintained throughout the entire duration of a turn for one main reason: when one or both of the legs turns in, the force of the spin is invariably lost, and the turn will grind to an early halt. In addition, a turned-in position is classically incorrect and unaesthetic in appearance.

There are many different kinds and sizes of preparations for turns. The most common are those in demi-plié in 2nd, 5th, and 4th positions. However, turns may also be executed from grand plié, as well as from a jump, coupé, step-tombé, or piqué. All forms must be mastered. A well-executed preparation provides the correct impetus and force for a turn. One should never throw oneself into a turning movement without a moment of thought and a consciously controlled preparation, regardless of how speedily it is executed. Failure to think and prepare is dangerous and will leave the success of the subsequent turn in the hands of the gods, rather than in the control of the dancer. Details on how to correctly execute the preparations for all turns shown on the following pages appear in the captions under the photographs. Additional information is in chapter 1, "Basic Concepts," on pp. 36–37.

Finally, a dancer must learn how to finish a turn with aplomb and control. This is as important a part of technique as is turning itself. Falling out of a pirouette is a guaranteed method for destroying its effect, regardless of how perfectly it is performed. Dancers should be encouraged to finish properly **every** turn they execute in class, "no matter what." Many variables affect turning technique: floor surface, nerves, and stamina, as well as basic skills and placement; so, more often than not, a turn may be a little "off." Dancers must learn to compensate by "saving" a turn with the execution of a good finish. This is important preparation for what will be expected of them onstage. Many classical variations end with a virtuoso display of pirouettes. A strongly executed final pose after a series of turns that happen to be a little "off" can save the day. Most of the time the audience will not even notice that things were less than perfect. It takes skill and split-second timing to save a series of fast turns gone awry. Onstage, nervous, blinded by lights, often somewhat disoriented and exhausted at the end of a variation, a dancer has only his or her reflexes to rely upon. These reflexes, schooled to finish "no matter what," must be developed in the classroom.

# Pirouette

## Pirouette en dehors from 4th position

Prepare in 4th position demi-plié en face.

On the upbeat, deepen the plié and open the front arm halfway.

Relevé, closing both arms quickly to 1st position, executing a passé with the back leg to retiré devant and turning toward it. (Arms may also be placed in 4th or 5th position for the turn.)

## Several alternate preparations for pirouette en dehors from 4th position

4th position croisé.

For men only: wide, open 4th position.

4th position effacé with low 2nd arabesque arm.

Balanchine-style croisé lunge with a straight back leg and elongated front arm.

## Pirouette en dehors from grand plié

From 5th position, grand plié croisé, bringing the arms into the preparatory 3rd position for pirouettes.

**Without** lowering the supporting heel to the floor, straighten the supporting leg en demi-pointe, lifting the working leg to retiré devant and turning en dehors.

The turn is away from the supporting leg.

Finish closing the leg back into 5th position croisé plié with arms opening to demi-seconde, palms up.

In pirouettes the force for turning is provided by:

1. The **immediate** closing of the second arm at the moment of relevé (**not** by the opening of the first arm).
2. The supporting heel pressing forward at the moment of relevé.
3. The fast straightening of the knees from a generous plié position.
4. A slight rotation of the upper torso into the direction of the turn.

The pose in which a pirouette finishes is determined by the teacher. There are many possibilities, including poses on the knee, poses on both feet (in 4th or 5th), and poses in plié with one leg extended in pointe tendue or at various levels en l'air.

NOTE: Pirouettes from grand plié are most commonly performed in grand adagio exercises. They are often finished with a développé to an open pose (in any direction). They are also executed from 1st position and en dedans, but are rarely done from 2nd or 4th positions or with grandes pirouettes.

## *Pirouette en dedans from 4th*
*(bringing lifted foot directly to retiré)*

Execute a preparatory lunge position croisé, head en face.

On the upbeat, deepen the plié, opening the arm in 1st halfway out to 2nd.

## *Pirouette en dedans from 4th with fouetté to retiré*
*(also called pirouette tire-bouchon)*

Execute a preparatory lunge croisé, head en face.

On the upbeat, deepen the plié, throwing the back leg directly on a diagonal path to 2nd en face, opening the arms à la seconde.

Relevé retiré devant, raising the arms from 2nd to 5th en haut (or closing to 1st or 4th) and turning toward the supporting leg.

NOTE: If an en dedans turn is to finish in croisé with the eyes looking to the corner, then the "spot" will be to that corner, instead of en face (as pictured).

In demi-caractère pirouettes en dedans, the leg is often placed retiré derrière, with the supporting leg either straight or bent in a small plié.

Relevé retiré devant, turning toward the supporting leg and closing the arms to 1st (or 4th or 5th) position.

Finish closing the leg in front into 5th croisé plié, opening the arms demi-seconde.

 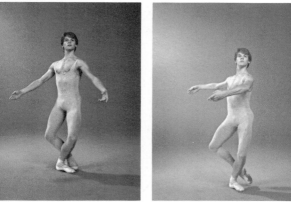

Finish closing the leg in front in 5th croisé plié, opening the arms to demi-seconde, **or—**

Alternate finish: Tombé coupé over to fondu sur le cou-de-pied derrière, lowering one arm directly to 1st from 5th, opening the other outward to 2nd.

## *Several alternate preparations for pirouette en dedans*

Lunge en face.

Lunge effacé.

Lunge upstage en diagonale. (If the turn finishes downstage, the "spot" must change on the first half-turn.)

# Examples of pirouettes finished in open positions

## Pirouette en dehors finished in croisé derrière at 90°

Relevé on the front leg, turning away from the supporting leg, lifting the back leg to retiré devant, and closing the arms to 1st.

## Pirouette en dehors finished in poses devant at 90°

Relevé on the front leg, turning away from the supporting leg, lifting the back leg to retiré devant, and closing the arms to 1st.

## Pirouette en dedans finished in 1st arabesque

On the upbeat, open the leg and arms à la seconde (as for tire-bouchon, p. 182) and relevé, closing both arms to 4th (side arm lifts directly to 5th) and turning en dedans with the foot in retiré derrière.

In the last quarter of the turn, lower the top arm through 1st and open to finish in the pose 1st arabesque plié.

In the final quarter of the turn, begin to pass the leg from front to back alongside the knee, in anticipation of the final pose in 3rd arabesque plié, **or**—

Alternate finish: attitude croisée derrière.

Finish with a fast développé to plié effacé devant, lifting the downstage arm to 5th and opening the upstage arm to 2nd, **or**—

Alternate finish: croisé devant.

## Pirouette en dehors finished with tombé

The en dehors turn is completed en face **en demi-pointe**, with a sharp opening of the lifted leg à la seconde.

Tombé de coté to finish, or to prepare for the next movement.

# Piqué Turns

*(jetés en tournant in Soviet syllabus, posé turns in English school)*

EN DEHORS

Prepare in pointe tendue croisée devant.

On the upbeat, tombé diagonally downstage into effacé derrière and brush back leg **directly** (without rond de jambe) to 2nd, deepening the plié and opening the arms à la seconde.

An immediate closing of both arms to 1st position at the moment of the piqué is essential to the smooth coordination of piqué turns en dedans. Opening the upstage arm to the side on the coupé-fondu, instead of to 1st arabesque as pictured, will result in a delayed closing of the arms that will impede the speed of the turn.

EN DEDANS

Prepare in pointe tendue croisée devant.

Plié on the upbeat, with a quarter-turn en dehors to effacé devant, opening the front arm to 1st arabesque.

Piqué onto the front leg, turning toward it, bringing the back leg retiré derrière and closing the arms to 1st.

## Three possible finishes for piqué turns en dedans

EXAMPLE 1

From retiré derrière, slip the foot forward past the knee, executing a failli to 4th arabesque à terre.

With an **immediate** exchange of weight from one foot to the other, piqué onto demi-pointe **in front of** the supporting leg through 5th (or a very small 4th) position, closing the arms quickly to 1st.

The turn is "away" from the supporting leg, with the lifted leg in retiré devant.

NOTE: This turn may be finished by passing the leg to the back to 5th plié, or with a lunge in 4th position, or with a tombé en avant or de côté.

Continue turning "toward" the supporting leg.

### EXAMPLE 2

### EXAMPLE 3

Lower supporting heel and développé plié to 1st arabesque.

Lower retiré leg through 5th position back into coupé under, finishing in plié dégagé effacé devant.

# Examples of piqué turns in open positions at 90°

## Piqué en dedans in attitude derrière

Begin in a preparatory pointe tendue pose. Plié, turning to effacé devant, then piqué, turning en dedans in attitude derrière. The leg is lifted by means of a grand battement to the full 90° height **without delay**. The leading arm opens strongly to 2nd into the direction of the turn while the other arm lifts directly to 5th on a slight diagonal trajectory in front of the shoulder.

# Pirouette en dedans–en dehors

## (without coming off pointe or demi-pointe)

From a preparatory pointe tendue pose—

Tombé en avant in effacé and execute a relevé fouetté turn (back leg to 2nd, then to retiré devant) en dedans on the front leg, closing the arms to 1st.

From this point, begin to lower the lifted leg.

NOTE: There are no pauses whatsoever during this movement. The first turn (en dedans) goes immediately into the second turn (en dehors).

## *Piqué en dedans à la seconde*

From a plié effacé devant preparation, piqué onto the front leg, simultaneously executing a grand battement à la seconde **through 1st position** and turning en dedans "toward" the supporting leg. The lifted leg must be thrown immediately around the body with the torso and leading arm opening strongly into the direction of the turn. The arms are placed in 2nd directly over the lifted leg. The level of the leg must not be allowed to drop during the turn.

Place the leg into a small 4th position croisé, staying en pointe.

Transfer the weight onto the downstage leg, lifting the other leg retiré devant and turning en dehors.

Finish taking the leg back to lunge in arabesque croisée (or open it to dégagé effacé devant en pointe, as preparation for tombé into the next movement).

## *Piqué emboîté en tournant by half-turns*

Plié on the upbeat, turning to effacé devant.

Piqué en dedans, executing a quarter-turn, bringing the back foot retiré front, and exchanging the arms across the body in low 3rd position.

# Tours Chaînés *(also called chaînés déboulés)*

These small, fast, linked turns are usually performed in a series and may begin with either a piqué or a tombé. Both versions are pictured here. The arms open on the preparatory plié, then close to 1st and remain there for the duration of the series of turns.

## *Chaînés with the second step in 1st position*

**INITIATED WITH A PIQUÉ**

From the preparatory pointe tendue pose, plié, turning to effacé to face the direction of the turns; then piqué onto the downstage leg, drawing the back leg forward through 1st position. The arms close to 1st.

## *Chaînés with the second step in 6th position (Soviet syllabus)*

**INITIATED WITH A TOMBÉ**

Tombé effacé devant.

Bring the back leg around en dedans.

Close to 6th position, continuing to turn upstage.

Lower the retiré leg to close in front in 5th (continuing to turn en dedans) and **simultaneously** lift the back foot to retiré devant, pulling the knee back and turning en dehors. The arms change across the body to the other low 3rd position.

To continue in a series from the point pictured above: step into the downstage effacé direction, staying en pointe, bringing the back foot to retiré devant, and turning en dedans. May be finished with a tombé en avant, or by lowering off pointe to plié while extending the lifted leg devant.

Step downstage into 1st position, continuing to turn upstage.

Transfer the weight onto the downstage leg in 1st, turning on it and drawing the other leg around it in 5th.

Open the leading leg and step downstage in 1st. Continue in a series.

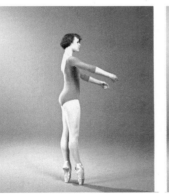

Transfer the weight onto the downstage leg, turning on it and drawing the other leg around it through 5th position.

Open the leading leg and step downstage in 1st. Continue in a series.

# Glissade en Tournant

From a preparatory pointe tendue pose—

Plié, turning to effacé devant.

Piqué onto the downstage leg, quickly bringing back leg to 5th croisé in front and closing arms to 1st.

NOTE: This step is also executed in the reverse (en dehors).

# Soutenu en Tournant

EN DEDANS

Tombé croisé en avant. Demi-rond the back leg en dedans to 2nd, bringing the body en face and opening the arms à la seconde.

Close the leg front into 5th croisé en relevé, closing arms to 1st and turning up-stage.

EN DEHORS

From the preparatory pose "B+" croisé, coupé under and tombé de côté to 2nd onto the back leg.

Relevé, drawing the leg in 2nd to the back in 5th, lifting arms in reverse to 5th, and turning upstage toward the back foot.

NOTE: Other variations of port de bras suitable for soutenu turns include 1st, 3rd, 4th, or simply leaving the arms à la seconde.

Transfer the weight onto the front foot, turning upstage toward the back leg, which readjusts around to 5th front.

Finish in plié in 5th croisé, opening the arms demi-seconde.

   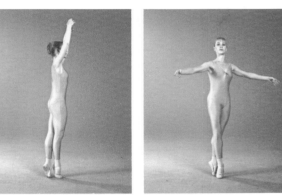

Transfer the weight onto the front foot, continuing to turn upstage, readjusting the back foot around to 5th in front, and lifting the arms to 5th en haut.

Finish in 5th en demi-pointe (or in plié), opening the arms en dehors to 2nd.

Transfer the weight onto the front foot and turn upstage, readjusting the other leg around to 5th front.

Finish in plié (or en demi-pointe) in 5th croisé, opening the arms en dehors to 2nd.

# Fouetté en Tournant

In fouettés en tournant, it is incorrect for the thigh of the whipping leg to move up and down during the opening and closing movements of the leg. Once the level of the thigh has been established in the retiré, it must not drop when opening forward, nor lift when closing for the turn. The level of the leg varies somewhat from dancer to dancer, ranging from 60° to 90°.

## Fouetté en dedans—en dehors

Tombé croisé en avant as preparation, and sharply demi-rond to 2nd on the upbeat, bringing the body en face and opening the arms à la seconde.

Fouetté en dedans, initially bringing the foot retiré devant, then slipping it to the back of the knee as the turn is completed.

## Fouetté rond de jambe en tournant

The precise coordination of the arms opening and closing with the whipping leg is essential to the smooth execution of these turns. They are usually performed in a series, such as the famous thirty-two fouettés in the female dancer's coda in the Black Swan pas de deux.

Both the pas de bourrée en tournant and the pirouette en dehors preparations are acceptable ways to begin **either** of the two fouettés en tournant below.

From pointe tendue croisée derrière, plié with demi-rond to 2nd en face and close the leg in 5th in front into pas de bourrée en tournant en dedans, as preparation for the fouetté turn.

Coupé under into plié croisé devant.

## Fouetté en tournant with working leg opening to the side (Soviet syllabus)

Begin with pirouettes en dehors from 4th position.

Coupé under through 5th behind, into extension croisé devant (just below hip level) in plié.

Demi-rond and fouetté en dehors.

To finish: close behind or extend croisé devant for tombé into the next movement.

Demi-rond to the side. Opening of front arm to the side is exactly coordinated with opening of leg.

Relevé fouetté en dehors, turning in retiré devant, with arms closing sharply to 1st position.

Fondu croisé devant; the upstage arm opens **directly** à la seconde. (Do not allow it to open in back of shoulder.)

Plié à la seconde.

Relevé retiré devant, turning en dehors.

Plié à la seconde.

# Grande Pirouette

Grandes pirouettes are advanced movements. They are commonly used in grand adagio combinations, in which they are executed in a smooth, sustained manner. They may be performed with single, double, or triple turns. Occasionally, male virtuoso dancers may perform a grande pirouette with more than three rotations from a single plié-relevé.

Grandes pirouettes are performed in all poses, turning both en dehors and en dedans. The manner in which any of these turns is finished is determined

## Grandes pirouettes à la seconde

EN DEDANS

From the preparatory croisé lunge, relevé with grand battement à la seconde, turning en dedans, "toward" the supporting leg. Do not rond de jambe the leg en dedans into 2nd position, but rather direct it diagonally upward through an open 1st position. Open the arms strongly to 2nd as the turn begins, then lift them directly to 5th en haut.

EN DEHORS

Execute a preparatory plié in 2nd (or use the standard 4th position plié for turns en dehors, in which case the leg to be lifted is placed behind in 4th).

Relevé with grand battement à la seconde, opening the leading arm, torso, and lifted leg strongly into the direction of the turn (upstage, "away" from the supporting leg).

From 2nd, both arms lift immediately to 5th.

NOTE: Grandes pirouettes à la seconde may also be performed with the arms remaining in 2nd position.

by the teacher or choreographer. There are many possibilities, a variety of which are pictured here.

When executing grandes pirouettes, the preparatory deepening of the plié, opening of the leading arm (and torso) into the direction of the turn, and succeeding relevé and grand battement are performed in **one smooth, unbroken, coordinated motion**. Any hestitation or pause during this succession of movements will destroy the force necessary to produce the spin.

Continue turning until the body comes en face, at which point the arms open en dehors to 2nd in anticipation of the finish.

Finish with a failli across to a croisé lunge. Alternate finish: plié en face in 2nd at 90° and then execute a soutenu en tournant en dedans.

Finish en face in demi-plié à la seconde, **or—**

From 2nd position en face en demi-pointe, lower supporting heel into plié while simultaneously executing a demi-rond de jambe en dehors to 4th arabesque.

# Grandes pirouettes in attitude

## Grande pirouette en dedans in attitude derrière

From the preparatory lunge croisé, deepen the plié, simultaneously opening the downstage arm à la seconde.

Immediately relevé with grand battement to attitude derrière, turning en dedans "toward" the supporting leg. The arm on the "closing" side of the body lifts directly to 5th on a diagonal trajectory slightly in front of the shoulder.

## Grande pirouette en dehors in attitude derrière

In this movement, the weight must be maintained well forward, with the lifted leg strongly pressed around in back of the body. It is incorrect to allow the supporting heel to "slip" (turn in) just before the relevé.

From the preparatory 4th position demi-plié, deepen the plié, opening the front arm à la seconde and spiraling the torso into the direction of the turn.

Immediately relevé with grand battement to attitude derrière, lifting the arms directly to 5th en haut.

## Grande pirouette en dedans in attitude devant

From the preparatory lunge croisé, deepen the plié, simultaneously opening the front arm à la seconde.

Immediately relevé with grand battement to 2nd. Demi-rond the leg en dedans to attitude devant, lifting the opposition arm directly to 5th en haut. The turn is en dedans, "toward" the supporting leg.

Continue to turn en dedans, keeping the weight well forward and maintaining the height of the leg at 90°. Finish the turn by lowering the supporting heel into plié while sustaining a 90° pose; or with a failli to croisé; or with a soutenu turn en dedans.

Continue to turn en dehors. Do not allow the level of the lifted leg to drop. Finish the turn by lowering the supporting heel into plié while sustaining a 90° pose, or by lowering the back leg to the floor into a 4th position lunge croisé.

Continue to turn en dedans, maintaining the leg crossed in front of the body at the 90° level. Finish the turn by lowering the supporting heel into plié while maintaining a 90° pose; or with a tombé en avant; or with a soutenu turn en dedans.

# Grandes pirouettes in devant and arabesque poses

## Grande pirouette en dehors in devant position

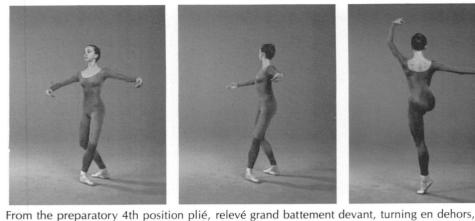

From the preparatory 4th position plié, relevé grand battement devant, turning en dehors, sharply opening the front arm à la seconde into the direction of the turn, and lifting the other arm directly to 5th en haut.

The hip of the lifted leg must not be allowed to rise. The upper body must be squarely placed over the hips and supporting leg.

## Grande pirouette en dehors in 3rd arabesque

In this movement, turn-out of the supporting foot must be strongly held throughout the preparation, relevé, and turn. It is incorrect to allow the supporting heel to "slip" (turn in) just before the relevé.

**Grandes pirouettes in arabesque are not "spotted."** The eyes look over the front arm in arabesque throughout the turn.

From the preparatory 4th position plié, deepen the plié and spiral the body into the direction of the turn.

Immediately, relevé grand battement to arabesque, extending the front arm forward and thrusting the lifted leg around in back of the body. The weight must be maintained well forward.

## Grande pirouette en dedans in 1st arabesque

From the preparatory croisé lunge—

Deepen the plié, opening the front arm, and spiral the body into the direction of the turn.

Grand battement relevé to 1st arabesque, continuing to open the body and front arm into the direction of the turn.

At the top of the relevé battement, bring closing side of body strongly into correct ("square") arabesque pose.

Continue turning "away" from the supporting leg. To finish the turn, tombé en avant from the effacé devant position to 1st arabesque. Try to travel out as far as possible, almost in the manner of grand jeté en avant. Alternate finish: lower the supporting heel into plié, maintaining the 90° devant pose.

Continue to turn en dehors, "away" from the supporting leg, maintaining the level of the lifted leg at 90°. Finish the turn by lowering the supporting heel into plié while sustaining the arabesque pose, or by lowering the back leg to the floor into a 4th position lunge.

Continue to turn "toward" the supporting leg, maintaining the 90° pose in arabesque with the weight well forward. Finish the turn by lowering the supporting heel into plié while holding the lifted leg in a 90° arabesque; or with a failli; or with a soutenu turn en dedans.

# Grandes pirouettes sautillées

Grandes pirouettes sautillées are hopped turns on one leg with the other leg held at 90°. They may be performed in all poses en dedans and en dehors, but are most commonly executed à la seconde or in arabesque (for example, Giselle's variation in *Giselle*, Act II).

In virtuoso male variations, they are often performed in a series with relevé turns. These are fast turns, in which successful execution depends upon a strongly held extension at 90° (staying at the same level throughout the sequence

## Grandes pirouettes sautillées en dehors à la seconde

From 4th plié preparation, execute pirouettes en dehors.

Plié développé à la seconde en face at 90°, opening the arms to 2nd.

## Adding relevé turns

After completing the desired number of hopped turns, a series of relevé turns may be inserted into the sequence. These may be executed as singles or doubles, and—upon occasion, by virtuoso male dancers—with as many as five turns from a single relevé.

From en face, relevé à la seconde, turning en dehors and strongly opening the leading elbow and lifted leg into the direction of the turn.

## Grandes pirouettes sautillées en dehors in 3rd arabesque

From 4th position preparation for turns en dehors—

Grand battement to 3rd arabesque, staying in plié and turning immediately en dehors with a series of little hops.

of turns) and a well-turned-out demi-plié. They may be performed with eight, four, or two (most advanced) hops for each full rotation.

A sequence of grandes pirouettes sautillées may be completed with either a pirouette en relevé in retiré (termed "closing in" by most dancers) or a soutenu relevé en tournant. These are executed in the same direction as the hopped turns.

Continue turning en dehors in 2nd with a series of small hops on the whole foot, staying in demi-plié. Only the heel releases from the floor, pushing forward with each hop.

The level of the lifted leg at 90° should remain constant, as should the level of the demi-plié. The arms must remain exactly opposite each other in 2nd and squarely placed above the lifted leg, with the shoulders parallel to the floor.

Continue to turn en dehors in 2nd for the desired number of rotations; then return to the hopping turns, or complete the sequence with a plié en face at 90°, followed by an en dehors pirouette in retiré finished in a 4th position lunge.

Maintain the weight well forward, and do not allow the back leg to drop.

# Grandes pirouettes finished with fouetté to another pose

## Grande pirouette en dedans finished with fouetté to 1st arabesque

**SHOWN À LA SECONDE**

Execute a grande pirouette à la seconde en dedans.

**SHOWN DEVANT**

With a small rond de jambe en dedans, relevé into grande pirouette in the devant pose, turning "toward" the supporting leg.

## Grande pirouette en dehors in arabesque finished with fouetté to effacé devant

**SHOWN IN 3RD ARABESQUE**

Execute a grande pirouette en dehors in 3rd arabesque, turning "away" from the supporting leg.

Execute one-and-a-half turns.

Begin the fouetté when the lifted leg arrives in écarté derrière.

Staying en relevé, sharply turn the body into 1st arabesque, pressing the lifted leg back in line with the shoulder, opening the arms outward from 5th to the arabesque line. Finish in plié at 90°.

Execute one-and-a-half turns en dedans.

Begin the fouetté through 2nd as the toe approaches the upstage corner.

Bring the top arm down through 1st and sharply turn the body en relevé to 1st arabesque, opening the arm forward and finishing in plié at 90°.

Execute one-and-a-half turns.

Begin the fouetté when the body, turning, faces the upstage corner. Turn en relevé through écarté into effacé devant, opening the front arm sharply to the side, lifting the other arm in reverse to 5th en haut, pulling the working hip back, and aligning the toe of the lifted leg with the center of the body. The entire adjustment must be executed as one fast, coordinated movement. Finish in plié at 90°.

In *Romeo and Juliet* in the U.S.S.R., Galina Shlyapina executes a grand battement développé à la seconde as a preparation for grand fouetté relevé en dedans. Photo: Juri Barikin.

# 9 ✑ Turning Movements Used in Adagio

Several advanced turning movements commonly used in adagio exercises in upper-level classes are pictured in this chapter. They involve difficult coordinations and must be executed with high extensions and considerable control en relevé. They are among the most challenging and strengthening of all exercises in the centre. Most should be practiced first with slow promenades on the whole foot, so that students can become well acquainted with each of the components in every movement.

Because of the technical difficulty of these exercises, most students will have a tendency to "cut corners" when first performing them "up to tempo" en relevé. The unfortunate result of passing too quickly through some of the positions (i.e., not executing each one to its fullest extent) is that the overall shape of the step becomes blurred. When the movements are performed in the correct, fully detailed fashion with complete control en relevé, they have a breathtaking quality of suspension.

Students often find these exercises extremely frustrating, but they should be urged to persevere. The ability to perform them, although it does not come easily, is proof of considerable technical prowess.

In class, Galina Shlyapina practices a Vaganova renversé en dehors. Photo: J. Tomas Lopez.

# Grand Fouetté Relevé

## EN DEDANS, SHOWN WITH HALF-TURN TO 1ST ARABESQUE

    →

Prepare in pointe tendue derrière with the arms in 2nd.

Brush through 1st position demi-plié, lowering the arms en bas.

Grand battement relevé devant, lifting the arms through 1st to 5th. Lean back slightly at the top of the battement in order to anticipate the forward body placement in arabesque at the end of the fouetté.

## EN DEHORS, SHOWN WITH HALF-TURN TO EFFACÉ DEVANT

    →

Prepare in pointe tendue devant with the arms in 2nd.

Brush through 1st position demi-plié, lowering the arms en bas.

Grand battement relevé derrière, lifting the arms to 1st and maintaining the upper back well in front of the hips.

## EN DEHORS, SHOWN WITH THREE-QUARTER TURN TO CROISÉ DEVANT

    →

Prepare in effacé devant.

Brush through 1st position demi-plié, opening the top arm en dehors to 2nd.

Continue lowering the upstage arm through 5th en bas, then lift it forward, simultaneously executing a grand battement relevé to 3rd arabesque with a quarter-turn en dehors.

Fouetté through écarté derrière to 1st arabesque, staying en demi-pointe. The arms open outward to the 1st arabesque line.

Finish at 90° with a controlled lowering of the supporting heel into demi-plié.

Fouetté, turning downstage through écarté to effacé devant, first opening the arms outward to the side, then lifting one arm in reverse to 5th.

Finish with a controlled lowering of the supporting heel into demi-plié.

When the arabesque toe reaches the downstage corner, fouetté through écarté, opening the arms to the side. Finish in croisé devant en demi-pointe, lifting the upstage arm to 5th in reverse.

Lower the supporting heel into demi-plié, maintaining the leg at 90°.

# Grand fouetté effacé en face *(Soviet syllabus)*

EN DEHORS

Prepare in "B+" croisé.

With the back leg, step to the side into plié attitude effacée devant at 45°, with body inclined slightly forward to lifted leg, downstage arm in 1st. Deepen the plié, extending the arm and leg forward en diagonale.

Relevé à la seconde, turning en face, lifting the leg to full height and the front arm to 5th.

EN DEDANS

Begin in pointe tendue croisée derrière.

Close foot through relevé 5th en face, reversing the upstage arm to 5th en haut and turning to effacé.

Coupé over into plié attitude effacée derrière at 45° in a slight backbend, lowering the arm to 1st.

Deepen the plié, extending the leg and downstage arm.

# Grand fouetté Italien

SHOWN EN DEHORS

Begin in pointe tendue croisée derrière.

Fondu sur le cou-de-pied derrière, opening the arms demi-seconde.

Coupé under en demi-pointe, lowering the arms en bas.

Plié développé devant to attitude at 45°, lifting arms through 1st to low 3rd, inclining body slightly forward.

NOTE: This exercise may be performed en dedans in the exact reverse of the sequence pictured here.

Exchange the arms overhead, pressing the leg behind in line with the shoulder as the body rotates to effacé derrière en demi-pointe.

Finish the fouetté **en demi-pointe** in attitude effacée derrière (or arabesque), then lower with control to plié at 90°.

Relevé à la seconde, turning en face "toward" the supporting leg and opening the arms to 2nd.

Continue to rotate the body into effacé devant, lifting the downstage arm in reverse to 5th, pulling the upstage hip and shoulder back, and finishing **en demi-pointe.** Complete the movement by lowering with control to plié at 90°.

Relevé, straightening the leg with demi-rond en dehors to 2nd, lifting the front arm from 1st to 5th.

Staying en demi-pointe, exchange the arms overhead, passing the top arm down through 1st into the arabesque line as the leg executes a demi-rond en dehors to arabesque.

Lower into demi-plié en face in arabesque.

# Grand fouetté relevé en tournant

### EN DEDANS, SHOWN TO ATTITUDE CROISÉE DERRIÈRE

Prepare pointe tendue croisée devant.

Tombé croisé en avant, finishing en face in fondu sur le cou-de-pied derrière, bringing the arms en bas and up to 1st.

Relevé développé à la seconde en face, opening the arms to the side.

Lower the leg, turning toward the supporting leg and lowering the arms en bas.

### EN DEDANS, SHOWN TO ARABESQUE EFFACÉE DERRIÈRE

Prepare pointe tendue croisée devant.

Tombé croisé en avant, finishing en face in fondu sur le cou-de-pied derrière, bringing the arms en bas and up to 1st.

Relevé développé à la seconde en face, opening the arms to the side.

Lower the leg, turning en dedans to face the upstage corner and brushing the leg through 1st plié. The arms come en bas and lift to 1st.

### EN DEHORS, SHOWN TO CROISÉE DEVANT

Prepare pointe tendue croisée derrière.

Coupé under to fondu sur le cou-de-pied devant, moving the upstage arm en bas and up to meet the other arm in 1st.

Relevé développé à la seconde, opening the arms strongly to the side.

Lower the leg, brushing through 1st in demi-plié, lowering the arms en bas, and turning en dehors, "away" from supporting leg.

Brush through 1st position demi-plié, continuing to turn en dedans to face the up-stage corner. The arms lift to 1st.

Grand battement relevé devant, lifting arms en haut to 5th and leaning back slightly at the top of battement.

Fouetté through écarté, finishing in attitude croisée derrière en demi-pointe. Lower with control to demi-plié at 90°. (May also finish in 3rd or 4th arabesque.)

Relevé grand battement devant, lifting the arms en haut and turning one-quarter en dedans. As the toe points to the up-stage corner, lean back slightly.

Fouetté through écarté to effacé derrière en demi-pointe. Lower with control through the supporting foot to demi-plié at 90°. (May also finish in 1st or 2nd arabesque.)

Grand battement relevé to 3rd arabesque (continuing to turn en dehors), lifting the arms up through 1st and extending them to arabesque.

When the toe reaches the downstage corner, fouetté through écarté, opening the arms to 2nd. Finish in croisé devant en demi-pointe, lifting the upstage arm overhead to 5th. Lower with control to demi-plié at 90°. (May also be completed by adding a final quarter-turn to the pose effacée devant.

# Renversé

## Standard Western version

Prepare in pointe tendue croisée derrière.

Relevé with a quarter-turn en dedans into a low arabesque, opening the arms à la seconde. Failli croisée to fondu sur le cou-de-pied derrière, bringing the downstage arm en bas and up to 1st.

Coupé under to fondu croisé devant at 45°, bringing the side arm en bas and up to 1st to meet the other arm.

## Renversé en dedans through ecarté to 4th arabesque
### (Soviet syllabus; also called tire-bouchon)

This is a fast, brilliant movement. Its force is provided by the coordinated closing of the arms and legs, the sharp sideways inclination of the body, and the forward thrust of the supporting heel into the direction of the turn.

From 4th arabesque—

Plié, swiveling one-quarter turn en dedans on the whole foot, bringing the back leg through a high passé with the body leaning downstage into the lifted knee. Arms go en bas and up to 1st.

Switch the body sharply with a turn upstage, lifting the arms through 1st.

Relevé with grand rond de jambe en dehors at 90° through 2nd to écarté derrière. The arms lift to 5th.

Continue the rond en demi-pointe to the back. Finish in plié attitude croisée derrière, increasing the bend of the body sideways. Complete the renversé with a pas de bourrée en tournant en dehors (not shown), returning the body sharply upright. The arms open en dehors to 5th en bas and lift to 1st during the pas de bourrée turn.

Finish en relevé with développé écarté derrière, arms in 5th, leaning downstage.

Lower the supporting heel and step upstage en diagonale into the position fondu sur le cou-de-pied devant, arms opening en dehors and lifting en bas to 1st.

Step forward to 4th arabesque.

The renversés shown on these two pages are among the most difficult movements in the classical vocabulary. They combine a turn of the torso in a backbend with a pas de bourrée en tournant en demi-pointe. (The body must never bend sideways during these movements.) Stability is maintained by proper coordination of the port de bras, strongly pulled-up thighs, and the exact replacement of one foot with the other in pas de bourrée. Failure to adhere to these three principles will cause the dancer to stagger out of control.

## *Vaganova renversé en dehors (Soviet syllabus)*

From 3rd arabesque—

Plié, bending the back leg into attitude, inclining the body slightly forward, curving the arms into low 3rd.

Elongate the hands and relevé en attitude, with a slight backbend.

Simultaneously execute the following movements: coupé under onto the attitude leg, bringing the other foot cou-de-pied devant, increasing the backbend, and rotating one-quarter of a turn upstage. The downstage arm closes to 1st.

## *Renversé en dedans from devant pose through écarté*
### *(Soviet syllabus)*

From croisé devant—

Plié, bending the front leg to attitude and leaning forward slightly while lowering the side arm en bas, then lifting it up to 1st to meet the top arm lowering from 5th. (In an alternate version, the lifted leg remains straight.)

Relevé with a sharp quarter-turn upstage, opening into the écarté line with a slight backbend, eyes looking downstage **behind** the lifted arm.

  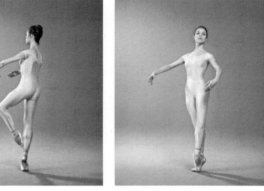 

Coupé over onto the front leg, bringing the other leg with a low passé to cou-de-pied devant, continuing to turn and lowering the top arm to 1st. The body begins to come upright.

Bring the body sharply upright, completing the turn toward the front foot. Close to 5th front in croisé. To finish, demi-plié in 5th, opening the arms demi-seconde.

Increase the backbend, closing the leg in front, lifting the back leg cou-de-pied derrière, and opening the arms à la seconde.

With the back foot, coupé over by executing a small passé to the front and lifting the other foot to cou-de-pied derrière. Simultaneously execute a quarter-turn, bringing the body upright and the arms sharply en bas.

Finish closing the foot behind into 5th croisé plié, opening the arms demi-seconde.

Pennsylvania Ballet principals Melissa Podcasy and Marin Boieru prepare to tombé en avant in *Water Music Suite*. Photo: Steven Caras.

# 10 ∿ Linking Steps

The movements on the following pages are primarily used to create smooth transitions between individual steps in ballet combinations. Often they play the role of preparatory steps, providing the necessary thrust and impetus to propel the dancer into and through another movement. In addition, if used at the end of an enchaînement, they may provide a smooth finish to a movement, often helping to absorb the force of a landing from a jump or to stop the spin of a turn.

All linking steps are first studied as separate exercises. The basic ones, such as pas de bourrées, chassés, balancés, and glissades, are among the first moving steps in the centre to be studied by beginners. All involve a transition of weight from one leg to the other, some by simply stepping, others by a small jump. Considerable time should be spent mastering the individual linking steps before they are used as preparatory steps for other movements.

Linking steps function most importantly as preparatory movements for jumps. Executed accurately, with the correct sense of timing and form, they propel the body into the air in a way that enables the dancer to perform a jump with ease, elevation, and aplomb. Executed in an uncoordinated manner, they can destroy the effect of the jump.

Particularly important is that special group of linking steps that precede large jumps. I have found it beneficial to teach moving combinations of these linking steps (e.g., pas couru, glissade en avant, chassé-coupé-glissade) in combination with running, balancés, and simple sautés arabesques, to intermediate-level students in place of a grand allegro combination at the end of class. Students at this level are not yet technically ready to attempt big jumps such as grands jetés; however, learning the preparations for them is not only good advance practice for the day when they will study grand allegro, but also is beneficial for learning to move across the floor in a broad, expansive manner. Indeed, I believe that many advanced dancers do not execute grand allegro movements as well as they might simply because they perform the preparatory steps leading into these large jumps in an uncoordinated manner. Unfortunately, many dancers seem confused by or unaware of the differences among the variety of linking steps that can precede large jumps. Their ability to excel in these jumps may simply be a matter of clarifying and perfecting their preparations.

In Tbilisi, U.S.S.R., fourth-year students practice failli to 4th arabesque. Photo: G. Warren.

# Pas de bourrée

## Pas de bourrée de côté

DESSOUS ("UNDER")

From fondu sur le cou-de-pied derrière—

Coupé under onto a straight leg en pointe (or demi-pointe), lifting the front foot to cou-de-pied and closing the arms to 1st.

Take a small step to the side with the front foot.

DESSUS ("OVER")

From fondu sur le cou-de-pied devant—

Coupé over onto a straight leg en pointe (or demi-pointe), lifting the back foot to cou-de-pied and closing the arms to 1st.

Take a small step to the side with the back foot.

## Pas de bourrée en avant and en arrière

SHOWN EFFACÉ

From fondu sur le cou-de-pied derrière croisé—

Coupé under with a quarter-turn en dehors, closing the arms to 1st position.

Step forward with the front foot to a small 4th position.

Draw the back foot forward to an **overcrossed** 5th position.

The pas de bourrées pictured are demonstrated en pointe with the feet "picked-up" in the cou-de-pied position. They are also commonly done en demi-pointe; men usually execute them without the "picked-up" foot action.

They may also be performed without changing the feet, in which case a pas de bourrée initiated with the front foot and a coupé over is called a pas de bourrée devant; initiated with the back foot and a coupé under, it is called a pas de bourrée derrière. Small, fast pas de bourrées without "picking up" the feet are a common linking step in petit allegro enchaînements.

Bring the other foot **immediately** to cou-de-pied devant.

Coupé over to fondu sur le cou-de-pied derrière, opening one arm to the side. (Or close in 5th plié, opening the arms demi-seconde.)

Bring the other foot **immediately** to cou-de-pied derrière.

Close in 5th plié, opening the arms demi-seconde. (Or coupé under to fondu cou-de-pied devant.)

Coupé under into fondu pointe tendue effacée devant, opening arms to a low 3rd position.

To execute this movement in reverse: draw the foot backward to 5th (coupé over), step en arrière with the back foot through 4th position, draw the front foot backward through 5th position (not pictured), and coupé over into fondu pointe tendue effacée derrière.

# Pas de bourrée en tournant

EN DEHORS

From fondu sur le cou-de-pied derrière, coupé under with a sharp quarter-turn upstage, bringing the other foot cou-de-pied devant and immediately closing the arms to 1st.

EN DEDANS

From fondu sur le cou-de-pied devant, coupé over with a sharp quarter-turn upstage, bringing the other foot cou-de-pied derrière and immediately closing the arm to 1st.

# Pas de bourrée piqué

This variation of pas de bourrée is generally performed by women only, usually en pointe. It may be done dessus, as well as en tournant.

SHOWN DESSOUS

From fondu sur le cou-de-pied derrière, coupé under onto pointe, simultaneously lifting the front leg to retiré devant at 90°.

Take a small step to the side onto pointe onto the front foot.

Execute a half-turn with coupé under through 5th, bringing the back foot forward to cou-de-pied devant.

Continue turning to croisé and close front in 5th plié, opening the arms demi-seconde.

Execute a half-turn with coupé over through 5th, bringing the front foot to the back to cou-de-pied derrière.

Continue turning to croisé and, as an alternate to closing 5th plié, coupé under to fondu sur le cou-de-pied devant.

**Immediately** transfer the weight to the side, sharply lifting the other foot to retiré devant.

Coupé over to fondu sur le cou-de-pied derrière.

# Glissade

Glissades (from glisser, "to glide") are terre à terre steps in which the toes barely leave the floor. They are performed in all directions and are most commonly used as the preparatory step leading into jumps. They may be employed in a broad, legato form in grand adagio or in a more dynamic, widely traveled manner in grand allegro.

A glissade is executed in one smooth, continuous motion. The legs are thrown outward on the upbeat, with the accent "in" (on the count) on the closing to 4th or 5th position. A soft, pliable demi-plié at the beginning and at the end of a glissade is **essential** to the correct look of this step. At no time must it ever look brittle or be executed "in pieces," without flow.

The term "glissade precipitée" refers to a tiny, fast, almost airborne glissade in any direction. For a description of glissade en avant through 4th position, as used for preparation in large jumps, see p. 236.

## Glissade de côté

This movement may be executed toward either the front or back foot, with or without changing feet. Note the use of épaulement in the beginning and ending plié poses.

SHOWN DESSUS
("OVER," OR CHANGÉE),
TOWARD THE FRONT FOOT

From 5th plié—

Extend front leg to the side, staying in plié. Arms open sideways.

Strongly stretch both legs, pushing body upward and to the side, with toes barely leaving the floor. Arms continue to lift to the side with intake of breath.

## Glissade en avant (with port de bras)

SHOWN IN CROISÉ

From 5th plié croisé with arms in high 3rd—

Extend front foot forward, staying in plié.

Immediately stretch both legs, pushing body upward and forward, with toes barely leaving the floor. Top arm opens to 2nd.

# *Failli* (standard Western version)

Prepare in pointe tendue croisée derrière with arms in low 3rd.

Relevé in arabesque at 45° with a quarter-turn en dedans, opening arms to demi-seconde. This may also be jumped (see note).

Pass back leg through 1st, lowering from relevé. Downstage arm follows movement of leg forward.

Finish sliding foot forward to finish in 4th arabesque plié à terre (or 4th position demi-plié), with front arm curved in 1st.

NOTE: Failli is also commonly executed from 5th plié with a jump on the initial opening to the low arabesque pose. Pas failli as a separate allegro movement (p. 296) appears in the Soviet syllabus but is rarely used elsewhere.

Transfer weight to the side onto leading leg into plié. The other leg remains stretched, toe on floor, in 2nd.

Slide leg in and close front into 5th plié, lowering arms en bas.

Transfer weight over onto plié on front leg, with other leg stretched croisé derrière. Downstage arm begins to lift to 5th.

Slide back foot in and close to 5th behind in plié, completing port de bras to high 3rd (looking under front arm).

# Balancé *(the ballet waltz step)*

## Balancé de côté

*Waltz*
$\frac{3}{4}$ ♪ | ♩ ♩ ♩ | ♩ ♩ ♩ |

Prepare—     and ♪     one ♩     and- ♩

From "B+" croisé with the arms in low 3rd—

Execute a small rise, extending the back leg in a low développé side and opening the arms with a breath.

Tombé sideways onto the leg, turning into croisé in cou-de-pied derrière and bringing one arm to 1st.

Coupé piqué under, lifting the croisé leg devant and extending the arms to a low arabesque position.

## Balancé en avant and en arrière

*Waltz*
$\frac{3}{4}$ ♪ | ♩ ♩ ♩ | ♩ ♩ ♩ |

Prepare— ♪     one ♩     and- ♩     ah ♩

From croisé, extend the back leg forward en diagonale with a small rise, opening the arms outward to a high 1st arabesque. Tombé downstage to cou-de-pied derrière.

Coupé piqué under, extending the front leg devant; then coupé piqué over, lifting the back leg to cou-de-pied derrière.

## Pas de basque en avant en tournant

*Polonaise*
$\frac{3}{4}$ ♩ ♩ ♫ | ♩ ♩ ♩ |

one ♩     two ♩     three ♪     and- ♪

Step en avant in effacé, brushing the leg through to croisé devant. Open arms outward to high 3rd allongé.

Step forward with 2 steps in 4th position (croisé and effacé) en demi-pointe, traveling downstage en diagonale.

Bring the back leg through, turning upstage, and tombé downstage en diagonale en écarté (back to the audience).

*ah* ♩

Coupé tombé over onto the front foot, **staying en demi-pointe** and releasing the back leg slightly off the floor.

**Balancé de côté en tournant** is executed in the above manner with the turn to the new direction on the initial coupé dégagé (shown with a quarter-turn).

*two* ♩          *and-* ♩

Extend the leg in a low développé effacé and tombé en arrière upstage en diagonale, passing the front leg to cou-de-pied derrière. Increase the bend of the body forward over the arm in 1st.

Coupé piqué under, lifting the croisé leg slightly devant, and tombé over (not shown) to cou-de-pied derrière.

*ah* ♪     *one* ♩     *two* ♩     *three* ♩

Bring the foot cou-de-pied derrière, swiveling en dehors, and développé in low 2nd arabesque in plié.

Step downstage, continuing to turn the body toward the audience. Closing the arms to 1st, bring the second foot through to step downstage diagonally into 4th position croisé.

# Linking Steps from the Bournonville School

## Pas de bourrée de côté to 2nd from échappé sauté

This is a very fast movement, with the pas de bourrée executed on the upbeat in 2/4 time between counts 1 and 2.

*Polka*

*Prepare—*          *and-ah* ♫          *one* ♪          *e* ♪

From 5th plié—

Échappé sauté à la seconde, landing with the weight placed slightly in the direction of the movement.

Draw up to the leading foot, closing behind in 5th en demi-pointe.

## Bournonville glissade de côté precipitée

*Polka*

This fast terre à terre step almost has the look of a low cabriole à la seconde. It is done with relaxed knees en demi-pointe, with the leading leg seeming to beat against the closing leg before stepping out into the final tendu pose. It travels swiftly to the side in one motion.

*Prepare—*          *e* ♪

From 5th plié, extend the front foot à la seconde, pushing the weight to the side toward the leading leg with the feeling of a little jump.

## Bournonville contretemps

*eight*          *and-* ♪          *ah* ♪          *one* ♩.

Plié effacé derrière and coupé chassé en avant diagonally downstage through 5th en l'air, finishing by transferring the weight forward onto the leading leg into effacé derrière in plié. The arm opens from 5th outward to 2nd.

*and-* ♪     *ah* ♪ ——————————————————————————→ *two* ♩

Continue the pas de bourrée under, using an overcrossed 5th position on the 3rd step to increase the distance traveled de côté.

Step out de côté with the back leg into plié and **immediately** straighten into pointe tendue à la seconde.

*and-* ♪     *ah* ♪     *one* ♩

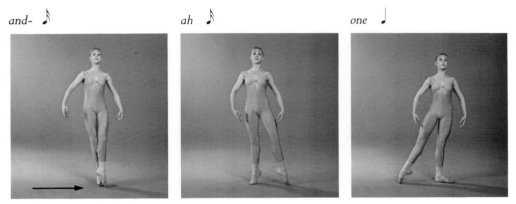

Draw the closing leg to 5th and quickly extend the front leg to the side, falling on it sideways into plié and immediately straightening into the final pointe tendue pose à la seconde.

*e* ♪     *and-* ♪     *ah* ♪     *two* ♩

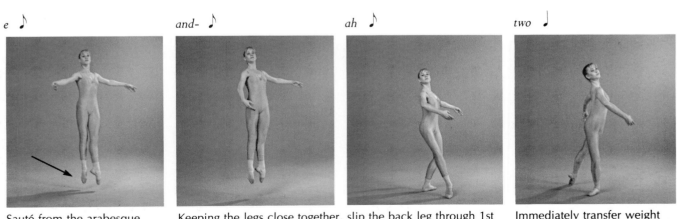

Sauté from the arabesque plié position, **immediately** closing the back leg toward 5th position en l'air.

Keeping the legs close together, slip the back leg through 1st position in the air and open it forward, landing on the back leg from the jump. The downstage arm lowers en bas and lifts to 1st, following the movement of the leg forward.

Immediately transfer weight forward to croisé leg. Bring downstage shoulder forward, twist back to audience.

# Coupé

A coupé (from couper, "to cut") is a **movement** through 5th position, exchanging one supporting foot for the other. It may be executed staying in demi-plié; through 5th position on the whole foot; en demi-pointe; and through 5th position en l'air. Coupés are first studied at the barre (as pictured here) before being added as linking steps in enchaînements in the centre.

## Coupé from pointe tendue

DESSUS ("OVER")

From à la seconde, cut working leg across in **front** of supporting leg (by means of a small rise in 5th position), and tombé onto it into the position fondu sur le cou-de-pied derrière.

DESSOUS ("UNDER")

Working leg cuts across in **back** of supporting leg into the position fondu sur le cou-de-pied devant.

## Coupé en demi-pointe

SHOWN DESSUS,
FROM FRONT TO BACK

## *Coupé en l'air*

# *Tombé*

A tombé (from tomber, "to fall") is a fall into demi-plié that travels outward from an open position on one leg to any position on the other. It may be executed from the whole foot, or from demi-pointe (as shown). The term "step-tombé," from the Soviet syllabus, refers to a single step into a deep demi-plié on one leg. It is commonly used as a preparatory movement for jumping.

Tombé en avant in croisé from the pose croisée devant at 90° on the demi-pointe to plié 3rd arabesque.

In the Vaganova school in Leningrad, U.S.S.R., students tombé en avant into 3rd arabesque. Photo: Paul B. Goode.

# Sissonne Tombée *(Soviet syllabus)*

This movement is often completed with a pas de bourrée or an assemblé. It may be executed traveling in all directions.

SHOWN TRAVELING
EN AVANT IN EFFACÉ

Jump from 5th plié, executing a small développé devant **to the floor** with the front foot. The arms lift through 1st and open in low 3rd upon landing.

# Chassé

The term "chassé" (from chasser, "to chase") is often used to describe a single sliding movement of one foot (with the knee in demi-plié) along the floor, transferring the weight outward; the foot in this case is flat on the floor. Pas chassé (pictured) is a composite movement that combines sissonne développée with a tombé, followed by two or more traveled jumps in 5th and finishing with an assemblé par terre (not pictured). It is executed traveling in all directions.

# Pas chassé *(Soviet syllabus)*

SHOWN DE CÔTÉ

Jump from 5th plié, executing a small développé à la seconde to the floor. The arms lift to 1st to open to the side.

# Temps levé chassé *(English school)*

This step may be completed with an assemblé or pas de bourrée, continuing to travel in the direction of the chassé. It may be performed in all directions.

SHOWN EFFACÉ EN AVANT

From 5th plié, jump in 5th and land in 5th. The arms lift to 1st.

Deepen the plié, sliding the pointed foot forward along the floor. Transfer the weight forward through 4th position plié to finish on one leg in arabesque plié. The downstage arm opens demi-seconde.

Deepen plié, sliding pointed foot out along the floor in 2nd, leaning slightly away from it. Transfer weight to the side onto leg into plié and jump, drawing back leg up to close behind in 5th en l'air. Land on back leg, sliding front leg out again to the side, and repeat the jump in 5th. Continue thus in a series, concluding with an assemblé par terre.

Immediately slide front foot forward in 4th plié. Transfer weight forward into low arabesque plié, opening arms to 2nd.

# Contretemps

The entire sequence of movements in contretemps is performed on the upbeat of the music, with the final tombé occurring on the count.

## Demi-contretemps

*Waltz*
$\frac{3}{4}$ ♪♫ | ♩ ♩ ♩ |

*Prepare—*  　　　　　*e* ♪  　　　　　*and-* ♪

Jump from 5th plié croisé, bringing the back foot to cou-de-pied derrière and turning the body effacé. The arms lift to 1st. (The head should remain turned toward audience, over the downstage shoulder, throughout *entire* sequence.)

## Full contretemps

*Waltz*
$\frac{3}{4}$ ♪♫ | ♩ ♩ ♩ |

*Prepare—*  　　　　　*e* ♪  　　　　　*and-* ♪ ————————→

From pointe tendue croisée derrière, rond de jambe the back leg en dedans with a very small terre à terre jump, to face the opposite diagonal downstage. The arms close in 1st. (May also be performed without a jump on the initial rond de jambe—coupé.)

## Contretemps en tournant  $\frac{3}{4}$ ♪♫ | ♩ ♩ ♩ |

*Prepare—*  　　　　　*e* ♪ ————————————————————————→

From pointe tendue croisée derrière, plié and jump, executing a rond de jambe en dedans, which closes in front as the body makes a complete turn in 5th en l'air. The arm close to 1st.

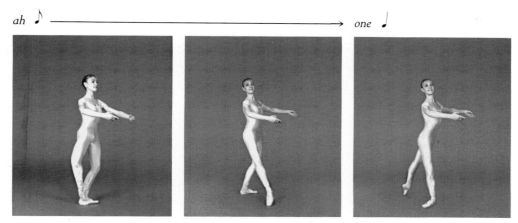

Land in effacé and immediately pass the back foot forward (keeping it close to the ankle of the supporting leg), to tombé en avant in croisé. The upstage arm opens to 2nd. The eyes look over the downstage shoulder at the audience.

Exchange the legs quickly en l'air and land in effacé devant, opening the upstage arm à la seconde. Immediately transfer the weight forward into tombé effacé en avant, opening the downstage arm à la seconde.

As the body rotates en face, exchange the legs, bringing the back leg forward to effacé devant. Land, opening the upstage arm à la seconde; immediately transfer the weight forward into a tombé effacé en avant, opening the downstage arm to 2nd.

# Linking Steps preceding Large Jumps

Many different jumps may follow these preparatory steps. A selection of possibilities is pictured below.

## Tombé, développé croisé, glissade

(into grand jeté 2nd arabesque)

$\frac{3}{4}$ 𝅗𝅥. | ♩ ♩ ♩ | ♩ 𝅗𝅥 |

*Prepare—*          *one* 𝅗𝅥. ——————————————→    *two* ♩

From 5th croisé en relevé, release the back leg sideways to a low écarté derrière position (not shown) and tombé upstage into fondu sur le cou-de-pied devant. The arms open en dehors to 5th en bas and lift to 1st.

Relevé (or sauté) développé croisé devant at 45°, opening the arms to 2nd.

Tombé croisé devant.

## Pas couru en avant

(into grand jeté croisé en avant)

$\frac{3}{4}$ 𝅗𝅥. ♪♩ | ♩ ♩ ♩ |

This movement consists of three steps en avant in 4th position. In movement quality, the first two steps are lighter and quicker, almost off the floor, and the third step slower, pressing into a deep plié to gather force for the takeoff. Pas couru may also be executed with five or seven little running steps, all of which take place on the count preceding the jump.

*Prepare—*      *eight* 𝅗𝅥.      *and-* ♪      *ah* ♩

From croisé, tombé en avant.

Glissade precipitée en avant, with the tops of the toes just clearing the floor. The body inclines to the upstage side.

*and-* ♩      *ah* ♩      *three* ♩      *and-* ♩

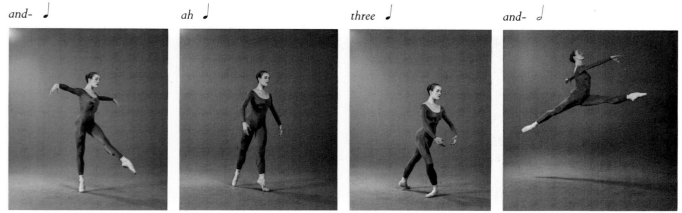

Glissade en avant through 4th position, with the arms lowering en bas and lifting to 1st as the glissade finishes.

Grand battement the upstage leg through 1st into a grand jeté en avant (or another large jump, such as assemblé volé).

*one* ♩      *and-* ♩ ⟶      *ah* ♩

From the glissade, land on the croisé leg (not shown) and immediately bring the upstage leg through into tombé effacé en avant. The arms come en bas.

Brush the back foot forward with grand battement sauté into grand jeté croisé en avant in 3rd arabesque, landing on the following count.

# Tombé, coupé chassé, glissade
*(into grand jeté 1st arabesque)*

$\frac{3}{4}$

 seven $\downarrow$.

 eight $\downarrow$. ⟶ and- ♪

From relevé développé effacé devant, tombé and execute a chassé en avant.


# Coupé chassé, coupé en tournant
*(into grand jeté effacé)*

$\frac{3}{4}$

Prepare—     eight $\downarrow$ ⟶

From pointe tendue croisé derrière—

Jump, drawing the feet together in 5th en l'air and turning the body to effacé.

Land on the back leg.

*ah* ♩        *one* ♩        *and-* ♩ ⟶

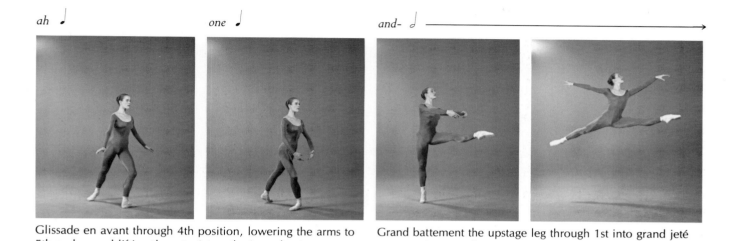

Glissade en avant through 4th position, lowering the arms to 5th en bas and lifting them to 1st as the jump begins.

Grand battement the upstage leg through 1st into grand jeté en avant in 1st arabesque.

*and-* ♪        *ah* ♩ ⟶        *one* ♩

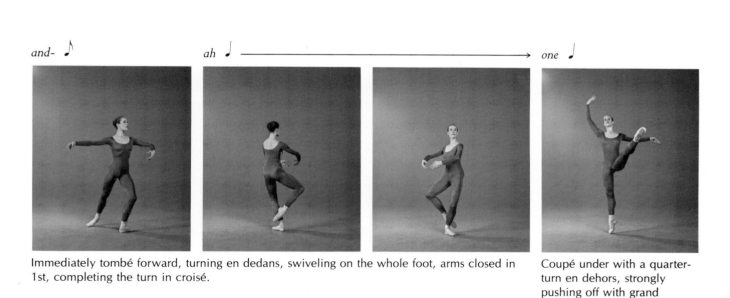

Immediately tombé forward, turning en dedans, swiveling on the whole foot, arms closed in 1st, completing the turn in croisé.

Coupé under with a quarter-turn en dehors, strongly pushing off with grand battement effacé devant into grand jeté en avant (not shown) with the arms in high 3rd.

# Hop-step-coupé
## (into grand jeté en tournant)

$\frac{2}{4}$ ♫ | ♫ ♩ |

*Prepare* —   *and-* ♪   *ah* ♪ ————————————→

Plié 3rd arabesque.

Execute a small preparatory hop in arabesque. Land with the palms turned up, reaching for the downstage corner, pulling backward toward the lifted leg, and deepening the plié.

Step upstage with a quarter-turn en dedans into fondu sur le cou-de-pied derrière in écarté. Simultaneously, lower the arms en bas and lean downstage, looking over the shoulder.

# Tombé, temps levé développé en tournant

This is a quick movement in which the initial tombé occurs on the count, with the swivel turn and développé occurring on the following upbeat, and the final tombé en avant on the next count. The whole step is performed as one unbroken movement, without a pause in any of the positions.

$\frac{3}{4}$ ♩ | ♩. | ♩ ♩ ♩ |

*Prepare* —   *e* ♩ ————————————→

From effacé, tombé en avant, executing a rond de jambe en dedans with the back leg slightly off the floor.

Turning upstage, coupé over with the rond de jambe leg into fondu sur le cou-de-pied derrière, closing the arms to 1st position.

Coupé under into the jump, throwing the front leg in an arc and turning the body en l'air to the downstage corner.

Land in arabesque croisée.

Continue turning in the fondu position (on the ball of the supporting foot, with the heel slightly off the floor). The lifted knee must decisively open and pull back.

The foot in cou-de-pied slips around the supporting ankle from the back to the front.

Execute a small hop, simultaneously extending the front leg in a low développé croisé devant. The arms open to demi-seconde with palms up, and the head turns downstage toward the audience.

Tombé en avant in croisé, lowering the arms to 5th en bas and lifting them to 1st. From this point it is most common to execute a glissade or pas couru en avant.

# 11 ～ Allegro

Jumping, or allegro, movements in classical ballet are divided into three categories: petit allegro, medium allegro, and grand allegro. Small jumps (petit allegro) are the least strenuous and the first to be studied. After acquiring sufficient technical ability, students move on to the more difficult medium allegro movements, which provide an important strength-building link between small and big jumps. The big jumps, or grand allegro, are the last to be learned and should be attempted only by advanced dancers.

The allegro portions of upper-level classes contain jumps in all three categories; the dancers begin with small jumps, using them for warm-up, and gradually progress to larger ones. Intermediate-level classes, however, contain only small and medium jumps, and beginners practice only small jumps.

There is a logical progression for the study of jumps. First to be learned, and easiest, are those small jumps that take off from two feet and land on two feet, such as temps levés. Next are jumps from two feet onto one foot; these require considerable control upon landing and include such jumps as petits jetés and sissonnes. At the same time, students learn jumps that take off from one foot and land on two, such as step-tombé assemblé. Finally, students are introduced to the most difficult allegro movements: those in which the dancer pushes off from one foot and lands on one foot. These include jumps such as temps levés on one foot and, later, ballottés and grands jetés, in which the dancer leaps from one foot to the other. Following is the recommended order for learning the allegro movements in the classical ballet vocabulary, based upon the method of the Soviet syllabus. A few jumps that are not in the Soviet syllabus have been included and are marked with an asterisk.

| | | |
|---|---|---|
| *Beginner* | Temps levé in 1st, 2nd, and 5th | Grand changement |
| | Changement de pied | Échappé à la seconde finishing on one leg |
| | Échappé sauté à la seconde | Grand échappé à la seconde |
| | Petit assemblé (to the side) | Petit and grand échappé to 4th |
| | Sissonne simple | Sissonne fermée at 45° |
| | Assemblé devant and derrière | Emboîté par terre in pointe tendue |
| | Double assemblé | Pas de chat |
| | Petit jeté (to the side) | |

| | | |
|---|---|---|
| *Intermediate* | Soubresaut | Pas chassé |
| | Temps levé on one leg (first in the position sur le cou-de-pied, later at 45°) | Emboîté at 45° (in place—later traveling) |
| | Italian changement* | Jeté passé at 45° |
| | Jeté porté | Grande sissonne ouverte (without traveling) |
| | Passé sauté | Échappé en tournant à la seconde |
| | Sissonne tombée | Assemblé porté |
| | Sissonne ouverte (à terre and at 45°) | Single tour en l'air (men) |
| | Sissonne doublée* | Compound form of échappé battu with beats on both jumps |
| | Ballonné (in place—later traveling) | Échappé battu to one leg |
| | Temps lié sauté | Entrechat trois |
| | Changement en tournant | Entrechat cinq |
| | Échappé battu | Assemblé battu |
| | Royale | Échappé to 4th en tournant |
| | Entrechat quatre | |

Assemblé en tournant
Double assemblé battu
Petit jeté battu
Ballonné battu (à la seconde)
Temps de cuisse*
Brisé en avant and en arrière
Rond de jambe en l'air sauté
Ballotté (first par terre, later at 45°)
Bournonville pas de basque en l'air*
Grande sissonne ouverte (traveling)
Sissonne fondue at 90°
Jeté fermé at 45°

Pas failli
Grande sissonne tombée
Grand temps lié sauté
Jeté fermé (jeté fondu) at 90°
Grand assemblé
Grand jeté en avant from step-tombé
    or step-coupé preparation
Grand emboîté
Sissonne simple en tournant
Sissonne ouverte en tournant
Sissonne tombée en tournant
Temps lié sauté en tournant

*Advanced*

Double rond de jambe en l'air sauté
Gargouillade
Cabriole at 45°
Brisé volé
Emboîté en tournant
Petit jeté en tournant (to the side)
Grand pas de chat
Soubresaut (with a bend of the body)
    Grand jeté en avant in all forms
    (including grand jeté développé
    en avant), from pas couru, pas
    de bourrée, glissade-type
    preparations
Jeté passé at 90°
Grand assemblé en tournant
Ballonné en tournant
Grande sissonne ouverte en tournant
Grand échappé en tournant (men)
Double tours en l'air (men)
Petit jeté battu with half-turns
Entrechat six
Ballotté at 90°
Pas de poisson (men)
Grand fouetté sauté
Grande cabriole
Grand battement sauté passé
    développé
Saut de biches*
Grand pas de chat développé à la
    seconde
Temps de flèche
Grand pas de basque sauté
Saut de basque
Grand jeté passé de côté
Grand jeté en tournant
Sissonne ouverte battue
Jeté passé battu
Grand jeté entrelacé
Sissonne fermée battue
Grand assemblé battu
Grand assemblé entrechat six de volée

Grand temps lié sauté at 90° en
    tournant
Chassé en tournant (performed fast
    in a series)
Double tour en l'air in retiré landing
    on one leg (men)
Pas ciseaux
Grand rond de jambe en l'air sauté
    double
Grande sissonne ouverte battue
Sissonne fondue battue at 90°
Grande cabriole fermée
Grand jeté elancé
Brisé en tournant
Grand assemblé six de volée en
    tournant (men)
Double saut de basque (men)
Saut de basque finished in 90° poses
    (men)
Revoltade (men)
Big jumps en manège (saut de
    basque, grand jeté entrelacé, etc.)
Grand jeté entrelacé battu (men)
Grand sauté à la seconde en tour-
    nant (men)
Grand assemblé en tournant with
    double tour (men)
Grande cabriole fouettée
Double cabriole (men)
Jeté passé devant with a double
    change of legs (men)
Grande sissonne ouverte with a
    double tour en l'air (men)
Grand jeté en tournant on an angle
    in series (manège) from coupé
    (men)
Demi-caractère form of double saut
    de basque with bent legs
    (men)
Entrechat sept
Entrechat huit (men)

It is important that jumps be introduced to students and mastered by them in the sequence listed above, for the following reasons. Each jump is designed to develop a particular strength. Jumps are like building blocks, one building upon another in a precise, gradual progression toward the grand allegro, for which a considerable amount of strength is necessary. It is dangerous and counterproductive to ask students to attempt jumps for which their bodies have not been properly prepared. A student who is not yet strong enough to attempt a jump (1) will not be able to get high enough in the air to assume the correct pose, (2) will introduce unsightly tension into the upper body, arms, neck, and face in straining to attempt the mechanics of the movement, and (3) will not be in control upon landing. A dancer without sufficient strength and control to land properly from a jump can have a bad accident.

Students learning a new jump naturally struggle a bit. Their coordination is somewhat shaky; it takes time and practice before the movement becomes strong and effortless-looking. Before moving on to another jump, however, they should always be able to exert control over their movements—to assume the correct pose in the air with correctly placed arms, fully pointed feet, adequate elevation, and sufficient control upon landing. It is useless for students to hop and flail about, approximating movements in a distorted, earthbound manner. I cannot emphasize enough how unproductive it is to require students who can barely execute a grand battement to 90° or a simple sissonne fermée at 90° to attempt movements such as grands jetés or tours jetés. Only through the careful, repeated study of the strength-building medium allegro movements is an easy, high-flying grand allegro technique acquired.

Timing is everything in jumping. The speed and technical accuracy with which a dancer pushes off the floor directly controls the success of any jump. For this reason, the musical accompaniment for jumping exercises is very important. Rhythm is a dancer's guide, into, through, and out of a movement. Teachers must choose the music for jumping exercises carefully, making sure that it provides the correct support for the dancers in tempo, meter, and quality. As a general rule, dancers, when jumping, are always in the air on the upbeat and down on the count. Time must be allotted in the music for the execution of preparatory pliés, as well as controlled landings from jumps.

When jumping, dancers should press their heels into the floor in a controlled and elastic manner at the beginning and end of every jump. The only exception to this is in the execution of very fast, terre à terre, petit allegro combinations in which they must transfer their weight extraordinarily quickly from one movement to the next. (The choreography of George Balanchine and Frederick Ashton often requires such speed.) For all other jumping movements, however, pressing the heels into the floor is essential for the following reasons: (1) it provides a greater surface (the whole length of the foot) from which to push off, and therefore produces a higher jump; (2) it forces the Achilles tendon to be engaged to the maximum extent (first stretched, and then contracted) in the push-off action, again resulting in a higher jump; (3) it creates a larger and more secure base for the dancer to balance upon when landing; and (4) the position of the ankle, important in both the preparatory and final plié position, is considerably more stable when the heel is on the floor. In other words, pushing off from the heels and landing "through" the whole foot is technically more efficient, producing higher elevation and more controlled landings. Students initially may find jumping in this manner quite strenuous, but eventually they will appreciate the strong allegro technique that results. Soviet and Danish dancers, whose training emphasizes this method of jumping, are particularly admired for their exemplary allegro techniques.

The jumping sequences in the photographs on the following pages illustrate only the most basic port de bras coordinations; they may of course be changed or embellished at the teacher's discretion. However, the following rule should be kept in mind: when the legs are flung apart in jumps, the arms usually are thrown open as well; conversely, when the legs are closed in the air, the arms are too, in 1st, 5th en bas, 4th, or 5th en haut. There is a logical reason for this rule. Movements of the arms help provide momentum in the take-off, lend stability to the pose upon landing, and create additional lift and force during movements performed in the air.

Another generally accepted maxim is that small jumps are accompanied by small, low arm movements and large jumps by higher, more expansive ones.

Finally, it is essential that the port de bras during jumps be performed without tension. Most dancers have the tendency to reflect the effort of a jump by showing unattractive tension in their arms, hands, neck, and shoulders. Teachers must note and discourage this practice before it becomes habitual. Tension in the upper body can make a jump appear belabored and earthbound, whereas an easy, tension-free port de bras gives a quality of freedom and airiness. Well-controlled arms can contribute a great deal to the desired appearance of suspension in the air, for which dancers are continually striving.

In an effort to show the interim position through which a jumping movement passes, the dancers in some of the allegro photographs appear to be jumping from the demi-pointe. Readers should not misconstrue the action in these pictures. A dancer should never jump from demi-pointe (though the foot may pass through this position as it moves away from the floor into the air).

In the sequential photographs of the larger jumps, space limitations prevented the inclusion of the preparatory (linking) steps that are almost always executed before these jumps. These steps are essential for providing dancers with the amount of momentum they need to gain the high elevation required by all grand allegro movements. They are pictured in all their various forms in the section entitled "Linking Steps preceding Large Jumps" on pp. 236–41.

Most small jumps, such as petits jetés, ronds de jambe en l'air sautés, and pas de chats, may also be executed turning in the air. The method for performing such jumps en tournant is described on p. 170. In addition, batterie may be added to many of the jumps on the following pages. The method for executing batterie, including photographic sequences of many beaten steps, is described in chapter 13, "Batterie," beginning on p. 320.

In the words of the great Russian prima ballerina Tamara Karsavina, "Natural elevation is a boon accorded to the few only; but where it is not granted by nature it can be developed by a systematic, well-planned training" (*Classical Ballet*, p. 68). In other words, anyone can learn to jump well. It is simply a matter of perseverance and proper training. Teachers are urged to refer to the suggestions for teaching allegro in chapter 3, "The Ballet Class: Notes for Teachers," and to allocate no less than twenty minutes of each hour-and-a-half classroom period for the study and practice of jumping movements.

# Temps Levé

Temps levés are the first and easiest forms of jumping taught to dance students. They begin and end on two feet and are most often performed as small jumps without high elevation. The importance of using generous demi-pliés and of "pushing off from the heels" cannot be overstressed in the practice of these jumps. Keep the back absolutely erect during the initial plié, as well as in the air and upon landing. Never lean forward with the upper body in order to facilitate the ascent from the floor; and be careful not to arch the torso when pushing away from the floor, which causes the weight to be thrown backward in the air.

## Temps levé in 1st position

INCORRECT INCORRECT

From demi-plié in 1st, spring upward, pulling the toes "under the heels." The legs are vertically aligned with the hips.

The heels are touching. The legs have been drawn too close together in the air.

The feet are too far apart. The legs were pushed apart on ascent, dissipating energy needed for the upward thrust.

## Temps levé in 2nd position

INCORRECT INCORRECT

From demi-plié in 2nd, spring upward, pulling the toes "under the heels." The width of the legs in the air should be approximately the same as the width of 2nd position on the floor.

The 2nd position plié is too wide. The heels are not aligned with the hips. The thigh strength necessary for push-off is considerably diminished by such a wide 2nd.

The legs are too wide apart in the air. They have been kicked outward on the ascent and will have to be brought inward in order to land in a safe 2nd position. This "in-out" leg action will diminish the dancer's ability to achieve maximum elevation.

# Temps levé in 4th position

From demi-plié in 4th, spring upward, drawing the legs inward so that one is directly in front of the other when seen en face. The feet must be adjusted outward for the landing in the initial 4th position plié.

The legs have been opened outward on the ascent.

American Ballet Theatre soloist Peter Fonseca executes a temps levé in 5th position in the Peasant pas de deux from *Giselle*. Photo: Mira.

## Temps levé in 5th position

From demi-plié in 5th, spring upward, drawing the legs tightly together. The front foot should be directly in front of the back foot. The feet must be readjusted outward for landing in the correct 5th position plié.

There is space between the legs in the air. The feet pushed straight up on the ascent without drawing together.

# Changement de Pieds

The heels pass each other in 1st at the height of the jump. The feet change from 5th to 5th.

## Grand changement

From demi-plié in 5th, spring upward, drawing the feet into a tightly held 5th en l'air, which is sustained briefly before changing the feet in anticipation of landing. Grand changement, a jump of maximum elevation, is the basic preparatory step for the study of tours en l'air.

# Échappé Sauté

Échappés sautés are small jumps from 1st or 5th position in which the legs are thrown equally apart on the ascent, achieving an open pose in 2nd or 4th in the air. The dancer lands on both feet in the open pose. A typical simple échappé sauté à la seconde involves jumping from 5th to 2nd and back to 5th again. If the échappé finishes with the feet in the opposite relationship in 5th position from the way they began, then the movement is called "échappé changé."

Following are two variations of échappé sauté. Both may also be performed in 4th position in croisé or effacé, as well as en face.

## Échappé to one leg

**SHOWN À LA SECONDE TO COU-DE-PIED DERRIÈRE**

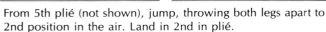

From 5th plié (not shown), jump, throwing both legs apart to 2nd position in the air. Land in 2nd in plié.

From plié in 2nd, spring upward, strongly stretching both feet in 2nd en l'air. Jump over onto one foot into fondu cou-de-pied derrière. (The step travels toward the leg in 2nd upon which the jump will land.)

## Grand échappé

**SHOWN À LA SECONDE**

As in grand changement, the initial 5th position en l'air is held briefly at the top of the jump before the legs open to 2nd and land.

# Temps Levés on One Leg

There are many forms of temps levés on one leg—jumps that begin and land on the same foot. They range from simple sautés (with the lifted leg maintained in the same cou-de-pied pose throughout the jump) to far more difficult movements such as those pictured on these two pages.

All temps levés on one leg require considerable strength, because the dancer uses only one leg to push the entire body weight off the ground. When landing, it is important to hold the ankle and thigh of the supporting leg absolutely turned-out. Good stability is required, since the impact is absorbed by only one supporting leg in plié.

Three advanced versions of temps levés on one leg are demonstrated here.

## Temps levé en tournant

SHOWN EN DEHORS CHANGING FROM COU-DE-PIED DERRIÈRE TO COU-DE-PIED DEVANT

From fondu sur le cou-de-pied derrière croisé with the arms in preparatory low 3rd position—jump, turning toward the back foot, changing it immediately to cou-de-pied devant, simultaneously closing the arm that was downstage in 2nd strongly to 1st.

Finish on demi-plié on one leg, with thigh of other leg well-lifted from underneath knee so that foot does not drop in cou-de-pied.

## Temps levé with grand rond de jambe

This step should be attempted only by strong, advanced dancers. It is rarely performed en dedans. Take care not to allow the leg to drop during the rond de jambe, especially as it moves from 2nd to arabesque.

SHOWN EN DEHORS
AT 90°, FINISHED
IN ARABESQUE CROISÉE

From a preparatory pose in fondu sur le cou-de-pied derrière, coupé under, executing a grand battement effacé devant as the coupé leg pushes away from the floor. Simultaneously, the upstage arm closes strongly to 1st.

# Temps levé at 90°

This step should be attempted only by strong, advanced dancers. It is primarily useful in technique classes as a strength-builder. There are many variations: with and without changing direction, maintaining the same pose, or with a change of pose (as shown).

SHOWN WITH A
CHANGE OF POSE

From plié effacé devant at 90°, spring upward, forcefully stretching the underneath leg and foot. Turn the body en dedans through the pose à la seconde at 90° en face, to land in plié in 1st arabesque at 90° en diagonale.

Stretching the underneath leg forcefully as it leaves the floor, execute a grand rond de jambe en dehors at 90° and land on one leg in plié arabesque at 90°.

# Italian Changement

   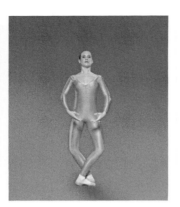

From 5th plié, spring upward with both knees bent, pulling the toes up under the torso. Sustain the position briefly in the air with the toes together (without having changed the feet); then change the feet on the descent, landing in 5th plié.

# Passé Sauté

From 5th plié, jump from both legs, drawing the front foot up the front of the straight back leg.

Arrive at the top of the jump in the passé position at the side of the knee. Try to keep the underneath leg as straight down under the torso as possible.

# Soubresaut

This step travels in 5th en l'air without changing the feet. It may be executed traveling in all directions.

Change the leg over the knee to the back and descend, sliding it down the back of the straight leg. Land on the front leg, almost simultaneously closing the back leg in 5th plié behind. The legs should appear to reach 5th at almost the same time.

Students at the Vaganova school in Leningrad, U.S.S.R., execute passés sautés.
Photo: Paul B. Goode.

# Emboîté

There are many variations of emboîtés sautés, jumps in which the body is transferred en l'air from a pose on one leg to a pose on the other. They may be performed with the extended leg pointed à terre, lifted to 45° or 90°, or in cou-de-pied (as shown below), or in attitude at any height. It is typical to repeat them in sequence, with a light, bouncing quality. The initial pose from which the dancer jumps may be different from the landing pose. Emboîtés may also be performed en tournant (see p. 304).

## Emboîté in cou-de-pied

SHOWN DERRIÈRE

From fondu sur le cou-de-pied derrière, spring upward, stretching both legs in a small 2nd position en l'air. Land in fondu sur le cou-de-pied derrière on the opposite leg from which the jump began.

## Emboîté at 90°

SHOWN IN ARABESQUE CROISÉE
CHANGING DIRECTIONS

  →

Jump from plié 3rd arabesque, bringing the body en face in arabesque and extending the arms in 2nd position (palms down).

# Emboîté at 45°

Jump from attitude croisée devant in plié, exchanging the legs in the air in attitude and landing in plié in attitude effacée devant. This movement in often performed in a series, traveling forward across the floor.

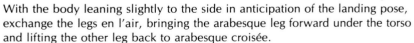

With the body leaning slightly to the side in anticipation of the landing pose, exchange the legs en l'air, bringing the arabesque leg forward under the torso and lifting the other leg back to arabesque croisée.

Land in 3rd arabesque in plié, facing opposite diagonal from which the jump began. The arms are in a high 3rd arabesque position, with the head toward the arm opened to the side.

# Assemblé

Correctly executed assemblés are the foundation upon which a strong allegro technique is built. They should be included as part of the warm-up jumps in **every** class, with the teacher emphasizing the importance of the strong, inward thigh action required to assemble the feet at the **top** of the jump. This same leg action will be required later in all beaten jumps.

Many dancers incorrectly assume that the high point of an assemblé is the open position to which the legs are thrown on the ascent of the jump. In fact, **at the highest point the legs should be in 5th position**. Achieving this is both difficult and strength-building.

Assemblés are executed in all directions and poses and with many variations in form. Shown elsewhere in this book are: assemblé en tournant (p. 302), grand assemblé porté (p. 258), grand assemblé six de volé (p. 342), and assemblé soutenu sur les pointes (p. 355).

The term "assemblé par terre" refers to a small type of assemblé that travels with the feet joined in 5th, barely off the floor. The effect is one of "skimming" the surface of the floor. It is executed from a tombé and is often used to complete another movement. An example is the finish of temps lié sauté en tournant (p. 316).

## Petit assemblé

SHOWN DESSUS

Begin in 5th plié, with épaulement to the front leg.

Pressing both heels firmly into the floor, deepen the plié on the push-off leg, simultaneously brushing the back leg to the side.

Ascend, fully stretching the working leg in a low position to the side.

NOTE: This step is also performed dessous, with the front leg brushing to the side and closing in back.

Johan Renvall executes an assemblé porté en avant in American Ballet Theatre's production of *Coppelia*. Photo: Mira.

As the ascent continues, both legs stretch forcefully en l'air with the push-off leg straight up and down **directly under the body**. The arms have opened to a small demi-seconde position.

At the peak of the jump, bring the brushing leg **inward** to join the underneath leg in a tight 5th position. Simultaneously close the arms to 5th en bas.

Land in 5th plié, with épaulement to the front leg.

# Assemblé from step-tombé

Tombé en avant in effacé and brush the back leg forward through demi-plié in 1st. The arms lower through 5th en bas and lift to 1st.

NOTE: This step is also performed traveling en arrière with the brush to the back, as well as à la seconde traveling sideways.

# Petit assemblé développé

This is a very quick, delicate, traveling terre à terre jump for female dancers only. The développé and jump occur on the upbeat, with the landing in 5th falling on the count. The legs remain rather relaxed throughout the movement, with the emphasis on the joining of the legs together in 5th at the end of the développé. The traditional Petipa choreography for *The Sleeping Beauty* uses this step in a series in Aurora's variation in Act II.

Jump from 5th plié, simultaneously executing a low développé écarté devant, traveling downstage toward the développé leg.

# Grand assemblé porté

This large traveling jump moves in the air in a tight 5th position at maximum elevation. It is usually preceded by either a pas couru or a glissade en avant.

From tombé en avant, brush the back leg through 1st plié, ascending with a battement devant to 45°. The arms lower through 5th en bas and lift to 1st.

Ascend, carrying the weight forward, the leg having brushed to croisé devant.

Immediately close the back leg to the front leg, traveling forward in the air in a tight 5th position. The arms open to low 3rd en l'air, with the eyes looking over the front arm.

Finish the jump in 5th plié croisé, maintaining the same low 3rd pose.

The body leans slightly downstage over the front leg, with the arms opened écarté allongé.

The toes are joined together in 5th as the jump begins to land.

Finish in 5th position demi-plié.

Quickly draw the back leg into a tight 5th en l'air and travel forward with the arms in 4th. Land in 5th plié on both legs simultaneously, maintaining the pose.

# Jeté

## Petit jeté

Petit jeté does **not** travel to the side. The brushing leg returns to the same spot where the jump originated. In jeté dessus (or dessous), the jump moves forward (or backward) only the width of one 5th position. (For variations of small jetés that do travel, see p. 262.)

The high point of petit jeté is a small, briefly held 2nd position en l'air. Achieving this position is essential to the look of lightness (ballon) that is desirable in this movement.

Petit jeté may also be executed en tournant, with the turn occurring as the leg brushes outward so that the dancer lands facing the new direction (see p. 176).

Jeté battu utilizes a royale type of beat: the leg brushes to the side, returns to beat in the same 5th position in which the movement began, opens, and lands with the feet having changed (see p. 332).

DERRIÈRE (DESSUS)

From 5th position demi-plié, brush the back leg à la seconde, jumping straight up with strongly stretched legs and opening the arms outward to demi-seconde.

DEVANT (DESSOUS)

From 5th position demi-plié, brush the front leg à la seconde, jumping straight up with strongly stretched legs and opening the arms outward to demi-seconde.

Susan Jaffe executes a grand jeté développé in American Ballet Theatre's production of *La Bayadère*. Photo: Mira.

Arrive at the highest point of the jump with the legs in a small 2nd position en l'air.

Bring the leg that brushed to the side back underneath the torso. Begin to bend the other leg in toward cou-de-pied derrière.

Land in fondu sur le cou-de-pied derrière with the thigh of the back leg well lifted, so that the foot does not drop with the force of the landing. The arms are in low 3rd in opposition.

Arrive at the highest point of the jump with the legs in a small 2nd position en l'air.

Bring the leg that brushed to the side in underneath the torso. Begin to bend the other leg in toward cou-de-pied devant.

Land in fondu sur le cou-de-pied devant with the thigh of the back leg well lifted, so that the foot does not drop with the force of the landing. The arms are in low 3rd in opposition.

## Jeté porté
### (Soviet syllabus)

Jeté porté means a "carried" jeté. The pose with one leg sur le cou-de-pied is quickly assumed upon takeoff, and the jump is executed traveling in this pose. It is a difficult, strength-building movement that is unique to the Soviet syllabus. It may be executed traveling in all directions and poses.

SHOWN EN AVANT

From 5th plié, brush front on ascent, quickly drawing the back leg to cou-de-pied derrière. The arms lift through 1st to a small demi-seconde.

# Two movements related to jeté

## Bournonville jeté de côté (completed with pas de bourrée dessous)

This is a fast terre à terre step in which the distance traveled sideways is more important than the elevation of the jump.

From 5th position plié, brush the back leg to the side and **travel** sideways in a low, wide 2nd position en l'air, with the arms thrown outward à la seconde.

## Bournonville pas de basque en l'air

When this movement is completed with a détourné turn after the final landing, it is called "pas de basque en l'air en tournant." A more difficult version (for men only) requires throwing the legs to 90° devant on the two battements.

From 5th plié croisé—

Push off with a dégagé croisé devant. Arms lift to 1st.

During the ascent, the body begins to turn en dehors toward the front leg.

The jump travels forward in this pose and lands in fondu sur le cou-de-pied derrière, the arms having opened fully to demi-seconde.

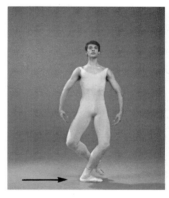  

Land, immediately bringing the second leg to cou-de-pied derrière and closing the arms en bas.

Execute a traveled pas de bourrée dessous to the side.

At the top of the jump the body has arrived in the pose effacée devant.

The second leg executes a slight rond de jambe en dedans, moving across the first leg into croisé devant.

The jump lands on the upstage leg, with the front (croisé) leg closing quickly to 5th in demi-plié. It is common to complete this movement with a détourné relevé (not shown).

# Jeté passé

This small jump may also be done without changing direction, in the following manner: begin with tombé effacé; coupé under and throw the front leg to effacé devant; exchange the legs en l'air in front of the body, and descend facing the same corner in croisé.

DEVANT

From fondu sur le cou-de-pied croisé derrière, coupé under into the air, throwing the front leg to effacé devant at 30°. The arms open outward to 2nd.

DERRIÈRE (ALSO CALLED
PAS DE PAPILLON),
FROM COUPÉ PREPARATION

From fondu sur le cou-de-pied croisé derrière, coupé under, brushing the front leg through 1st to effacé derrière as the jump ascends. The arms open out to 2nd.

FROM TOMBÉ
PREPARATION

Tombé en avant in effacé, taking both arms across the body and looking upstage. The back knee is relaxed in a low attitude allongée.

Jump, lifting both arms up.

At the height of the jump, exchange the legs in front of the body, leaning back slightly and opening the arms to a high à la seconde.

Land in croisé devant on the upstage leg.

At the top of the jump, bring the underneath leg up in back of the body, to meet and exchange places with the leg that initially brushed back.

Land in fondu sur le cou-de-pied croisé derrière, maintaining the arms in the allongée pose.

 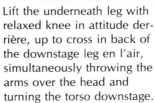

Lift the underneath leg with relaxed knee in attitude derrière, up to cross in back of the downstage leg en l'air, simultaneously throwing the arms over the head and turning the torso downstage.

Land in croisé plié on the front leg (the arms having completed the circle overhead to arrive in high 3rd), leaning slightly downstage, facing audience. Maintain the back leg in low attitude.

## Coupé, jeté passé derrière

Tombé en avant in effacé to fondu cou-de-pied derrière. The arms move to low 3rd with the body inclining over the supporting leg.

Coupé under (dessous), pushing off into the jump and turning the body sharply as the front leg brushes back into a low arabesque effacée.

## Jeté passé devant

This virtuoso step requires a great deal of elevation and is performed only by advanced male dancers.

From a step-tombé preparation (usually following a glissade), execute a grand battement sauté effacé devant, arms lifting from 5th en bas to 1st.

Quickly bring the underneath leg up to cross in front of the initial battement leg. The arms open simultaneously to high 3rd. The body is "piked," as if sitting in the air.

Re-open the legs.

At the top of the jump, exchange the legs through 1st in the air from effacé to croisé arabesque.

Land in plié on the downstage leg.

The arms are in high 3rd arabesque, with the head toward the arm opened to the side.

Re-cross the legs.

Re-open the legs and land in plié in the pose effacée devant at 90°, being careful not to tuck the pelvis under or to "roll over" on the supporting knee.

# Jeté fermé *(Soviet syllabus)*

This step has a soft, arcing quality and should be executed in a lyrical (never jerky) manner, finishing with a deep demi-plié and a generous cambré sideways over the leading leg. It is a wide, traveled jump rather than a high one, and can be executed dessous as well as dessus and in all directions.

SHOWN DE CÔTÉ DESSUS

From 5th plié, brush the front leg à la seconde and jump, leaning sideways away from the leading leg. The arms open directly out to the side from 5th en bas.

At the top of the jump, the body is upright with the legs spread wide à la seconde. This creates the arcing effect characteristic of the step.

Cynthia Harvey executes a grand jeté in 2nd arabesque in American Ballet Theatre's production of *Giselle*. Photo: Mira.

Traveling toward the leading leg, lift the body up and over to lean toward the other side.

Land on the leading leg, increasing the bend of the body to the side, and close the second leg in front in plié. The arms lower to 5th en bas.

Johan Renvall executes a Bournonville-style grand jeté croisé en avant in American Ballet Theatre's production of *La Sylphide*. Photo: Mira.

# Grand jeté

Large jumps demand a great deal of thigh and back strength. They should be attempted **only** by advanced dancers who are able to achieve accurate classical poses in the air and to finish the jumps with controlled landings. They are almost always preceded by one or more preparatory steps that help to provide the forward thrust necessary to lift the body into the air. For details on these preparatory movements, see pp. 236–41.

## Grand jeté en avant

SHOWN WITH ARMS
IN 2ND ARABESQUE

From the preparatory step-tombé en avant in croisé—

Jump, brushing the back leg through into grand battement effacé devant and lifting the arms from en bas to 1st. The upper body lifts forward over the battement leg.

## Grand jeté croisé en avant

SHOWN WITH ARMS OPENING
DEMI-SECONDE À LA
BOURNONVILLE

From the preparatory step-tombé en avant in effacé—

Jump, brushing the back leg through into grand battement croisé devant and lifting the arms from en bas to 1st.

Immediately battement the back leg to the level of the front leg, assuming the pose 2nd arabesque and carrying the jump forward through the air.

Land in 2nd arabesque plié with the weight well forward, without dropping the back leg.

Immediately battement the back leg up to the level of the front leg and carry the jump forward in the air, taking the arms to demi-seconde and opening the torso slightly downstage toward the audience.

Land on the front leg in arabesque plié with the weight well forward, without dropping the back leg, opening the arms fully to demi-seconde, palms up.

## Grand jeté de côté

SHOWN FINISHED IN
ATTITUDE CROISÉE DERRIÈRE

Tombé croisé en avant, lowering the arms from 2nd to 5th en bas.

Jump, brushing the back leg through to 2nd at 90°, bringing the body en face and thrusting it strongly sideways in the air. The underneath leg lifts immediately toward 2nd, and the arms are thrown à la seconde, palms down.

## Grand jeté passé

SHOWN À LA SECONDE FINISHED IN 4TH ARABESQUE

Tombé croisé. Brush the back leg à la seconde, jumping sideways through the air. The arms open directly outward to 2nd.

## Grand jeté passé développé

SHOWN À LA SECONDE FINISHED IN 3RD ARABESQUE

Tombé croisé, lowering the arms en bas and lifting them up to 1st.

Brush the back leg through 1st into grand battement sauté à la seconde, immediately bringing the underneath leg up to the level of the first leg and traveling sideways en l'air. The arms open strongly à la seconde on the sauté.

As the jump travels sideways in the air, both legs are stretched widely à la seconde at full height.

Reach for the floor with the leading leg and land, simultaneously executing a rond de jambe en dehors to attitude croisée derrière with the other leg. The leading arm lifts in reverse to 5th. The other arm closes across the body to 1st to complete the final pose in attitude with the arms in 4th position.

Land on the leading leg, immediately turning to face the diagonal as the other leg passes to the back through 1st into the final 4th arabesque pose in plié. The arms follow the movement of the leg, dropping to pass close to the sides of the body and immediately opening out into the arabesque line.

Reach for the floor with the leading leg, simultaneously bending the other leg in through passé. The body begins to turn toward the diagonal in anticipation of the landing pose.

Land, continuing the fast développé to 3rd arabesque. In the final pose, the eyes look over the front arm, the shoulders are pressed down, and the weight is maintained well forward over the plié leg.

# Jeté élancé

Jeté élancé is a fast, darting leap in which the emphasis is on the distance traveled rather than on elevation. With coupé en tournant (as shown below), these jumps are often performed en manège or in a series straight across the stage.

SHOWN WITH TOMBÉ-COUPÉ EN TOURNANT

Tombé effacé devant. Swivel upstage on the front foot, bringing the back foot to cou-de-pied derrière and closing the arms to 1st.

Coupé under, continuing to turn and opening the front leg forward.

# Grand jeté développé en avant *(also called pas de chat jeté)*

SHOWN WITH ARMS IN ARABESQUE À DEUX BRAS

Jump from tombé croisé, sharply bending the back leg and lifting it through a high, "turned-in" passé into a very fast développé devant at 90°. The arms lift from en bas through 1st and open forward into the arabesque à deux bras position. The torso must remain well forward throughout these three moves.

# "Stag" jeté en avant

Tombé croisé.

Jump, lifting the upstage leg in a parallel, bent-knee position, with the toe at the side of the knee of the push-off leg. The arms pass through 1st to arabesque à deux bras. Maintain upper body well forward. Briefly sustain the pose en l'air.

Jump, opening the body, front leg, and leading arm to the direction in which the jump will travel. The pose in the air is 1st arabesque. The front of the body must face the new direction as if placed in 4th position. The landing (not shown) is on the front leg.

Carrying the jump forward in the air, immediately battement the back leg up to the level of the front leg. Turn the head to look over the downstage shoulder.

Reach for the floor with the front leg and land, immediately bringing the back leg through 1st (in the manner of failli) and transferring the weight forward onto it in croisé. In the final pose shown here (one of many possibilities), the downstage arm opens straight back into 2nd as the upstage arm lowers to 1st. The body twists open to the front. The eyes look over the arm in 1st.

Release the bent leg, reaching down toward the floor; do not kick it outward.

Land on one leg in arabesque.

Bring the back leg through 1st to 4th position croisé and transfer the weight forward.

# Ballonné

## Three examples

### Ballonné dessus ("over")

From 5th position plié, brush the back leg to the side to 45°. At the height of the jump, bend it sharply at the knee and land sur le cou-de-pied devant. Never allow the thigh to drop on the descent; keep it well lifted from underneath the knee. This jump can also be done traveling to the side.

In ballonné **dessous**, brush the front leg to the side and land sur le cou-de-pied derrière. Ballonné à la seconde may also be done without changing the legs. Other variations of this step include ballonné en tournant (with the change of direction occurring on the brush outward) and ballonné battu (with either a royale or entrechat quatre type of beat). Ballonnés are also executed from one leg (with the other beginning in cou-de-pied); in this case they are done **without a brush**, but instead with a sharp développé on the ascent (see ballonné en arrière effacé, p. 277).

### Ballonné en avant effacé

**SHOWN FROM CROISÉ**

From 5th position plié croisé, brush effacé devant to 45°, traveling en avant en l'air. Land in fondu sur le cou-de-pied devant with both knees well turned-out. This movement could also begin from effacé.

## Ballonné en arrière effacé

**SHOWN JUMPING FROM ONE LEG**

Start from fondu sur le cou-de-pied croisé derrière. Jump, rotating the body a quarter-turn en dedans as the leg extends effacé derrière at 45° **without brushing**. Travel en arrière en l'air and land in fondu sur le cou-de-pied derrière in effacé.

# Sissonne

Sissonnes should be included in one form or another in every intermediate and advanced class. Sissonne simple, the first form to be studied, is the basic preparatory step for all jumps landing on one foot.

Sissonne fermée and sissonne ouverte (pp. 278–79) are the basic preparatory steps for grand allegro jumps. They are performed at 45° and 90° at both brisk (petit allegro) and slower, more measured (medium allegro) tempi; and in all poses and directions. They may also be executed with eighth, quarter, half, and three-quarter turns and (by men only) with a single tour en l'air.

## Sissonne simple

**SHOWN DEVANT**

From 5th plié, spring upward through a tight 5th en l'air and land on the back leg in fondu sur le cou-de-pied devant. The arms pass through 1st at the top of the jump and finish with one arm opening to the side to low 3rd.

# Sissonne fermée

### SHOWN CROISÉ EN AVANT TO 3RD ARABESQUE

Jump from 5th croisé, executing a strong grand battement to 3rd arabesque with the back leg, reaching forward with the front foot, and traveling en avant en l'air. Both legs spring outward simultaneously, without a brush. The arms lift through 1st position to 3rd arabesque.

Land on the front leg, **immediately** closing the arabesque leg to 5th plié in back. There should be no delay. The closing should appear to be almost simultaneous with the landing.

# Sissonne changée fermée

### SHOWN EN AVANT TO 1ST ARABESQUE

Jump from 5th croisé, taking the back leg forward and the front leg back into 1st arabesque en l'air. There is no brush. The legs pass close to each other through 1st position en l'air on the ascent. The arms lift through 1st position and open to 1st arabesque.

Land on the front leg, **immediately** closing the back leg to 5th plié in back.

# Sissonne ouverte

**SHOWN CROISÉ DEVANT EN ARRIÈRE AT 90°**

   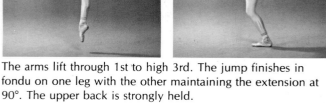

From 5th croisé, spring upward, traveling backward in the pose croisée devant. Both legs push away from the floor simultaneously, with the front leg executing a grand battement devant.

The arms lift through 1st to high 3rd. The jump finishes in fondu on one leg with the other maintaining the extension at 90°. The upper back is strongly held.

# Sissonne changée ouverte

**SHOWN EFFACÉ DEVANT EN ARRIÈRE AT 90°**

From 5th croisé, spring upward, traveling backward in the pose effacée devant. Both legs push away from the floor simultaneously. They exchange places through 1st en l'air, with the back leg executing a grand battement effacé devant. The arms pass through 1st to high 3rd. The jump finishes on one leg in fondu with the other maintaining the extension at 90°.

# Sissonne développée ouverte

This step does not travel. It may also be performed without développé. It is one of the major strength-building movements in intermediate allegro work.

**SHOWN À LA SECONDE AT 45°**

Jump from 5th plié, drawing the front foot up through cou-de-pied devant (arms to 1st). Extend en l'air à la seconde, opening arms to low 3rd. The jump finishes on one leg in fondu, the other in second at 45°. It is customary to follow this movement with an assemblé to 5th.

## Grande sissonne développée ouverte

This step may be executed with eighth, quarter, half, and three-quarter turns, and (by men only) with a single tour en l'air.

SHOWN À LA SECONDE
AT 90°

From 5th plié—

Retiré sauté devant, lifting arms to 1st.

Begin to développé à la seconde, arms lifting to high 3rd.

## Grande sissonne développée ouverte changée

This step may be executed with eighth, quarter, half, and three-quarter turns, and (for men only) with a single tour en l'air.

SHOWN FINISHED
IN EFFACÉ DERRIÈRE

From 5th croisé—

Passé sauté, taking the front leg to the back and lifting the arms to 1st.

Begin to développé effacé derrière, traveling forward en l'air. Arms open to high 3rd.

## Sissonne fondue (Soviet syllabus)

SHOWN IN 1ST ARABESQUE

From 5th effacé, spring upward, traveling en avant and opening the legs to a wide "split" position en l'air. The arms lift through 1st to arabesque. Note that the torso is carried well forward throughout the jump.

Complete the extension en l'air.

Land on one leg in fondu, with the other maintaining the extension at 90°.

The three types of sissonnes on these two pages are major preparatory steps for the study of grand allegro. They are essential for building the substantial thigh and back strength necessary to execute grands jetés with good elevation and control upon landing. The Soviet sissonne fondue is differentiated from sissonne fermée only in that it is performed at a slower tempo (in order to facilitate the higher extension and greater distance traveled). All sissonnes pictured may be executed in all poses and directions.

Land on the front leg in fondu, completing the extension effacé derrière simultaneously with the landing. (Strong male dancers may be able to fully complete the extension to arabesque before landing.)

Land on the front leg in arabesque, then close the back leg behind in 5th plié. This closing is somewhat more delayed than the fast closing executed in sissonne fermée. The 1st arabesque pose is maintained throughout.

# Compound Steps containing Sissonne

## Sissonne doublée *(also called sissonne retombée)*

SHOWN DESSOUS

Jump from 5th plié, executing a développé à la seconde. The arms lift through 1st (not shown) to high 3rd. The body inclines away from the lifted leg. Land on one leg in plié, with the other extended à la seconde.

## Temps de cuisse

Both forms of temps de cuisse should be mastered. The French form uses a petit passé to change the foot; the Italian form, a dégagé à la seconde. Temps de cuisse may be performed both dessous and dessus, and with the sissonne traveling in any direction. The arms are always held in a low, simple pose, since speed is essential in this movement. It is important to note that the little passé and the jump are performed **on the upbeat,** with the finish on the count.

### Italian form

SHOWN DESSOUS

From 5th plié (and **staying** in plié), execute a quick, low dégagé à la seconde, with the front foot closing behind in 5th plié.

### French form

SHOWN DESSUS

From 5th plié (and **staying** in plié), execute a quick, low passé, bringing the back foot over to close in 5th plié in front. Although the toes barely leave the floor in the little passé, take care to stretch the foot completely.

Sissonne doublée is a common compound step consisting of a sissonne ouverte, a coupé, and an assemblé. It may be executed with a grand battement instead of a développé (as shown); and also dessus (back foot coming to the front).

Close the lifted leg behind in 5th plié (coupé dessous), immediately brushing the front foot à la seconde into assemblé dessous. The body changes to incline to the opposite side as the top arm opens à la seconde. The arms close en bas on the assemblé.

Spring sideways, executing a sissonne fermée à la seconde without changing the foot (i.e., close the extended leg in 5th plié in back).

Spring sideways, executing a sissonne fermée à la seconde without changing the foot (i.e., close the extended leg in front).

# Ballotté

Ballotté means "tossed," which describes the light, rocking quality that is so difficult to achieve when attempting the movement. With the exception of the relatively easy ballotté par terre, all ballottés require considerable jumping strength.

Ballottés may be performed in sequence (dessous-dessus, as shown here), or singly in combination with another step (for example, a ballotté dessus followed by a ballonné devant). They may be executed in all directions and poses and may travel forward (ballotté dessous) or backward (ballotté dessus).

## Ballotté par terre

This simple form of ballotté utilizes a very low jump in 5th position and appears to barely skim the surface of the floor.

SHOWN DESSOUS-DESSUS
WITH STRAIGHT LEGS

From 5th plié croisé, jump through 5th position en l'air with a quarter-turn en dehors to land in plié effacé devant, with the toe of the extended foot à terre. The arms pass through 1st to low 3rd in opposition.

## Ballotté at 45°

This ballotté requires considerable strength in order to achieve the elevation necessary for executing the bent-leg 5th position en l'air. When this position is only approximated rather than fully achieved, the step will lack the light, tossed quality that it should have.

SHOWN DESSOUS-DESSUS
WITH DÉVELOPPÉ

Jump from 5th plié croisé with a quarter-turn en dehors, drawing the knees up slightly and crossing the feet in a tightly held 5th en l'air. Land in plié in effacé devant at 45°.

Jump, drawing the front foot back to join the other foot in an **overcrossed** 5th en l'air. Land on the front foot with the back foot pointed à terre in effacé derrière.

John Turjoman jumps with a petit passé in American Ballet Theatre's production of *Romeo and Juliet*. Photo: Mira.

Jump, drawing the front foot back to join the other foot in a crossed 5th en l'air with knees slightly bent. Land on the front foot in plié effacé derrière at 45°.

# Ballotté at 90°

Ballottés at 90° should be attempted **by advanced dancers only.** The key to success with this step is the execution of the coupé through a clean 5th position en l'air (with legs either bent or straight), with enough elevation to lift the body well off the ground. This is especially difficult to do in the second part of the step, in which the dancer is jumping from only one foot. There is no easy way to accomplish this movement, but it helps to maintain a strongly held upper back and coordinate the arm closings and openings with the legs.

## With développé with one leg

**SHOWN DESSOUS-DESSUS**

From croisé, coupé under, jumping through 5th en l'air with a quarter-turn en dehors and executing a développé effacé devant at 90°. Land in plié at 90°, being careful to maintain the turn-out of the supporting knee and the correct placement of the pelvis (without tucking it under).

## With développé with both legs

**SHOWN DESSOUS-DESSUS**

Jump from 5th croisé plié, bending both knees sharply and drawing the feet in a tight, crossed 5th up to the body; execute a quarter-turn en dehors in the air. Land, extending the front leg into effacé devant at 90°. The arms lift through 1st and open to low 3rd in opposition upon landing.

Jump, drawing the front leg back to 5th en l'air, and execute a développé effacé derrière. (The développé movement begins in the air and is completed upon landing in plié at 90°.) Maintain the weight well forward upon landing, with the back strongly held.

Jump, bending both legs en l'air and bringing the front leg back to join the other in a tightly drawn-up, crossed 5th position under the body. Land, extending the back leg into effacé derrière at 90°. The arms close directly to 1st and re-open in low 3rd in opposition.

# Rond de Jambe en L'Air Sauté

In this movement, the height of the leg extended à la seconde may be either 30° or 45°; only rarely, by extremely strong (usually male) dancers, is this step executed with the leg thrown to 90°.

It is important to remember that the object of the step is to show a clean single or double rond de jambe en l'air while still off the floor, with the working toe passing in clean circles **close** to the jumping leg. Both techniques for getting into the air (with and without brushing) are acceptable, and both should be mastered.

Rond de jambe en l'air sauté is also performed en dedans.

## Rond de jambe en l'air sauté without a brush

SHOWN EN DEHORS

From 5th position plié, jump in the manner of a sissonne (without any brush), stretching the back leg straight down underneath the body and opening the front leg to the side in a low 2nd. From 5th en bas one arm lifts to 1st, while the other opens straight out to the side.

## Double rond de jambe en l'air sauté with a brush

SHOWN EN DEHORS

From 5th plié, brush the front leg à la seconde, pushing up from the floor with the underneath leg, which should be strongly stretched and straight down underneath the body.

Sharply bend the leg at the knee, beginning a rond de jambe en dehors.

# Common errors in rond de jambe en l'air sauté

INCORRECT

INCORRECT

INCORRECT

The rond is too far from the jumping leg.

The knee is thrust too high, causing the hips to drop at the top of the jump.

The rond is being executed upon landing instead of en l'air.

During the jump the extended leg executes a single circle en dehors. The final few inches of extension à la seconde are completed simultaneously with the landing. The arms remain in low 3rd throughout; the head is turned with épaulement toward the rond de jambe leg.

Complete the first circle, opening the leg to an angle perpendicular to the knee.

Bend the leg in, to begin the second circle en dehors.

Land in plié, completing the last rond de jambe by extending the leg à la seconde.

# Pas de Chat

The name of this movement translates as "step of the cat." It can be performed either with or without changing the feet, at various tempi, and at all levels of elevation. It is also performed en pointe at low elevation.

## Standard Western version

SHOWN WITHOUT
CHANGING FEET

   →

Jump from 5th plié, lifting the back leg with bent knee to 90° and immediately drawing the other leg up to match it. The pose is briefly sustained en l'air, traveling slightly to the side.

## Soviet version

### Through 4th position

This version may be completed in either 4th or 5th position and is also performed en arrière, as well as en pointe at low elevation.

SHOWN EN AVANT

Jump from 5th croisé, executing a small passé with the back foot en avant, as if to 4th position. The eyes look over the leading arm in 1st.

### Through 4th position with feet flicking to the back

SHOWN EN AVANT

   →

From croisé, tombé en avant into a low attitude croisée derrière. The arms are in low 3rd with the eyes looking over the hand of the front arm.

Jump, exchanging feet in 1st in **back** of the body. **Both** knees remain bent in attitude in the air. Arms lift to arabesque à deux bras.

Reach for the floor with the first leg and land, immediately lowering the other leg through the retiré position to close 5th front in plié.

Draw both legs up in the retiré position in a small 4th en l'air.

Stretch for the floor with the front leg, bringing the other leg up and over the knee of the landing leg, and placing it en avant in 4th plié.

Land in a low attitude effacée derrière and immediately tombé through with the back leg to a small 4th position croisé.

# Grand pas de chat développé

## De côté

SHOWN FINISHED
IN 5TH POSITION

Tombé en avant croisé. The arms lower through 5th en bas and lift to 1st.

Jump, lifting the back leg through high retiré position into a fast développé à la seconde, immediately bending the knee of the underneath leg and tucking the foot up close to the torso. Arms are in 4th.

## From coupé

SHOWN FINISHED
ON ONE LEG AT 90°
CROISÉ DEVANT

From fondu sur le cou-de-pied derrière in croisé, coupé under (closing the side arm directly to 1st) and jump, turning the body into effacé, throwing the front leg forward with knee bent, then pulling the underneath leg up immediately to meet it en l'air.

# Grand Pas de Basque Sauté (Soviet syllabus)

SHOWN EN AVANT

From 5th croisé plié, throw the front leg forward with slightly bent knee in croisé and jump, straightening it and opening it simultaneously into grand rond de jambe en dehors to 2nd. The arms lift through 1st to 5th, with the body leaning away from the leg à la seconde.

Traveling sideways through the air, reach for the floor with the leading leg, land on it, and lower the other leg past the knee to close 5th plié in front. Maintain the arms in 4th position with épaulement throughout.

Straighten the first leg toward the floor and land on it, immediately executing a développé croisé devant and opening the arms to high 3rd in opposition. The step lands in approximately the same spot where it began. Maintain the upper back well lifted upon landing, without tucking the pelvis under.

Traveling through the air sideways, draw the underneath leg sharply up under the torso with knee bent. Reach for the floor with the leading foot and land on it, immediately executing a développé croisé devant with the other leg, as the arms open to high 3rd in opposition. Keep the upper back well lifted upon landing, without tucking the pelvis under.

NOTE: This step is usually completed by lowering the leg, sliding it forward along the floor, transferring the weight onto it, and executing a traveled assemblé derrière (en avant) to finish in 5th plié croisé (not shown).

# Gargouillade

Gargouillade is a difficult, virtuoso movement performed only by female dancers. It is a small, fast step that requires a strong, brilliant technique. It is initially practiced with a single rond de jambe en l'air, then with one single and one double, and eventually with both legs executing double ronds.

Jump from 5th plié, brushing à la seconde with a single rond de jambe en l'air en dehors.

## Gargouillade volée *(Cecchetti method)*

Jump from 5th croisé, brushing the back leg through 1st position to effacé devant.

With a circular en dedans movement, draw the effacé devant leg around in front of the underneath leg, with both knees bending. The arms are closed in 1st.

NOTE: This step may also be executed with a double rond de jambe en l'air on the initial en dedans movement.

While finishing the single rond outward, bend the other leg sharply at the knee and execute a double rond en l'air en dedans, landing as the leg passes the calf the second time. Close the foot directly down into the 5th position plié.

NOTE: In the Soviet syllabus, gargouillade is executed with *both* ronds performed en dehors (or, in reverse, en dedans). Instead of closing to 5th, the movement is completed in the following manner: at the end of the second rond, bring the toe forward to stretch along the floor croisé devant, transfer the weight onto it into plié, and execute a small traveling assemblé par terre en avant finished in 5th croisé in demi-plié.

From a small, crossed 4th position in the air, lift the back foot up and over the heel of the front leg.

Land, extending the leg to pointe tendue effacée devant, leaning over the front leg with the arms in low 3rd position.

# Pas de Poisson

The name of this movement translates as "step of the fish." It is performed almost exclusively by male dancers. The most famous example of it is in the Bluebird variation in Act III of *The Sleeping Beauty.*

From 5th plié, jump in place, strongly arching the back and throwing the feet in back of the hips in an overcrossed 5th position. The arms lift through 1st to 5th. The pose is sustained momentarily en l'air.

# Pas Failli *(Soviet syllabus)*

This is a compound movement made up of several different parts that are executed as one smooth, continuous, flowing sequence.

Demi-plié from 5th croisé, bending the body sideways toward the back leg, and jump with a quarter-turn in 5th, arms lifting to 1st. Just before landing, release back leg to a low arabesque en l'air, as arms open to demi-seconde, palms down. Land in this pose in plié.

# Pas de Ciseaux

The name of this movement translates as "scissors step." It should be attempted only by strong, advanced dancers.

From tombé croisé, grand battement effacé devant with a strong demi-plié, lifting arms to 1st; then jump, immediately lifting the underneath leg up toward the effacé leg.

Release the front leg and land in plié in 1st arabesque, with the weight well forward.

Without hesitation, draw the back leg through 1st (leaning back slightly with the upper body), and stretch the toe forward to slide along the floor in croisé devant.

Transfer the weight forward onto this foot and **travel** forward in assemblé croisé par terre, finishing in 5th plié. The downstage arm follows the movement of the leg, passing en bas with a softly bent elbow and lifting forward in a low arabesque croisé position.

The legs pass each other in the air at the top of the jump. As the upstage leg reaches for the floor, throw the croisé devant leg backward through 1st plié to arabesque. The jump finishes in plié in 1st arabesque.

# Temps de Flèche

The name temps de flèche ("arrow step") is derived from the fact that the leg action in this step resembles an arrow being shot through a bow. It is not a traveling movement.

From the preparatory step-tombé en avant in croisé, with the arms en bas—

Jump, brushing the back leg through 1st into grand battement effacé devant. The arms lift to 1st.

# Grand Battement Sauté Passé Développé

**SHOWN TO 3RD ARABESQUE**

This is not a traveling step. It may also be completed in other arabesque poses.

From the preparatory step-tombé en avant in croisé with the arms en bas—

Brush the back leg through into grand battement sauté effacé devant, lifting the arms to 1st.

# Grand Battement Sauté Enveloppé-Développé

*(also called saut de biche)*

**SHOWN TO 1ST ARABESQUE**

Saut de biche translates as "step of the deer." The step has a light, "tossed" quality. It may also be completed in other arabesque poses.

From the preparatory step-tombé en avant in croisé, with the arms en bas—

Jump, brushing the back leg through 1st into grand battement effacé devant, lifting the arms to 1st.

Sharply bend both legs en l'air, drawing the toes inward toward each other. The feet pass each other under the torso, the back one moving forward, the front one moving back.

Reach for the floor with the upstage leg as the other leg continues to execute a very fast développé croisé devant. The arms open to high 3rd.

Land in plié with the front leg completing the fast développé croisé devant. Maintain a strongly held upper back without tucking the pelvis under.

Draw the battement leg backward through passé en l'air.

Reach for the floor with the underneath leg, continuing to développé to 3rd arabesque. The arms begin to open to the arabesque line.

Land in plié in 3rd arabesque, maintaining a strongly held upper back with shoulders well pressed down and weight well forward over the plié.

Sharply bend both legs, pulling the feet under the torso.

Stretch the front leg to the floor and land on it, as the back leg continues to développé to 1st arabesque. Finish in plié in the arabesque pose.

Johan Renvall executes a grand jeté en tournant in American Ballet Theatre's production of *Coppelia*. Photo: Mira.

# 12 ᧗ Turning Steps en L'Air

Two basic petit allegro turns en l'air—chassé en tournant and emboîté sauté en tournant—are among the first traveling jumps with turns in the air to be studied by intermediate-level dancers. They are shown first in this chapter, followed by examples of medium and grand allegro turns in the air, which are more difficult and should be attempted only by advanced dancers.

The preparatory study for many of these movements includes practicing them without turning, or with only a partial turn. These jumps require not only strength and elevation but also landings that are executed with complete control (without which there is considerable potential for injury).

Several kinds of turns in the air are usually performed only by male dancers, whose powerful leg muscles make it possible for them to achieve the high elevation necessary. In the following photographic sequences, because of space limitations, most of the men's tour en l'air steps are demonstrated with only a single rotation in the air. As noted in the captions, however, these steps are more typically performed with double turns.

In teaching turning movements in the air, teachers should pay particular attention to the coordination of the arms. Precise control of the port de bras is not only essential for successful execution of these difficult jumps, but also adds grace and an element of "danciness" to their rather acrobatic appearance.

In Tbilisi, U.S.S.R., a second-year student practices changement en tournant, the preparatory step for tour en l'air. Photo: G. Warren.

# Assemblé en Tournant

The execution of this step is much facilitated when the dancer can achieve the feat of wrapping the front leg around the back leg in an overcrossed 5th position at the top of the jump. This action, along with a strong en dedans thrust by the closing side of the body, will provide the force to complete the turn.

### EN DEDANS (WITH SINGLE TOUR EN L'AIR)

Tombé en avant, as arms lower to 5th en bas.

Brush back leg forward through a strong 1st position demi-plié (as arms lift through 1st) to the devant position en l'air (as arms lift to 5th en haut).

### EN DEHORS (WITH SINGLE TOUR EN L'AIR)

Tombé en arrière, brushing the upstage leg to the back through 1st position demi-plié. The arms lower through 5th en bas and lift to 1st on the ascent.

### EN DEDANS (WITH DOUBLE TOUR EN L'AIR)

Tombé en avant, brushing the back leg forward through 1st position demi-plié into the ascent. The arms pass through 5th en bas.

Lift arms through 1st to 5th en haut. The brushing leg closes in front in a tight 5th position en l'air. The body turns strongly toward the back leg.

NOTE: In a virtuoso form of double assemblé en tournant, the body is almost parallel to the floor during the two rotations en l'air. An example occurs in the male variation in the Kingdom of the Shades in *La Bayadère*.

## WORDS OF CAUTION

1. Do not drop the head forward or look down at any point during these jumps.
2. Anything less than a **tight** 5th position of the legs will cause these turns to go out of control. The dancer must work against centrifugal force.
3. Take care **not** to lift the shoulders on the ascent.
4. Always take the underneath leg **up** to join the brushing leg, so the jump will have a "top," or peak of elevation. Joining the legs in 5th by bringing the brushing leg back to the underneath leg will cause a drop in elevation.

Pushing the hips up and forward into the air, join the back leg to the front leg in a tight 5th position en l'air, turning toward the back leg. As the turn is completed en l'air, the body becomes vertically erect. The eyes "spot" downstage. The jump finishes in 5th position croisé demi-plié.

Close the brushing leg behind in 5th, pulling the shoulders strongly around to the front. Land in 5th position croisé demi-plié, opening the arms simultaneously à la seconde.

The eyes "spot" downstage. The jump is complete after one-and-a-half rotations en l'air. The landing is in 5th croisé demi-plié.

# Chassé en Tournant

From 5th position demi-plié croisé–

Jump in 5th with a quarter-turn toward the front foot. The arms lower en bas and lift to 1st.

Land on the back leg, extending the front leg effacé devant. Immediately transfer the weight forward onto the front leg into 4th demi-plié. The downstage arm opens to 2nd.

# Emboîtes Sautés by Half-turn

SHOWN TRAVELING
EN DIAGONALE

From 5th position croisé demi-plié, jump with a half-turn toward the front foot, bringing the back foot to cou-de-pied devant by means of a small passé. The arms change from low 3rd to the opposite low 3rd without passing through 1st. The eyes "spot" directly over the shoulder to the downstage diagonal.

Jump, drawing the back leg into 5th in **back**, with a single tour en l'air toward the front foot (upstage). The downstage arm closes strongly to 1st simultaneously with the jump. Land on the back foot, extending the front leg forward, and tombé forward through 4th position demi-plié.

Jump in 5th with a half-turn, changing the back foot to the front through 5th en l'air and landing in croisé in cou-de-pied devant. The arms change from low 3rd to the opposite low 3rd without passing through 1st.

# Sissonne en Tournant

## Sissonne fermée en tournant

SHOWN DESSUS WITH A HALF-TURN

From demi-plié 5th position croisé, execute a grand battement à la seconde while simultaneously springing upward from both feet **without a brush.** The body turns sharply toward the leading foot (which began in front in 5th position) and travels upstage. The arms are in low 3rd, with the eyes looking over the elbow of the arm in front.

The jump lands on the leading leg, with the grand battement leg closing quickly after it through the pointe tendue position à la seconde to 5th plié. Note the manner in which the leading leg "reaches out" toward the direction in which the jump is traveling. Also note the strongly held upper back.

## Grande sissonne développée ouverte (with single tour en l'air)

SHOWN EN DEHORS
FINISHED IN
EFFACÉ DEVANT

Demi-plié in 5th, with the arms in preparatory 3rd position for turning en dehors.

Jump upward, turning toward the front leg and closing the side arm sharply to 1st. The front leg passes through 5th to the position cou-de-pied devant.

# Sissonne changée ouverte en tournant

SHOWN EN DEHORS TO 3RD ARABESQUE WITH THREE-QUARTER TURN

From 5th position demi-plié croisé, spring upward, sharply turning the body upstage toward the back leg while executing a grand battement to arabesque. Finish the jump on one leg in 3rd arabesque. The arms pass through 1st in the air and open to the arabesque pose upon landing.

The closing side of the body must be strongly thrust en dedans to bring the body around and downstage. The weight of the body must land forward over the front of the supporting foot in demi-plié, so that the full height of the arabesque leg can be maintained. Landing with the weight back to any degree will cause the back leg to drop.

The leg reaches the position retiré devant as the turn continues en l'air.

Land on the back leg, releasing the retiré leg into développé effacé devant and opening the arms to the high 3rd position.

WORDS OF CAUTION: It is essential to maintain the small arch in the lower back upon landing in the effacé devant pose. Tucking the pelvis under in an effort to increase the height of the front extension at this moment can cause the supporting knee to roll in and give way, a dangerous accident for a dancer.

# Saut de Basque

This step is commonly performed by men, with a double tour en l'air. It is also often executed while lifting the arms to 5th en haut on the jump.

From croisé, tombé diagonally forward in effacé onto the front leg, brushing the back leg through 1st position demi-plié. The side arm lowers through en bas and lifts forward, following the movement of the battement leg. The other arm opens à la seconde.

# Demi-caractère Double Saut de Basque with Legs Bent *(for men only)*

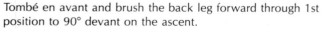

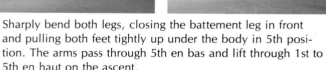

Tombé en avant and brush the back leg forward through 1st position to 90° devant on the ascent.

Sharply bend both legs, closing the battement leg in front and pulling both feet tightly up under the body in 5th position. The arms pass through 5th en bas and lift through 1st to 5th en haut on the ascent.

Continue extending the leg forward as the body turns upstage, jumping into écarté with the back to the audience. The arms are opened widely to the side, palms down.

Immediately draw the second leg up to retiré devant position, closing the arms sharply to 1st, as the body continues to turn en l'air.

Land on the back leg in croisé in fondu sur le cou-de-pied devant, opening the back arm à la seconde.

Execute two rotations in the air, "spotting" the downstage diagonal.

Release the back leg in preparation for landing. Land on the front leg in a wide 4th position lunge, opening the arms outward into the desired final pose (the character pose from *Le Corsair* is shown here).

# Grand Jeté Entrelacé *(also called tour jeté)*

## SHOWN FINISHED IN 1ST ARABESQUE

Tombé en avant, lowering the arms to 5th en bas.

Jump, brushing the back leg forward into grand battement devant, as the arms lift through 1st.

At the peak of the jump, the body has turned into a full 2nd position at 90°, with the arms in 5th en haut.

## *Grand jeté entrelacé with fouetté*

SHOWN FINISHED
IN EFFACÉ DEVANT

Tombé en avant, lowering the arms from 2nd to 5th en bas.

Jump, brushing the back leg forward into grand battement devant and lifting the arms to 1st.

At the peak of the jump, the body has turned into a full 2nd position at 90° with the arms in 5th en haut.

The body continues to turn as the battement leg lowers and passes the underneath leg through 1st en l'air.

The underneath leg executes a grand battement derrière. The body reaches the pose 1st arabesque **en l'air** and maintains this pose upon landing on one leg in demi-plié.

NOTE: Take care to avoid a circular, "over-the-barrel," rond de jambe action of the legs en l'air. The legs should pass each other **in a straight line** through the 1st position. The weight must be placed well forward over the final plié, so that the arabesque leg does not drop with the force of the landing.

Exchange the legs through 1st in the air as the body continues to turn.

From the arabesque pose en l'air, fouetté the body en dehors, opening the arms outward and finishing in plié in the pose effacée devant.

WORDS OF CAUTION: Take great care to insure the stability of the landing in the final pose of this movement. Pay particular attention to the turn-out of the supporting knee in plié in effacé devant; failure to do so can result in serious injury. This movement should be attempted by advanced dancers only.

# Grand Fouetté Sauté

EN DEDANS
FINISHED IN
ARABESQUE EFFACÉE

Tombé en avant, lowering the arms through 5th en bas. Jump, bringing the back leg through
1st into grand battement devant and lifting the arms through 1st.

EN DEDANS
WITH HALF-TURN
TO ARABESQUE
CROISÉE

Tombé en avant, lowering the arms through 5th en bas. Jump, bringing the back leg through
1st into grand battement devant and lifting the arms through 1st.

# Grand Jeté en Tournant

From 3rd arabesque in plié, step backward with a quarter-turn en dehors into
fondu sur le cou-de-pied derrière, lowering the arms to 5th en bas and looking
over the downstage shoulder.

Coupé under into grand battement
sauté devant, lifting the arms to 1st
and turning the head toward the leading shoulder.

At the peak of the jump, the body is à la seconde at 90° with the arms in 5th en haut.

Turn en dedans into the pose arabesque effacée **en l'air**. Land on one leg in plié in this pose, maintaining the height of the arabesque leg with the weight well forward and the upper back strongly held.

At the peak of the jump, the body is à la seconde at 90° with the arms 5th en haut.

Bringing the closing side of the body around forcefully, turn sharply into the pose 3rd arabesque en l'air, reaching forward with the underneath leg. Land with the weight well forward in the arabesque pose, maintaining the height of the lifted leg and keeping the shoulders well pressed down.

The leading leg "fans" around, bringing the grand jeté downstage into 3rd arabesque. The second (closing) side of the body must be brought strongly en dedans, with the front arm directed **exactly to the downstage diagonal** in the 3rd arabesque line. This insures that the jump will travel both **around and en avant** in the air.

# Revoltade

## With one leg bent

**SHOWN FINISHED IN ARABESQUE CROISÉE**

Tombé en avant, bringing the arms through 5th en bas up to 1st.

Execute a grand battement sauté devant.

As the jump ascends, bring the underneath leg up toward the battement leg.

NOTE: This step is generally performed only by male dancers.

## With both legs straight

**SHOWN FINISHED IN 1ST ARABESQUE**

From fondu sur le cou-de-pied derrière croisé—

Coupé under with grand battement sauté devant, with a slight grand rond de jambe movement en dehors. The arms lift to 1st.

Immediately battement the underneath leg up and over the leading leg. The arms lift to 5th en haut. The body leans back.

Sharply turn the body over en l'air, passing the second leg over the top of the battement leg in a high passé position.

In preparation for landing, straighten the passé leg, reaching for the floor. The arms begin to open.

Land in plié in 3rd arabesque, in approximately the same spot where the jump began (i.e., do not travel).

Flip the body over en l'air, reaching for the floor with the top leg.

Begin to open to the pose 1st arabesque en l'air.

Land in plié in 1st arabesque in approximately the same spot where the jump began.

# *Temps Lié Sauté en Tournant* *(Soviet syllabus)*

### EN AVANT (WITH SINGLE TOUR EN L'AIR)

From a preparatory plié position in 5th croisé, execute a tour en l'air en dehors in cou-de-pied devant.

At the moment of landing, the lifted leg executes a small développé croisé devant directly to the floor to pointe tendue. The arms open to low 3rd.

### DE CÔTÉ TOWARD THE FRONT FOOT (WITH SINGLE TOUR EN L'AIR)

From a preparatory plié position in 5th croisé, execute a tour en l'air en dehors in cou-de-pied devant.

At the moment of landing, the lifted leg executes a small développé à la seconde directly to the floor. The arms open to the side.

NOTE: The above step may be reversed by executing a tour en dedans in cou-de-pied derrière, traveling sideways toward the back foot and closing behind.

### EN ARRIÈRE (WITH SINGLE TOUR EN L'AIR)

From a preparatory 5th position croisé, execute a tour en l'air en dedans in cou-de-pied derrière.

At the moment of landing, back leg executes a small développé croisé derrière directly to the floor. Arms open to low 3rd, and body leans slightly forward.

This advanced step may be executed without a turn, using a simple sissonne tombée (see p. 232). In advanced men's classes it is performed with a double tour en l'air. Temps lié en tournant, the preparation for this step, is executed without a jump, with single or double pirouettes from 5th instead of the tours en l'air.

As the landing plié deepens, the pointed toe slides out along the floor and the weight is transferred forward over it, into a wide 4th lunge.

Jump, drawing the back foot into a tight 5th, and **travel** en avant en l'air (as in assemblé par terre) with the arms in 3rd arabesque.

Land in 5th plié croisé, lowering the arms directly en bas.

As the landing plié deepens, the toe slides out along the floor and the weight is transferred over onto it, in a wide lunge à la seconde.

Jump, drawing the pointed foot **in front** into a tight 5th. Travel sideways en l'air with the arms à la seconde, and the head turned with épaulement toward the direction **from which** the step has come.

Land in 5th croisé plié, bringing the arms directly en bas and maintaining the épaulement.

As the landing plié deepens, toe slides backward along the floor and weight is transferred back, into a wide lunge in the pose croisé devant. The body leans slightly back.

Jump, drawing the front leg into a tight 5th, and **travel** en arrière with the arms in 3rd arabesque.

Land in 5th plié croisé, lowering arms directly en bas.

TEMPS LIÉ SAUTÉ EN TOURNANT  317

# Men's Tours en L'Air

Tours en l'air are virtuoso feats essential to the technique of male dancers. They are rarely performed by women. Only single tours are pictured here, but most of the different forms are commonly performed with a double rotation.

## Tour en l'air changing legs

When the change of feet occurs is a matter of personal preference for each dancer. Some make the change immediately upon takeoff. Others believe that pushing upward in a tight 5th, as for grand changement, and then changing at the height of the jump, is the best way to achieve the high elevation required (especially for double tours).

Tours en l'air changing legs usually finish in 5th position demi-plié, but may also finish in 2nd or 4th plié.

## Tour en l'air to arabesque

SHOWN EN DIAGONALE WITH TOMBÉ-COUPÉ-ASSEMBLÉ PREPARATION

Tombé en avant.

Coupé under into petit assemblé devant, finishing in the preparatory plié position for turning en dehors.

## Grand sauté en tournant

SHOWN EN DEDANS À LA SECONDE

Chassé en avant and tombé into the preparatory lunge for takeoff.

# *Tour en l'air to retiré devant* (without changing legs)

From a preparatory 5th position plié, spring upward, lifting the front foot through 5th en l'air to retiré devant and turning toward the front foot.

This tour lands on one foot and may be finished in any number of poses.

Jump, **immediately** taking the front leg to the retiré position at the **back** of the knee. The arms lift through 1st to 5th.

Land in the retiré pose and **immediately** extend leg to arabesque. (Landing and extension should appear almost simultaneous.) Arms open outward from 5th to 1st arabesque.

Jump, turning en dedans; simultaneously execute a grand battement 2nd. (The leg executes a slight rond en dedans as it lifts to 90°.) Arms open initially to the side, then lift in reverse to 5th. Tour may be finished in plié at 90° in 2nd; or with soutenu turn en dedans.

# 13 ❧ Batterie

Many of the jumps in classical ballet may be executed with beats—small movements in which the legs swiftly move in and out of 5th position in the air. In most beaten steps, this leg action involves a crossing or exchanging of the legs from one 5th position to the other. In the case of cabrioles, however, the legs simply beat against each other rather than exchanging places.

Adding the element of batterie to any movement makes it more complex, both in execution and appearance. (Choreography that involves beaten steps is intricate and busy-looking.) Simple beats (such as entrechats quatres), which land on two feet and involve only one crossing of the legs in the air, are learned at the intermediate level. Beats involving more than one change of legs in the air and those that land on one leg are considerably more difficult. Movements such as entrechat-six or entrechat-sept, grand assemblé six de volée, double cabriole, and any of the grand allegro leaps involving batterie are strictly in the technical domain of advanced, and usually virtuoso, dancers.

No student should attempt any form of batterie until he or she has already developed good elevation and a strong jumping technique. The correct order for learning steps with beats is included in the list indicating the order in which allegro movements should be studied, on pp. 242–43.

Speed and clarity are essential in batterie. Most dancers spend no more than a fraction of a second in the air. If they wish to cross their legs more than once while they are up there, they must increase the speed at which they move the legs in and out of the beating positions. The ability to do this comes after much practice. Batterie, by nature, is a display of virtuosity. Although it is occasionally added to a movement by choreographers to communicate confusion or excitement, it is most often performed simply to exhibit a dancer's technical prowess. It would therefore defeat one's purpose to execute beats in any except the cleanest, most dazzling manner. Each crossing of the feet should be neatly positioned and clearly visible, with the final landing poses controlled, well-shaped, and secure.

All beats are performed with both legs straight and actively involved in the beating action. Students should be urged to cross their feet **past** the usual position of 5th in the air (as used in temps levé or soubresaut) and not to just hit them together. In addition, all beats must be performed utilizing a maximum degree of turn-out from the top of both legs (from the hips). This will insure that the beating action will occur sideways, through small openings in 1st position, rather than incorrectly by means of a forward-backward motion of the legs in the air.

The desired crossed-feet action en l'air, which produces the interlaced appearance of the legs that is characteristic of batterie, is more easily mastered by some dancers than others. Dancers with slightly bowed legs usually have the fewest problems, while those with hyper-extended legs may find that the only way to produce the required effect is to relax their knees slightly during the beats.

When attempting to keep the leg pattern of beats clear in their minds, students may find it helpful to think of one "leading" leg. Thinking, for instance, that the front foot beats back and lands front again may help them perform an entrechat quatre more easily than if they try to think about what both legs are doing simultaneously. It is also useful to face and hold onto the barre when first studying all beats, a practice that gives students an extra moment to think about and control what their legs are doing in the air. Care must be taken to land safely from beaten jumps, particularly those in which the dancer lands on one leg, such as entrechat cinq or cabriole ouverte.

For purposes of clarity, the picture captions refer to only one foot when describing how the feet change in a beaten step. Though dancers often think of one "leading" leg, particularly in complicated batterie enchaînements, they must remember that **both** legs are active in beats. The legs **share equally** the in-out beating action in the air.

Finally, the arms must be held relaxed and well positioned during beaten movements and must not reflect tension or jerk involuntarily.

All beaten steps are based upon one or the other of the two basic forms of beats. An entrechat quatre type of beat is one in which the feet begin and end in the same relationship to each other as when they began. A royale type of beat finishes with the feet in the opposite relationship from which they began. Therefore all beaten jumps may be divided into categories pertaining to the placement of the feet in their initial and final poses on the floor. For instance, a jump in which the foot beginning in front in 5th finishes, after beating, in the back is said to be "a beat that changes." Knowledge of which beaten jumps fall into which category can be an important tool for helping students to sort out the complexities of these intricate movements. Following are lists of the beaten jumps included in each category.

## Beaten Jumps

### —that do not change the feet

| | |
|---|---|
| Entrechat quatre | Cabriole |
| Entrechat cinq | Sissonne battue en avant and en |
| Entrechat huit | arrière |
| Brisé | |

### —that change the feet

| | |
|---|---|
| Royale | Assemblé battu |
| Entrechat trois | Grand assemblé six de volée |
| Entrechat six | Entrechat sept |

### —that may or may not change the feet

| | |
|---|---|
| Échappé battu | Ballonné battu |
| Petit jeté battu | Sissonne battue (à la seconde) |

# Entrechat Quatre

From 5th plié, spring upward, changing the front foot to the back through a small 1st en l'air.

## *Royale* (changement battu in English school)

This jump is named "royale" for King Louis IV, an enthusiastic amateur dancer. According to legend, he invented it as a substitute for the entrechat quatre, which was apparently too difficult for him.

From 5th plié, spring upward, opening the legs slightly to the side.

In the Vaganova school in Leningrad, U.S.S.R., students strive for perfect 5th position demi-pliés as they land from jumps. Photo: Paul B. Goode.

Beat the legs together, crossing them in 5th.

Re-open the legs, bringing the back foot to the front through a small 1st en l'air.

Land in 5th plié, with the feet in the same relationship to each other as when they began the step.

Re-join the legs, beating them in a crossed 5th with the same leg in front that began in front.

Re-open the legs, taking the front leg to the back through a small 1st en l'air. Land in 5th plié with the legs in the opposite relationship to each other from which they began.

# Entrechat Trois

The action of the legs in entrechat trois is the same as that in a royale (i.e., the feet change). Upon landing, it is important to hold the ankle and thigh of the supporting leg absolutely turned-out.

DERRIÈRE

From 5th plié, spring upward, opening the legs slightly to the side.

DEVANT

From 5th plié, jump, opening the legs slightly to the side.

# Petit Battement
# Battu Sauté

From fondu sur le cou-de-pied derrière, jump, forcefully stretching both legs downward on ascent, bringing the back leg to the front.

NOTE: This movement may also be executed from fondu sur le cou-de-pied devant, taking the front foot behind to beat in back in 5th.

Re-join the legs in a crossed 5th, with the same leg in front that began in front.

Re-open the legs, taking the front leg to the back through a small 1st en l'air, and land with this leg placed in fondu sur le cou-de-pied derrière. Simultaneously, the arms open to low 3rd with épaulement to the front leg, the torso is held vertical without any leaning to the side, and the back leg is strongly supported under the thigh so that the foot does not drop in cou-de-pied.

Re-join the legs in the same 5th position in which they began, then re-open them and bring the back leg to the front, to land in fondu sur le cou-de-pied devant.

Beat in front in an overcrossed 5th. Re-open the legs, taking the front one to the back. Land in the same fondu sur le cou-de-pied derrière pose in which the step began.

# Entrechat Cinq

In this step the feet beat in the manner of an entrechat quatre (i.e., without change).

DEVANT

Jump from 5th plié, passing the front leg to the back through a small 1st en l'air. The arms begin to lift to 1st on the ascent.

Beat the legs in 5th (in the opposite relationship from which they began).

DERRIÈRE

Jump from 5th plié, passing the back leg to the front through a small 1st in l'air. The arms begin to lift to 1st on the ascent.

Beat the legs in 5th (in the opposite relationship to each other from the way they began).

# Entrechat Six

This is an advanced step requiring more elevation than entrechat quatre or royale beats. In entrechat six, the feet change—i.e., the foot that begins in front is in back at the end.

Jump from 5th plié, passing the front leg to cross in 5th in back through a small 1st en l'air.

Re-open them, and bring the back leg in front to land sur le cou-de-pied devant in fondu.

Re-open them, and bring the front leg to the back to land sur le cou-de-pied derrière in fondu.

Following are descriptions of three other advanced forms of beats. All are difficult and are usually reserved for superior displays of male virtuoso technique.

**Entrechat sept** is performed with the same number of beats as entrechat six, but lands on one leg in fondu with the other placed sur le cou-de-pied in the manner of entrechat trois. It may be performed devant or derrière.

**Entrechat huit** is performed in the manner of entrechat six, beginning and ending in 5th plié, but adds one more change of the legs. The feet land in the same relationship to each other as when they began.

**Entrechat dix** is performed in the manner of entrechat huit, beginning and ending in 5th plié, but adds one more change of the legs. The feet land in the opposite relationship to each other from which they began.

Re-open the legs, bringing the back leg to cross in front in 5th through a small 1st en l'air.

Re-open the legs, taking the front leg to land in 5th behind through a small 1st en l'air.

# Échappé Battu

In simple échappé battu, the legs beat either on the initial jump from 5th **or** on the final closing of the legs from 2nd to 5th. Either an entrechat quatre or a royale beat may be used.

In compound échappé battu, the legs beat both on the initial jump from 5th **and** on the final closing of the legs from 2nd to 5th. Either an entrechat quatre or a royale beat may be used; the same type of beat does not have to be used both times.

In both the simple and the compound form, multiple beats (usually two, as in entrechat six) may be used; these are most typically performed by male dancers. The number of beats executed on the initial jump need not be the same as the number performed on the final closing.

Échappé battu may also be executed in 4th position.

## Simple échappé battu changé (with royale beat)

From 5th plié, spring upward, opening the legs à la seconde en l'air. The arms lift through 1st to open to 2nd.

NOTE: In another version of this movement, a royale beat is executed on the initial jump, with the legs closing at the end from 2nd to 5th without a beat.

## Compound échappé battu (with entrechat quatre beat)

From 5th plié, spring upward, opening the legs through a small 1st en l'air and taking the front leg to beat behind in 5th. The arms lift to 1st.

Open the legs and arms to 2nd en l'air.

In the Vaganova school in Leningrad, U.S.S.R., students perform échappés battus à la seconde. Photo: Paul B. Goode.

Land in plié in 2nd position.

Jump in 2nd.

Draw the feet inward to cross in 5th, with the same foot in front as when the step began.

Re-open the legs, taking the front one to the back to land in 5th plié.

Land in plié in 2nd position.

Jump from 2nd, drawing the feet inward to cross in 5th, in the opposite relationship from which they began.

Re-open the legs, bringing the back leg forward through a small 1st en l'air, to land in 5th plié in front with the feet in exactly the same position as when the step began.

# Assemblé battu

SHOWN DESSUS

From 5th plié, brush the back leg à la seconde and jump as for assemblé (see p. 256). The arms open outward to demi-seconde, palms down.

# Pas de Basque Battu *(Cecchetti method)*

From 5th croisé plié, jump with quarter-turn en dehors, brushing front foot to effacé devant.

# Ballonné Battu

Ballonné battu may be executed either (1) from 5th position with a brush or (2) from fondu sur le cou-de-pied, in which case the leg is thrown outward without a brush. It may also be executed in the manner of an entrechat quatre, with the legs exchanging places on the beat, then returning to finish in the same relationship to each other as when they began. For instructions on how to control the landing of ballonné battu, see p. 332.

SHOWN DERRIÈRE
(DESSOUS)
WITH ROYALE BEAT

Jump from 5th plié, brushing the front leg à la seconde. The arms open outward to 2nd.

At the top of the jump, cross the legs in 5th in the same ralationship as when they began (i.e., the back foot beats in back).

Re-open the legs, bringing the back leg to the front to land in 5th plié, with the feet in the opposite relationship from which they began. The arms close 5th en bas.

Immediately lift the underneath leg up to beat in back of the effacé leg, exchange the legs in l'air, land in plié on the upstage leg, and close the croisé devant leg to 5th plié.

At the top of the jump, close the leg that brushed outward under the body to beat in front in 5th.

Re-open the leg that brushed to the side and land, placing it sur le cou-de-pied derrière in fondu. The arms are in low 3rd, with épaulement to the front leg. The torso is strictly erect, with the supporting knee well turned-out in plié.

# Jeté Battu

When landing from either jeté battu or ballonné battu, it is important to remember the following points:

1. Hold the torso strictly erect, avoiding the tendency to lean sideways.
2. Both the supporting knee in plié and the lifted leg in cou-de-pied must be well turned-out.
3. Counteract the force of the landing by strongly lifting up under the thigh of the lifted leg so that the foot does not drop in cou-de-pied.

## Petit jeté battu

SHOWN DERRIÈRE
(DESSOUS) WITH CHANGE

Jump from 5th plié, brushing the back leg à la seconde. Arriving at the top of the jump, stretch the underneath leg in a small 2nd position en l'air. The arms open directly outward to 2nd from 5th en bas.

## Coupé jeté battu

SHOWN DERRIÈRE
(DESSOUS)
WITHOUT CHANGE

From fondu sur le cou-de-pied derrière, coupé under, throwing the front leg à la seconde without a brush and jumping toward a small 2nd position in the air. The arm in 1st opens directly out to 2nd.

Draw the legs together to beat in 5th, with the feet in exactly the same relationship as when the step began.

Re-open the legs, bringing the back leg forward to land in front with the other leg raised in back in cou-de-pied. The arms are in low 3rd, with épaulement to the front leg.

The front leg closes to beat in back in 5th.

Re-open the legs, with the leg that first beat in back coming to the front to land in the same position fondu sur le cou-de-pied derrière in which the step began. The arm returns to 1st, with épaulement to the front leg.

## Two stylistic variations of jeté battu:

### Bournonville jeté battu *(brushing slightly écarté derrière)*

From 5th plié, brush the back leg to the side and slightly to the back. Throughout the jump the arms are held in the Bournonville 5th en bas, with fingers at the sides of the thighs.

### Balanchine jeté battu *(with body inclination)*

From 5th plié, brush the back leg à la seconde, open the arms outward, and ascend, throwing the upper body sideways toward the leg that brushed.

From the high point of the jump in a small 2nd, return the leg that brushed to beat in an overcrossed 5th in back. Re-open the leg and land on the leg that brushed, with the other leg sur le cou-de-pied derrière.

Leaving the leg that brushed out to the side, bring the underneath leg across to beat in front.

Re-open the front leg just enough to change it to the back to cou-de-pied derrière **en l'air** and land, inclining the body over the fondu leg. The arms are in a stylistic variation of a high à la seconde.

In the finale of Balanchine's *Symphony in C*, New York City Ballet dancers execute petits jetés battus in the Balanchine style. Photo: Steven Caras.

# Brisé

Although students are sometimes taught to execute brisés traveling sideways with the leg brushing to écarté, the generally accepted correct manner for studying them is as shown here: **traveling forward and backward through 4th position**. The inclination of the body forward (brisé en avant) and backward (brisé en arrière) helps the dancer to travel in those directions.

In order to achieve the desired interlaced effect of the legs in the beat, the overcrossed 5th position en l'air is essential. This is difficult, because the legs beat in an effacé rather than a croisé position. Dancers with hyper-extended legs may have to relax the knees slightly in order to be able to cross the feet.

Brisés may also be executed in sequence, traveling in a small circle (en tournant). The body always turns into the new direction on the initial outward brush (see p. 176).

EN AVANT

From 5th croisé plié—

Brush the back leg forward through 1st plié. The upstage arm lifts to 1st, and the other opens outward to 2nd.

Jump with a battement to 45° effacé devant. The body inclines forward, eyes looking over the arm in 1st.

Bring the underneath leg up to meet the battement leg. The feet must be overcrossed in 5th, with the toes appearing to meet.

EN ARRIÈRE

From 5th croisé plié—

Brush the front leg backward through 1st plié. The downstage arm lifts to 1st, and the other opens outward to 2nd.

Jump with a battement to 45° effacé derrière. The upper body leans slightly back. The eyes look downstage over the shoulder.

Bring the underneath leg up to meet the battement leg. The feet must be overcrossed in 5th, with the toes appearing to meet.

In American Ballet Theatre's production of *La Sylphide*, Johan Renvall executes a perfect entrechat six de volée. Photo: Mira.

Traveling forward in the air, release the legs from 5th, exchanging them in the air and reaching for the floor with the upstage leg.

Land on the upstage leg, **immediately** closing the croisé leg to 5th plié. The legs should appear to land almost simultaneously. Maintain the inclination of the body over the front arm.

Traveling backward in the air, release the legs from 5th, exchanging them in the air and reaching for the floor with the croisé (downstage) leg.

Land on the downstage leg, **immediately** closing the back leg to 5th plié. The legs should appear to land almost simultaneously. The body is erect.

# Brisé volé

Brisés volés are usually executed in a series, which may be performed either staying in place or traveling forward (as in the famous Bluebird variation from Act III of *The Sleeping Beauty*). There are three acceptable positions in which the lifted leg may be held upon landing: in a low attitude (shown here), in cou-de-pied (fully pointed, not wrapped), and fully extended at 30° croisé devant or derrière.

From 5th plié, brush the back leg forward through 1st plié. The arms lift to low 3rd.

Jump as the upstage leg executes a battement to effacé devant, immediately bringing the underneath leg up to join it in an overcrossed 5th position. The body inclines forward over the legs.

Release the legs from 5th, exchanging them in the air, and land on the upstage leg in plié, with the front leg lifted in a low attitude croisée devant.

# Bournonville brisé

These brisés have a light, loping quality and are usually performed en diagonale in a series. The emphasis is on speed and distance traveled, rather than on elevation; they are extremely terre à terre. The landing on the leading leg is immediately followed by a transfer of weight forward onto the croisé leg into a small 4th position. (This is quite different from the standard allegro brisé, which lands in 5th position.)

Step forward in 4th. The arms are in low 3rd, with the body slightly inclined forward over the arm in 1st.

Battement the back leg through, jumping in effacé devant.

Lift the underneath leg up to join the battement leg in an overcrossed 5th, traveling forward in the air.

Brush the front leg back through 1st plié, bringing the torso upright and opening the upstage arm to 2nd.

Jump as the downstage leg executes a battement to effacé derrière, immediately bringing the underneath leg up to join it in an over-crossed 5th position. The upstage arm lifts to high 5th allongée, as the body arches back and twists slightly downstage.

Release the legs from 5th, exchanging them in the air, and land in plié on the downstage leg, with the back leg lifted in a low attitude croisée derrière. The body inclines slightly sideways (downstage).

Release the legs from 5th, exchanging them in the air, and land on the upstage leg, lowering the toe of the front leg to 4th position on the floor.

Immediately transfer the weight forward onto the front leg in 4th plié.

# Sissonne Battue

## Sissonne ouverte battue

SHOWN CROISÉE DERRIÈRE,
TRAVELING EN AVANT

Jump from 5th plié croisé, bringing the back leg forward to beat in front in 5th (as in entre-chat quatre). The arms lift to 1st.

## Sissonne ouverte changée battue

SHOWN EFFACÉE DEVANT,
TRAVELING EN ARRIÈRE

Jump from 5th plié, beating the front foot in front in 5th (as in royale). The arms lift to 1st.

## Sissonne fermée changée battue

SHOWN DESSUS,
TRAVELING DE CÔTÉ

Jump from 5th plié, beating the front foot in front in 5th (as in royale). The arms lift to 1st.

Take the front leg to the back, executing a grand battement croisé derrière traveling forward in the air, opening the arms to 3rd arabesque. Land on the front leg in plié with the weight well forward, without dropping the lifted leg.

Exchange the legs in the air, bringing the back leg forward with grand battement effacé devant and traveling backward in the air.

The arms lift to high 3rd in opposition. Land in plié effacé devant at 90°, with the supporting knee well turned-out and without tucking the pelvis under. There should be a small but strong arch in the lower back, with the torso well lifted above the waist.

Open the back leg with grand battement à la seconde, traveling sideways toward the original front leg and opening the leading arm to 2nd, with épaulement over the arm in 1st.

Land on the leading leg, quickly closing the battement leg to 5th in front through a pointed position on the floor.

# Grand Assemblé Entrechat Six de Volée

Tombé en avant croisé and jump, brushing the back leg through 1st to effacé devant. The arms lift to 1st.

Join the feet together at the top of the jump, bringing the underneath leg up to close in back of the battement leg. The body turns into écarté with arms in écarté devant allongé. Look up past the top arm.

Open the legs, taking the front one to the back.

# Grand Fouetté Battu en Tournant

Execute a tombé croisé, facing up-stage. The arms lower en bas.

Jump, bringing the back leg through with grand battement devant, lifting the arms to 1st.

Immediately lift the underneath leg up to beat in back of the battement leg. The arms lift to 5th, with the body leaning back.

# Grand Jeté Entrelacé Battu

Execute a tombé croisé, facing up-stage. The arms lower en bas.

Jump, bringing the back leg through with grand battement devant, lifting the arms to 1st.

Immediately lift the underneath leg up to beat in back of the battement leg. The arms lift to 5th, with the body leaning back.

Beat in back in 5th.

Re-open the legs, bringing the back leg forward to land in front in 5th position demi-plié. Maintain the upper body pose.

Turn the body over in the air (toward upstage), taking the front leg to the back in 5th.

Continue turning the body while opening the arms outward and releasing the croisé leg toward the floor.

Land in plié in 3rd arabesque at 90°, with the supporting foot well turned-out and the weight well forward over the plié.

Turn the body over in the air (toward upstage), taking the front leg to the back in 5th.

Continuing to turn the body, bring the back foot to the front. Lower it toward the floor, opening the arms outward.

Land in 1st arabesque plié at 90° with the weight well forward, without dropping the arabesque leg.

# Cabriole

The correct execution of all cabrioles **requires that the underneath (beating) leg come up to join the initial battement leg in 5th.** Bringing the top leg down to meet the push-off leg will result in an undesirable drop in elevation at the top of the jump.

## Cabriole fermée

SHOWN À LA SECONDE
DESSUS

From tombé croisé, brush the back leg through 1st, jumping with grand battement à la seconde. The arms lower en bas and lift through 1st into low 3rd with épaulement.

## Cabriole ouverte

SHOWN IN
1ST ARABESQUE AT 45°

From pointe tendue croisée derrière, bring back leg forward and tombé en avant into plié in 1st arabesque at 45°. Jump, lifting underneath leg up and back toward the leg in arabesque.

## Grande cabriole ouverte

SHOWN IN
EFFACÉ DEVANT

From tombé croisé, brush the back leg through 1st into grand battement effacé devant as the jump ascends. The arms lift to 1st.

Open arms to high 3rd in opposition, as bottom leg lifts toward battement leg.

NOTE: Cabrioles with multiple beats are performed only by male dancers. They are virtuoso feats, in which the legs beat together very quickly two or three times in 5th at the top of the jump. The opening between the legs in these beats is very small, with the legs remaining in the same relationship in 5th.

Bring the underneath leg up to join the battement leg, closing it behind in an overcrossed 5th.

Release the underneath leg, landing on it with the other leg still lifted à la seconde. Quickly close the lifted leg to 5th plié in front. Maintain the upper body pose throughout.

Close the underneath leg in front in an overcrossed 5th position.

Release the underneath leg, reaching for the floor. Land in plié in 1st arabesque with the weight well forward and the upper back strongly held in 1st arabesque. Special effort is required to keep the back leg from dropping with the force of the landing.

Close the underneath leg behind in an overcrossed 5th at the top of the jump.

Release the underneath leg, reaching for the floor. Land in plié at 90° in the pose effacée devant, without tucking the pelvis under and with a strongly held upper back.

# Advanced variations of cabriole:

## Grande cabriole fouettée

There are two acceptable methods for executing this step. In one, the beat at the top of the jump occurs in front (with the initial battement leg on top) before the body fouettés (or turns) en l'air. In the other (shown here) the beat occurs behind, just after the fouetté.

The second method is generally preferred by most male dancers. When it is performed with a double beat, it may be executed with the first beat in front before the fouetté and the second beat behind after the turn, or with both beats behind in the arabesque position after the fouetté.

**SHOWN EN DEDANS TO 1ST ARABESQUE**

Execute a tombé croisé, bringing the arms en bas and lifting them to 1st.

Jump, brushing the back leg through into grand battement effacé devant.

## Grande cabriole fouettée with double beat

**SHOWN EN DEDANS TO 4TH ARABESQUE**

Tombé upstage, bringing the arms en bas and up through 1st.

Jump, brushing the back leg through into grand battement devant. The arms continue to lift toward 5th.

Execute the first beat by drawing the push-off leg up to close behind the battement leg in 5th.

Turning the body away from the battement leg, draw the push-off leg up to close underneath so that it appears as if the beat is occurring in arabesque. The arms lift to 5th en haut.

Open the arms and legs outward and land in plié in 1st arabesque.

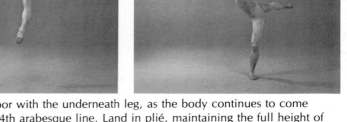

Turn the body upstage en l'air, changing the front leg to beat behind in 5th and opening the arms outward to arabesque.

Reach for the floor with the underneath leg, as the body continues to come around into the 4th arabesque line. Land in plié, maintaining the full height of the extension in arabesque with a strongly held upper back.

Cheryl Yeager piqués to arabesque en pointe in American Ballet Theatre's production of *Don Quixote*. Photo: Mira.

# 14 ✎ Pointe Work

Dancing on the tips of the toes evolved during the Romantic period in the early nineteenth century, as a means of elevating the female dancer above the floor in order to give her an airborne, ethereal quality. It requires special footwear: satin shoes with stiffened, reinforced toes, the tips of which are squared off to provide a small platform on which the dancer is able to balance. Gradually, the pointe shoe developed into a tool for virtuosity; it is effectively used by contemporary dancers to display their ability to spin and balance on its tiny tip. Pointe work also has the much-desired aesthetic effect of lengthening the line of a dancer's legs.

Pointe work, by tradition, is usually performed only by female dancers. The study of pointe work is begun only after a student has acquired proper placement and a considerable amount of technical strength on the demi-pointe. It takes many years of daily practice to develop a strong, graceful, and painless pointe technique. It should be undertaken only by someone who is seriously committed to the study of classical ballet (see p. 81). Additional illustrations of the correct manner in which to wear a toe shoe are on p. 12.

In lower-level classes, when the students' placement, legs, and feet are deemed sufficiently developed, pointe work can be introduced, beginning with approximately ten minutes en pointe at the end of the class. First, simple rises and relevés on two feet are performed slowly, facing the barre. Later, as stability and strength improve, similar exercises, as well as bourrées, can be performed in the centre. For instance, contrary to appearance, courus (little runs) across the floor in 6th position are a rather easy movement for young dancers, and one that they particularly enjoy.

Gradually, as students reach the intermediate level, their feet can tolerate longer and longer periods of pointe work and they can begin the study of all movements en pointe, including the more difficult ones such as relevés on one leg and pirouettes.

At the advanced level, pointe class (usually forty-five minutes to one hour in length) is an intensive session in which excerpts from female variations from the classical repertoire are studied and virtuosity en pointe is mastered.

Pictured on the following pages is a selection of the most common movements associated with pointe work. The vocabulary of possible movements en pointe, however, is certainly not limited to these few steps. All turning movements that are first learned en demi-pointe are later studied en pointe, including pirouettes, piqué turns, fouettés, and chaînés déboulés. Many of these are pictured en pointe in chapter 8, "The Traditional Turns of Classical Ballet," beginning on p. 177. In addition, dancers often perform small jumps, such as assemblés, en pointe.

The ultimate goal of dancing en pointe is to make it seem effortless. Ideally, the pointe shoe should appear to be a natural extension of the foot. The action of going up en pointe and coming down should be so controlled and smoothly executed as to be barely noticeable. A dancer should be able to dance allegro movements en pointe with sharpness and brilliant attack, and adagio movements with softness and fluidity. The mastery of these two extremes undoubtedly provides the greatest challenge in developing pointe technique.

There are two acceptable ways to rise en pointe: (1) by executing a relevé that employs a slight spring and displacement of the toes, and (2) by simply "rolling up" through the foot without moving the toes at all. The rolling-up method takes considerable strength and is used in adagio movements, such as fondu relevé, and in very fast movements, such as a series of relevé passés in which the speed of the choreography makes it impossible to slide the toes in and out or to fully transfer the center of the body's weight over the toe on each relevé. Although this chapter deals primarily with the types of relevés in which the toes are displaced, both methods of rising en pointe must be practiced and mastered.

# Rolling Up through the Feet without a Spring

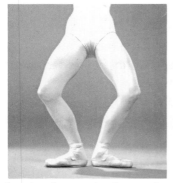 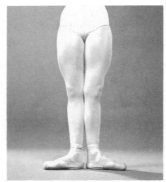  

Leaving the toes in place, roll up en pointe (and down), passing smoothly through a high demi-pointe position.

# Relevés from Both Feet (with a spring, sliding the toes)

The quality of movement used in these relevés lies somewhere between a jump and a smooth, rolling-up movement through the feet. There is a slight spring, but the toes never leave the floor. Instead, they slide inward, coming under the heels as the knees straighten.

Relevé is always a fast, bright movement, the effort of which must never be reflected in the upper body. To return to initial plié position, the dancer uses another slight spring to come off pointe, during which the toes readjust outward.

## Relevé in 1st position

Plié in 1st and spring upward, straightening the knees and simultaneously drawing the toes of both feet inward under the heels. (The feet must move equal distances). The toes must readjust outward to return to the initial plié position.

# Relevé in 2nd position

Plié in 2nd and spring upward, straightening the knees and simultaneously drawing the toes of both feet inward under the heels. The toes must readjust outward to return to the initial plié position.

NOTE: If 2nd position en pointe is too wide, the dancer will not be able to stand directly on top of the toes.

# Relevé in 4th position

Plié in 4th and spring upward, straightening the knees and simultaneously drawing the toes across into a straight line front to back, aligned with the center of the body. The toes must readjust outward to return to the initial plié position.

# Relevé in 5th position

Plié in 5th and spring upward, straightening the knees and drawing the toes together under the center of the body. There must be no space between the feet. Only one foot is completely visible from the front. The toes must be readjusted outward to return to the initial plié position.

Échappé relevé (from échapper, "to escape") is one of the most common exercises en pointe. From 5th plié, the feet "escape" to an open position (either 2nd or 4th), rising quickly onto pointe with a slight spring, then return, quickly sliding off pointe into 5th plié. Both the outward and the inward movements of the legs are relatively fast. The feet must achieve the open position en pointe at the same time and close to 5th at the same time; and they must travel equal distances out and in.

Simple échappé relevé involves just the outward movement onto pointe and the inward movement to 5th plié. Occasionally, as an exercise to heighten a student's awareness of turn-out, échappés may also be performed from 1st position to 2nd. Two forms of échappé are pictured here: échappé double in 2nd, which is also commonly performed in 4th, and échappé in 4th, which is also performed à la seconde.

## Échappé double

SHOWN À LA SECONDE CHANGÉE

Plié in 5th.

Slide both feet out to the side; they arrive en pointe simultaneously.

Plié à la seconde.

Slide both feet inward to 5th en pointe. (The feet move equal distances.)

## Échappé in 4th position

INCORRECT

SHOWN EN CROISÉ

Plié in 4th and spring upward, sliding both feet outward to arrive simultaneously en pointe with the toes **in a straight line** front to back, aligned with the center of the body. In croisé both legs are fully visible.

Because the toes were not drawn across in front of the center of the body, the legs are in an open position; one of them is almost hidden behind the other, and the desired crossed effect of croisé is lost.

# Détourné

This movement is like a changement en pointe.

From 5th plié, spring onto pointe, turning toward the back leg and immediately exchanging the legs in 5th. Finish, after three-quarters of a turn, in 5th plié croisé. The arms close to 1st to facilitate the turn.

# Sous-sus

SHOWN EN AVANT

Relevé from 5th plié, simultaneously **traveling** forward en croisé to finish in 5th en pointe. The arms lift forward to arabesque à deux bras. The torso inclines slightly forward. (May also be executed en arrière.)

# Relevé passé

SHOWN DESSOUS

From 5th plié, spring upward, drawing the toe of the front leg up the front of the shinbone of the supporting leg, past the knee at 90°, and down the back of the supporting leg to close with a slight spring off pointe into 5th plié behind. (The toe of the supporting leg must readjust outward to come off pointe). The arms are in low 3rd.

NOTE: This movement may also be executed dessus, and with épaulement (not shown).

# Sissonne relevée

Sissonnes relevées are performed traveling in all directions and in all poses at both 45° and 90°.

SHOWN IN
2ND ARABESQUE AT 45°

From 5th plié croisé, spring up and forward with a one-quarter turn en dedans, **traveling** forward diagonally to finish in a low 2nd arabesque line. The leading (supporting) toe slides out to pointe in the manner of an échappé. The torso must be carried well forward over the supporting hip.

# Rond de jambe en l'air relevé

SHOWN EN DEHORS

From 5th plié croisé, spring upward, **brushing** the front leg à la seconde as the body comes en face. Immediately execute a rond de jambe en l'air en dehors, finishing en pointe. The arms are in low 3rd, with épaulement to the rond de jambe leg. (May also be executed en dedans and with double rond de jambe en l'air.)

# Retiré relevé (sissonne simple relevée in Soviet syllabus)

This movement may also be executed derrière, and with petit retiré to the level of cou-de-pied.

SHOWN DEVANT

From 5th plié, spring upward, drawing the toe of the front leg up the front of the shinbone of the supporting leg, to finish in front under the knee at 90°.

# Relevés from one foot

## Assemblé soutenu

**SHOWN DESSUS**

  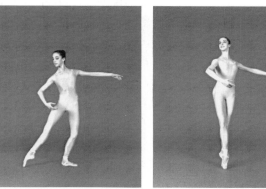

From 5th plié—

Slide the back foot to pointe tendue à la seconde, maintaining the fondu on the supporting leg and inclining slightly toward the extended leg. The arms are in low 3rd, with the eyes looking over the elbow of the arm in 1st.

Relevé en pointe, drawing the extended foot in to close in front of the supporting leg and finishing in 5th sur les pointes. The body straightens as the leg closes.

NOTE: Assemblé soutenu may also be executed dessous, as well as in all directions devant, derrière, and to the side without changing the legs.

## Ballonné relevé

**SHOWN CHANGING DIRECTIONS FROM EFFACÉ DEVANT TO 2ND POSITION EN FACE**

Execute a fondu sur le cou-de-pied effacé devant, with the back strongly held and the shoulders pressed down, and the arms in low 3rd in opposition.

Relevé, sliding the supporting toe forward to **travel** (approximately 6 inches) downstage as the lifted leg extends sharply 45° effacé devant.

With a slight spring to come off pointe, bend the knee, sharply changing direction to finish fondu sur le cou-de-pied devant en face.

Relevé in place, opening arms and leg à la seconde.

# Successive relevé turns on one foot at 90°

These turns, for advanced dancers only, require the following elements for successful execution: (1) a deep demi-plié over which the weight is maintained constantly forward; (2) forcing the supporting heel forward on each relevé; and (3) a slight opening and closing of the torso in the direction of the turn on each relevé. Take care to maintain the lifted leg at the same level throughout the turns.

**SHOWN EN DEDANS IN 1ST ARABESQUE**

Plié 1st arabesque at 90°.

Relevé, turning the body en dedans.

Plié off pointe, pressing the supporting heel well forward.

Relevé again, continuing to turn in the same direction. The amount of rotation is optional; quarter, half, and full turns are acceptable.

At the School of American Ballet in New York City, students bourrée under the watchful eye of their teacher, Alexandra Danilova. Photo: Steven Caras.

# Bourrées

In this movement the toes never leave the floor. The legs appear to ripple and are **always crossed.** The dancer thus appears to glide in perpetual motion across the floor. Bourrées sideways always move toward the front foot. They may also be performed sur la place, as well as traveling en avant and en arrière. The arms are shown here in high 3rd, but a variety of port de bras, either static (as shown) or in motion, may be used.

## Pas de bourrée suivi

From 5th position en pointe, alternately flexing and straightening the knees, move the back foot sideways behind and past the front foot, in the direction traveled. Slide the front foot sideways in the same way. Continue in this manner, traveling to the side toward the front foot, alternating the sliding movements (first the back foot, then the front).

## Pas de bourrée couru

### EN AVANT

With the feet almost parallel in a barely turned-out 1st position, run forward sur les pointes, keeping the knees relaxed and the weight well forward. The arms are shown here in arabesque à deux bras, but a variety of port de bras, either static or in motion, may be used.

### EN ARRIÈRE

In the same manner as pas couru en avant (described above), run backward sur les pointes. The body leans slightly back. As noted above, a variety of port de bras, either static or in motion, may be used.

# Piqué *(jeté in Soviet syllabus)*

Piqués are performed in all directions and poses, at both 45° and 90°.

## Piqué at 90°

**SHOWN EN AVANT TO 1ST ARABESQUE**

From fondu at 45°, maintaining a strongly held back with the weight centered over the demi-plié, step forward directly onto pointe, immediately lifting the other leg in the manner of a grand battement to arabesque. The body must effect a full and immediate transfer of weight from one leg to the other.

## Coupé piqué ballonné

**SHOWN DESSOUS**

From fondu sur le cou-de-pied derrière, coupé under, stepping directly onto pointe through 5th behind, throwing the front leg à la seconde at 45°, and opening the arms to 2nd. Maintain the integrity of the supporting side of the body without any inclination whatsoever. The shoulders are directly over the hips.

Finish with a spring off pointe, sharply bending the extended leg to finish in back in cou-de-pied and closing the arm on the side of the supporting leg to 1st with épaulement.

NOTE: These may also be performed dessus.

# *Piqué en tournant at 90°*

From a preparatory plié effacé devant, step directly onto pointe, turning in the direction of the supporting leg. Execute a strong grand battement to attitude derrière, taking the head and torso into the direction of the turn and closing the second side of the body. The front arm opens à la seconde and the other arm lifts from 2nd in reverse to 5th, passing diagonally in front of the head. The shoulders must be placed well in front of the hips.

> NOTE: Piqué turns at 90° en dedans are performed in many poses devant, derrière, and à la seconde. They are rarely performed en dehors.

# *Piqué soutenu (or glissade) en tournant*

SHOWN EN DEDANS

Prepare in pointe tendue croisée devant.

Fondu, opening the leg effacé devant.

Step directly onto pointe to the downstage diagonal, immediately drawing the other leg across in front in 5th croisé and closing the arms to 1st.

Turn toward the back leg, exchanging the feet in 5th to finish after three-quarters of a turn in croisé.

> NOTE: This turn is also performed en dehors, stepping to the side, closing in back, and turning toward the back foot to finish in croisé.

# Demi-caractère Steps

## Piqué fondu *(also called pas marché)*

This step should have a very gentle, pliable quality. It is also performed en arrière.

SHOWN EN AVANT

From "B+" croisé execute a fondu, bringing the back foot forward with passé développé effacé devant at 45°. The body inclines to the upstage side, with arms in a relaxed demi-seconde.

## Pas de polka

With hands on hips in demi-caractère style, execute a small hop and piqué en avant to 4th en pointe.

Slide the back foot forward to close 5th in back en pointe. Transfer the weight back onto it and step forward again in 4th with the front leg.

## Pas de basque

This step is performed in three-quarter time, most commonly with a mazurka. The leg is thrown in an arc on the upbeat. The step forward with développé croisé occurs on the first count. The piqué en avant is on count two, the coupé on count three.

From "B+" croisé, fondu coupé under, throwing the front leg en dehors in an arc to effacé devant. Note the placement of the hands on the hips, with the wrists down and the elbows pressed well forward in the demi-caractère style.

Step forward, transferring the weight directly onto pointe and bringing the back leg through passé at the cou-de-pied level into fondu développé croisé devant. The body changes over to incline downstage. **The lowering off pointe at the moment of développé must be performed by softly rolling through the foot with control.**

Hop en pointe on the front leg, executing a passé développé to croisé devant with the back leg (at the level of cou-de-pied).

Transfer the weight forward onto the croisé leg en pointe and slide the back foot in to 5th behind.

Step diagonally forward (downstage) onto the effacé devant leg and, staying in plié, simultaneously execute a passé développé croisé devant with the back leg.

Piqué en avant in croisé, drawing the back foot in to cou-de-pied derrière. Coupé under, extending the front leg croisé devant.

# Jumps en Pointe

When standing en pointe in demi-plié (at the beginning or end of a jump), pull the heel back a bit so that the ankle, **which must be strongly held,** is slightly flexed. **Never** try to push over into an arched position when jumping en pointe.

## Small jumps

All small jumps (temps levés, échappés, petits assemblés, petits jetés, etc.) may be performed en pointe. Only one example is shown below.

### Changement de pieds

From 5th plié, spring onto pointe directly into demi-plié, holding the feet securely in 5th and pulling back slightly at the ankles.

Jump, straightening the knees en l'air and changing the front foot to the back. Land in plié en pointe.

## Hops on one foot en tournant

These hops are usually performed in a series, with each hop rotating approximately one-quarter of a turn. They may be performed in all poses, as well as en dehors, and at 45°. Two virtuoso forms of hops on one leg commonly performed in classical variations are: (1) those in which the dancer, hopping forward en diagonale, simultaneously executes a series of small ronds de jambe en l'air; and (2) those in which the dancer, hopping in place in a circle, slowly changes the lifted leg from one pose to another, usually by means of a passé développé.

SHOWN IN ATTITUDE DERRIÈRE EN TOURNANT EN DEDANS AT 90°

From fondu effacé devant preparation, piqué **directly onto a bent supporting leg** in attitude derrière, opening the arms to the side. With the ankle securely held, execute a small hop, barely leaving the floor and turning the body toward the supporting leg. Maintain the height of the attitude leg throughout, keeping the shoulders placed well in front of the hips.

Melinda Roy hops en pointe in attitude in the New York City Ballet production of *Rubies*. Photo: Steven Caras.

# Turning en Manège

Both male and female dancers often finish virtuoso variations with a fast series of turns performed in a circle around the periphery of the stage.

During a manège of turns by a female dancer (usually consisting of combinations of piqué turns, chaînés déboulés, and/or jetés with coupé en tournant), the dancer must constantly readjust her "spot." With each new step en avant, she focuses to a new point around the outer edge of the stage. In the following series of pictures, the dancer demonstrates the method of changing the spot in a manège of piqué turns en dedans.

## Piqué turns en dedans in a circle

Piqué en avant, turning en dedans with the foot at the back of the knee.

Coupé under, changing the head to spot to the new direction. Piqué turn en dedans, stepping toward the new direction.

# Emboîté sur les Pointes

These brilliant little walks traveling downstage (cutting the legs "over" each other) are very common in pointe variations. They were used extensively by Petipa, most notably in *The Sleeping Beauty,* Act II (by Aurora's Friends). When executed traveling en arrière (with the legs cutting "under"), the step is called déboîté sur les pointes.

SHOWN EN AVANT

From 5th position en pointe, dégagé the back foot sharply à la seconde and close it in front in a slightly overcrossed 5th en pointe. At the moment of closing, the other leg immediately executes a dégagé à la seconde, so that **the weight is never on both feet for more than a moment**. The effect is one of throwing the weight from one foot to the other while brilliantly executing low battements to the side.

## *Floor pattern of a full circle manège*

The arrows indicate the new direction toward which the dancer steps with each turn. To counteract the pull of centrifugal force toward the inside of the circle, the dancer **always steps toward the outside of the circle.**

The spaces between the points of the circle must be equally divided among the total number of steps to be executed. Each piqué steps to a new point, and each must travel the same distance around the circular pattern.

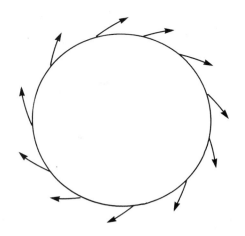

Continue in the circular pattern. With each coupé under, the body faces the new direction and the spot changes. Each turn is approximately one-and-a-quarter rotations. The arm that opens to the side must never open behind the shoulder, and the body must face each new direction (as in 4th position) before stepping into the turn.

Continue to move downstage with a series of dégagés dessus, each closing in an overcrossed 5th. The distance traveled in each step is a little more than the width of one 5th position. The arms are held forward in a low demi-seconde (as if poised over the edge of an imaginary tutu), the body inclines slightly forward, and the head changes from side to side, following the movement of each dégagé à la seconde.

# 15 ✑ Révérence

Révérence ("bow") is the final exercise in the ballet class. It should not be trivialized, nor should it ever be omitted from class. It is a traditional port de bras based upon classic mime gestures and is used by students to show respect and gratitude to their teacher and piano accompanist. On stage, the same graceful movements are used by the performer to say "thank you" to an applauding audience.

In the past, learning to bow and curtsy was an integral part of every person's social upbringing. Since this is no longer the case, the practice of these movements often seems silly or superfluous to contemporary students. The importance of cultivating a gracious, sincere, and natural-looking bow, however, cannot be overemphasized; it is the final visual impression with which the performer leaves the audience.

## Standard Women's Révérence

Extend one leg pointe tendue à la seconde and step over onto it to the side (not shown), bringing the other foot behind into "B+" (knees together!). Gesture with the palm up downstage at a 45° angle, first toward the direction of the supporting foot, then toward the other downstage diagonal.

## Standard Men's Révérence

Extend the back leg to the side, opening the arms outward. Step over onto it, lifting one arm as if in greeting, palm facing away from the audience. Draw the second leg in with relaxed knee, heel slightly off the floor, to a small, barely turned-out 1st position.

Lift both arms, bringing the head and torso directly en face. Bow, bending both knees, releasing the back foot as shown, and dropping the chin and eyes as the arms lower to demi- seconde, palms down. Maintain a straight back.

To bow lower, deepen the plié and tip the back and head **slightly** forward.

Extend the arm forward toward the audience.

Drop the arm to the side of the thigh. Lower the chin and eyes.

Variation: bring the arm across the chest and bow over it.

Students at the Ballet Aspen Summer Dance School bow to their teacher at the end of class. Photo: Daniel Kaczor.

# A Final Note:
# Classroom Etiquette

An aspect of training that should never be neglected is the practice of proper classroom etiquette. The traditional, prescribed modes of dress and behavior for ballet class are important preparation for the discipline and demeanor expected of all professional dancers. Students who are respectful and courteous toward the other dancers, the teacher, and the accompanist in class are training themselves to function much more successfully in a professional ballet company than those who are selfish and ill-mannered. Professional companies are large machines in which the expertise of many people other than the dancers is essential to the success of the performances. Courteous dancers are aware of the importance of people such as technicians, designers, musicians, and ballet masters and work with them in a gracious and professional manner. They appreciate the fact that a dance performance is a group effort, one in which every participant is important, and they are helpful and supportive toward their fellow dancers.

Students must understand that displays of temper and rudeness are as self-destructive and unacceptable in the classroom as they are in the profession. Teachers should always remember that their own behavior in class provides a role model for the students. A teacher who is abusive toward an accompanist is in effect saying to students that it is permissible for them to be so. Teachers who are insensitive, cruel, or disrespectful toward their students create an atmosphere of undesirable tension in the classroom, one in which students will not flourish. Such behavior not only provides a bad example but is the antithesis of the gracious manners and mores of the seventeenth century, in which all ballet tradition is firmly rooted. Teachers should keep in mind that a few words of encouragement to a student usually produce much better results than endless diatribes.

Practice clothes should be comfortable, neat, clean, and close-fitting. A teacher cannot accurately correct a student without seeing all parts of the student's silhouette. Given the sweaty nature of dancing and the fact that dancers work in close proximity to each other in class, cleanliness is imperative. Safety pins and jewelry such as rings, bracelets, and pierced earrings can be dangerous not only to the wearer, but also to other students who may inadvertently come in contact with them. (Jewelry is especially to be avoided in partnering or pas de deux classes.)

A large part of dance training includes the study of turns. Classroom apparel that is loose or left hanging (belts, shoe ribbons, dangling earrings) will fly about when a dancer is turning, striking the body with each rotation and inhibiting the ability to spin. Everything worn in class must stay close to the body. This includes women's hairdos, which should be sleek and well secured, up and away from the face and neck. A student who is meticulous in dressing for class will bring the same care to dressing in costume for the stage. Artistic directors and costume designers are very particular about grooming and always appreciate a dancer who is careful and sensitive to detail in this regard. If teachers express a preference regarding classroom apparel, their wishes should be respected. Some find it less distracting or easier to look at all members of a class on an equal basis, if everyone is dressed alike.

It is important for students to remain in their assigned places or formations—at the barre, in lines in the centre, and in groups moving across the floor. In this way they do not crowd each other and can avoid accidental and potentially dangerous collisions. Keeping in line or formation is also excellent practice for the challenge of corps de ballet work, an extremely difficult convention of classical ballet choreography. Students should strive to be constantly aware of where they are in space and of what is around them. The stage can be a dangerous and unpredictable place. Scenery may be placed slightly differently from night to night. Other dancers, in error, can suddenly appear when and where they are not expected. A professional dancer must always be on guard for the unexpected and be able, on a moment's notice, to make whatever spatial readjustments are necessary.

No one except the teacher should ever instruct the accompanist to change tempo in a ballet class. If the dancers feel that the music is too slow or too fast, they should inform the teacher, who may or may not agree. Students should remember that the teacher may have selected a tempo that is slightly uncomfortable in order to challenge them, and that by struggling with it they may acquire greater skill or strength.

It is improper for a student ever to question a teacher's authority in class. The time to do this, in a civilized fashion, is after class in private consultation with the teacher.

Chewing gum, eating, drinking, smoking, talking, sitting down, wandering in and out of the room, or leaning against the wall are as unacceptable during a ballet class as they would be on stage in front of an audience. Teachers should not allow students to indulge in any of these practices.

Students who arrive late for class usually should not be permitted to participate. Although teachers may occasionally make exceptions to this rule, it should be remembered that the barre exercises are designed to be done in a carefully regulated progression in order to warm up the body safely and slowly. A student who misses the initial pliés and tendus risks discomfort and injury by starting the barre work when faster and more strenuous exercises are being performed.

No student should ever leave class early without first informing and thanking the teacher. This is a common courtesy expected by all ballet teachers and should be done in a discreet manner so as not to disrupt the class. Whenever possible, a student who needs to leave early should request permission from the teacher before class begins.

Students should never be allowed to stop before completing an exercise unless they have sustained an injury. Giving up is defeatist and counterproductive. In addition, a student who leaves the floor before an exercise is finished causes an annoying and potentially dangerous distraction to those still dancing. Students should be reminded that a professional dancer would **never** consider cutting short a variation on stage, even if he or she were suddenly in great pain. This kind of mind-over-body discipline is considered de rigueur in the dance world. Students must learn to endure and to wait until they are off the floor to give in to fatigue or frustration.

Teachers and students alike should regard the ballet class as a ritual to be treasured. They should undertake their activities in the classroom with the same serious, responsible, and disciplined demeanor with which professionals approach dancing in front of an audience. It is a place to study, to grow, to discover, and to excel.

# Pronunciation Guide

## Key to phonetic pronunciation

All sounds are as in English except as noted below.

zh = **s** as in mea**s**ure, lei**s**ure
ew = **u** as in c**u**pid
eh = **ai** as in p**ai**r
oh = **o** as in r**o**le

oo = **oo** as in sh**oo**t, z**oo**
ahn = **on** as in c**on**cert
ohn = **on** as in l**on**g
ohm = om as in c**ome**

**À**   ah
**Allongé(e)**   ah-lohn-ZHAY
**Arabesque**   ah-rah-BESK
**Arrière, en**   ah nah-RYEHR
**Assemblé**   ah-sahm-BLAY
**Attitude**   ah-tee-TEWD
**Avant, en**   ah na-VAHN

**Balancé**   bah-lahn-SAY
**Balançoire**   bah-lahn-SWARR
**Ballonné**   bah-luh-NAY
**Ballotté**   bah-luh-TAY
**Bas, en**   ahn bah
**Battement**   baht-MAHN
**Battements divisés en quarts**   baht-MAHN
   dee-vee-ZAY ahn kar
**Batterie**   bah-TREE
**Battu(e)**   bah-TEW
**Bourrée**   boo-RAY
**Brisé**   bree-ZAY
**Brisé volé**   bree-ZAY voh-LAY

**Cabriole**   kah-bree-ohl
**Chaîné**   shay-NAY
**Changé(e)**   shahn-ZHAY
**Changement**   shahnzh-MAHN
**Changement de pieds**   shahnzh-MAHN duh pyay
**Chassé**   shah-SAY
**Cinq**   sank
**Cloche, en**   ahn klohsh
**Contretemps**   kohn-truh-TAHN
**Côté, de**   duh koh-TAY
**Cou-de-pied**   koo-duh-pyay
**Coupé**   koo-PAY
**Couru**   koo-REW
**Croisé**   krwah-ZAY

**Déboulé**   DAY-boo-LAY
**Dedans, en**   ahn duh-DAHN
**Dégagé**   DAY-gah-ZHAY
**Dehors, en**   ahn duh-OR

**Demi**   duh-MEE
**Demi-caractére**   duh-MEE ka-rak-TEHR
**Demi-contretemps**   duh-MEE kohn-truh-TAHN
**Demi-plié**   duh-MEE plee-AY
**Demi-pointe**   duh-MEE pwant
**Demi-rond**   duh-MEE rohn
**Demi-seconde**   duh-MEE suh-GOHND
**Derrière**   deh-RYEHR
**Dessous**   duh-SOO
**Dessus**   duh-SEW
**Détourné**   DAY-toor-NAY
**Deux bras, à**   ah duh brah
**Devant**   duh-VAHN
**Développé(e)**   DAYV-luh-PAY
**Diagonale, en**   ahn dya-guh-NAL
**D'ici-delà**   dee-SEE duh-LAH
**Double**   DOO-bluh
**Doublé(e)**   doo-BLAY

**Écarté(e)**   AY-kar-TAY
**Échappé**   AY-shah-PAY
**Effacé(e)**   ay-fah-SAY
**Élancé**   AY-lahn-SAY
**Élevé(e)**   AY-luh-VAY
**Emboîté**   ahn-bwah-TAY
**En**   ahn
**Entrechat**   ahn-truh-SHAH
**Entrechat cinq**   ahn-truh-SHAH sank
**Entrechat dix**   ahn-truh-SHAH deess
**Entrechat huit**   ahn-truh-SHAH weet
**Entrechat quatre**   ahn-truh-SHAH KA-truh
**Entrechat sept**   ahn-truh-SHAH set
**Entrechat six**   ahn-truh-SHAH seess
**Entrechat trois**   ahn-truh-SHAH trwah
**Enveloppé(e)**   ahn-vuh-law-PAY
**Épaulé**   AY-poh-LAY
**Épaulement**   AY-pohl-MAHN

**Face, en**   ahn fahss
**Failli**   fah-YEE
**Fermé(e)**   fehr-MAY

**Flic-flac**  fleek-FLAK
**Fondu(e)**  fohn-DEW
**Fouetté(e)**  fweh-TAY
**Frappé**  frah-PAY

**Gargouillade**  gahr-goo-YAHD
**Glissade**  glee-SAHD
**Glissé**  glee-SAY
**Grand, grande**  grahn, grahnd
**Grand jeté**  grahn zhuh-TAY
**Grand jeté entrelacé**  grahn zhuh-TAY
  ahn-truh-lah-SAY
**Grande pirouette**  grahnd peer-WET
**Grandes pirouettes sautillées**  grahnd peer-WET
  soh-tee-YAY
**Grand plié**  grahn plee-AY

**Haut, en**  ahn oh

**Italien**  ee-tah-LYEN

**Jeté**  zhuh-TAY

**L'air, en**  ahn lehr

**Manège, en**  ahn ma-NEZH

**Ouvert, ouverte**  oo-VEHR, oo-VEHRT

**Par terre**  pahr tehr
**Pas**  pah
**Pas chassé**  pah shah-SAY
**Pas couru**  pah koo-REW
**Pas de basque**  pah duh bahsk
**Pas de bourrée**  pah duh boo-RAY
**Pas de bourrée suivi**  pah duh boo-RAY swee-VEE
**Pas de chat**  pah duh shah
**Pas de cheval**  pah duh shuh-VAL
**Pas de ciseaux**  pas duh see-ZOH
**Pas de papillon**  pah duh pah-pee-YOHN
**Pas de poisson**  pah duh pwah-SOHN
**Pas failli**  pah fah-YEE
**Pas marché**  pah mar-SHAY
**Passé**  pah-SAY
**Penché(e)**  pahn-SHAY
**Petit, petite**  puh-TEE, puh-TEET
**Piqué**  pee-KAY
**Pirouette**  peer-WET
**Plié**  plee-AY
**Pointé**  pwan-TAY
**Pointe, en**  ahn pwant
**Pointes, sur les**  sir lay pwant
**Pointe tendue**  pwant tahn-DEW

**Port de bras**  por duh brah
**Porté(e)**  por-TAY
**Précipité(e)**  pray-see-pee-TAY
**Promenade**  pruhm-NAD

**Quart, à**  ah KAR
**Quatre**  KA-truh
**Quatrième, à la**  ah lah ka-tree-EM

**Relevé(e)**  ruhl-VAY
**Relevé lent**  ruhl-VAY lahn
**Renversé**  rahn-vehr-SAY
**Retiré**  ruh-tee-RAY
**Retombé(e)**  ruh-tohm-BAY
**Révérence**  RAY-VAY-RAHNSS
**Revoltade**  ruh-vuhl-TAHD
**Rond, en**  ahn ROHN
**Rond de jambe**  rohn duh ZHAHNB
**Royale**  rwah-YAL

**Saut de basque**  soh duh BAHSK
**Saut de biches**  soh duh BEESH
**Sauté(e)**  soh-TAY
**Sautillé(e)**  soh-tee-YAY
**Seconde, à la**  ah lah suh-GOHND
**Serré**  seh-RAY
**Sissonne**  see-SUN
**Soubresaut**  soo-bruh-SOH
**Sous-sus**  soo-SEW
**Soutenu**  soot-NEW
**Sur le cou-de-pied**  sir luh kood-PYAY

**Temps**  tahn
**Temps de cuisse**  tahn duh KWEES
**Temps de flèche**  tahn duh FLESH
**Temps levé**  tahn luh-VAY
**Temps lié**  tahn LEEYAY
**Temps relevé**  tahn ruhl-VAY
**Tendu(e)**  tahn-DEW
**Tendu double**  tahn-DEW DOO-bluh
**Tendu en tournant**  tahn-DEW ahn toor-NAHN
**Tendu pour batterie**  tahn-DEW poor ba-TREE
**Terre, à**  ah TEHR
**Tire-bouchon, en**  ahn teer-boo-shohn
**Tombé(e),**  tohm-BAY
**Tour**  toor
**Tour en l'air**  toor ahn LEHR
**Tour lent**  toor LAHN
**Tournant, en**  ahn toor-NAHN

**Volé(e), de**  du vuh-LAY

# Glossary of Common Ballet Terms

Movements defined in the text are not included in the glossary. Their definitions can be found by referring to the index.

**Accent**   That which is emphasized, usually a particular musical beat.

**Adagio**   Slow, sustained movement.

**Alignment**   The arrangement of the parts of the body in relation to each other according to the rules of classical ballet.

**Allegro, grand**   Combinations of expansive and widely traveled jumping movements that incorporate large, advanced-level leaps such as grands jetés.

**Allegro, petit**   Sprightly combinations of small jumping movements performed at a quick tempo.

**Allongé** (*fem.*, allongée)   Extended, outstretched, as opposed to bent or curved.

**Aplomb**   The poise and assurance exemplified by a dancer in complete control of his or her movements.

**Arabesque**   The position of the body when supported on one leg with the other extended to the back with the knee straight.

**Arrière, en**   Traveling backward.

**Attitude**   The position of the body when supported on one leg with the other lifted to the front, the side, or the back, with the knee bent.

**Avant, en**   Traveling forward.

**Backbend**   An arch of the body in which the dancer bends the upper body backward from the waist.

**Balanchine, George** (1904–1983)   The founder of the School of American Ballet and the New York City Ballet. Considered the leading neoclassic choreographer of the twentieth century, Balanchine was born in Soviet Georgia and trained at the Imperial Russian Ballet School in St. Petersburg. He choreographed his first major works for the Diaghilev Ballets Russes in the 1920s and emigrated to the United States in 1933, where he choreographed for the New York City Ballet for fifty years.

**Balançoire, en**   Literally, "like a seesaw." Used to describe the swinging of the working leg forward and backward through 1st position, as in grands battements en balançoire.

**Ballerina**   A principal female dancer in a ballet company.

**Ballet master/mistress**   The person in a ballet company who rehearses the repertoire and teaches company class.

**Balletomane**   An enthusiastic ballet fan.

**Ballon**   A term encompassing the desirable qualities of lightness, ease, and rebound when jumping.

**Barre**   The long, pipe-shaped bar (usually fastened horizontally to the wall of a ballet studio) that dancers hold onto for support when warming up. The word is also used to refer to the set of exercises performed at the barre at the beginning of every class.

**Bas, en**   Used to refer to any position in which the arms are held at hip level, as in 5th position en bas.

**Batterie**   Jumping movements in which the legs beat, or exchange places with each other, in 5th position in the air one or more times before landing. The effect is one of interlacing or crisscrossing the legs in the air.

**Beat**   To hit the legs together, moving them in and out of 5th position in the air so that they appear to crisscross. All batterie is composed of "beaten" movements.

**Beveled**   An incorrect position of the pointed foot in relationship to the ankle, in which the dancer angles the foot sideways outward from the ankle.

**Bournonville, Auguste** (1805–1879)   The great Danish ballet teacher and choreographer whose legacy includes such ballets as *Napoli* and *La Sylphide*. His uniquely musical classroom exercises are still used today by many teachers. In particular, he is credited with elevating the role of the male dancer in the 1800s to new importance through the creation of virtuoso solos for the leading men in his ballets.

**Cambré**   A bend of the body from the waist, forward, sideward, or backward.

**Cecchetti, Enrico** (1850–1928)   The illustrious Italian ballet teacher who counted among his pupils such famous dancers as Pavlova, Karsavina, Nijinsky, Massine, and Danilova. He developed a system for training dancers called the Cecchetti Method, based upon a routine set of daily exercises for each day of the week; it is still used by many teachers today. From 1890 to 1902 he was the teacher for the Imperial Russian Ballet in St. Petersburg, then taught for many years in England and Italy.

**Centre barre**   The exercises that are performed in the middle of the room without the support of the barre and that are directly related in form to the ten standard barre exercises. Examples: pliés, tendus, ronds de jambe, fondus.

**Centre work**   All exercises in a ballet class that are performed in the middle of the room without the support of the barre.

**Changé** (*fem.*, changée)   Literally, "changed." A term used to indicate that the feet change position in relationship to each other during the execution of a step (i.e., the foot that begins in the front finishes in the back, or vice versa).

**Character dance/style**   A stylized type of dancing derived from folk-dance forms but based upon classical ballet technique. Most of the large classic ballets such as *Swan Lake* or *Coppelia* include character dances, and all serious ballet students are required to study character dance as part of their training. Typical character dances are those based upon the Hungarian czardas, the Polish mazurka, the Italian tarantella, and the Spanish flamenco styles. In addition, the term can refer to any dance based on movements associated with a particular profession, personality, or life-style, such as a sailor's dance. A specific example is the clog dance for Mother Simone in Frederick Ashton's *La Fille Mal Gardée*.

**Choreography**   The arrangement of the steps and patterns in a dance composition.

**Cloche, en**   Literally, "like a bell." Refers to swinging movements of the working leg forward and backward through the 1st position in steps such as battements dégagés en cloche.

**Coda**   The finale of a dance; usually fast and showy.

**Combination**  A number of steps grouped together to form an exercise.

**Corps de ballet**  The dancers in a ballet company who do not perform solo roles. Typical of corps de ballet work is the performance of choreography in which the dancers move in large groups in unison while changing formation and creating beautiful spatial patterns across the stage.

**Côté, de**  Traveling to the side.

**Cou-de-pied**  On the "neck" (*cou*) of the ankle. The position of the working foot when lifted and pointed in front of, in back of, or wrapped around the ankle of the supporting leg.

**Croisé** (*fem.*, croisée)  Crossed. Refers to a direction of the body in which the legs of the dancer appear, from the audience's viewpoint, to be crossed one in front of the other. Examples: croisé devant (crossed with the working leg extended to the front) or arabesque croisée (crossed with the lifted back leg being the upstage leg). See pp. 42–43.

**Croix, en**  In the shape of a cross. Refers to a ballet convention in which the same movement is performed in sequence to the front, the side, the back, and again to the same side.

**Danseur, premier**  The leading male dancer in a ballet company.

**Danseur noble**  A male dancer who is tall, elegant, and aristocratic in appearance and dances leading roles such as the Prince in *Swan Lake* or the poet figure in *Les Sylphides*. He must be an excellent soloist and partner and possess pure classical line.

**Dedans, en**  Inward. Characterizes any circular or turning movement in which the working leg moves, or the body turns, toward the supporting leg.

**Dehors, en**  Outward. Characterizes any circular or turning movement in which the working leg moves, or the body turns, away from the supporting leg.

**Demi**  Half.

**Demi-caractère**  A term describing a type of classical ballet choreography that is heavily flavored with character-style or folk-dance references. An example of a demi-caractère divertissement is the *Don Quixote* pas de deux, with its many poses drawn from Spanish dancing. A demi-caractère dancer is one who is better suited to performing demi-caractère roles than strictly classical ones for reasons having to do with his or her physique, line, or natural quality of movement. A male dancer who is shorter than average, for instance, will be better cast in the demi-caractère role of the Jester in *Swan Lake* than in the danseur noble role of the Prince.

**Demi-pointe**  The position of the foot when the heel is raised from the floor and the dancer is poised on the ball of the foot. The term is often used synonymously with the term "relevé"—i.e., a dancer en relevé is also en demi-pointe.

**Derrière**  To the back.

**Dessous**  Under. Describes a movement in which one foot steps behind or cuts across in back of the other, sometimes replacing it, as in coupé dessous, when the back leg replaces the front leg.

**Dessus**  Over. Describes a movement in which one foot cuts across in front of the other, sometimes replacing it, as in coupé dessus, when the front leg replaces the back leg.

**Deux**  Two.

**Deux bras, à**  With two arms. This term usually refers to the Cecchetti 3rd arabesque pose, in which both arms are stretched forward in front of the body at shoulder level, with one raised slightly higher than the other.

**Devant**  To the front.

**Diagonale, en**  Traveling in a diagonal line across the stage or studio.

**Divertissement**   A suite of short dances designed to display the technical prowess and charm of the dancers.

**Downstage**   The area of the stage that is closest to the audience, i.e., the front of the stage. The term is derived from the period of the sixteenth and seventeenth centuries in European theatrical history, during which all stages were raked, or slanted, downward toward the audience, giving them a better view of the floor patterns made by the dancers. Dancers often use this term to indicate their location or direction of movement on the stage.

**Écarté** (*fem.*, écartée)   One of the nine directions of the body, in which the dancer's legs are in 2nd position with the body placed diagonally, as opposed to en face, in relationship to the audience (see p. 46).

**Effacé** (*fem.*, effacée)   One of the nine directions of the body, in which the dancer's legs appear open, as opposed to crossed, in relationship to each other from the audience's viewpoint (see p. 44).

**Élancer**   To dart. Used primarily to refer to a type of fast leap that is executed traveling forward, close to the floor (i.e., with minimal elevation).

**Elevation**   Height off the floor. A dancer who jumps high has good elevation.

**Enchaînement**   A combination of steps choreographically linked to form a phrase. For example, an allegro exercise that is composed of several jumps and their linking steps is referred to as an enchaînement.

**Entrechat**   A beaten jump in which the legs cross in 5th position in the air.

**Épaulement**   Shouldering. Refers to the manner in which a dancer slightly twists the torso when facing straight ahead, bringing one shoulder forward of the other. Épaulement is very important for lending dimension to a dancer's body (see p. 26).

**Extension**   The height of a dancer's working leg when lifted from the floor. High extensions in développés and grands battements are particularly desirable for female dancers.

**Face, de**   Refers to the position of a dancer's body when directly facing the audience.

**Face, en**   Same as "de face."

**Fermé** (*fem.*, fermée)   Closed, as in sissonne fermée (a jump in which the legs finish closed in 5th position).

**Fondu** (*fem.*, fondue)   Literally, "melted," from the verb fondre, "to melt, dissolve." This term is often used synonymously with the word "plié." It means on, or with, a bent supporting leg (i.e., in plié as opposed to straight). It may be used as a verb ("Fondu!") or as an adjective, as in arabesque fondue (arabesque with the supporting leg bent in plié). The term "battement fondu" refers to a specific exercise at the barre.

**Grand** (*fem.*, grande)   Large. Describes movements in which the legs are lifted to a height of 90° or above, as in grand battement.

**Haut, en**   High. Describes the height of the arms when they are being held above the level of the head, as in 5th position en haut.

**L'air, en**   In the air. Used to indicate that one or both feet are off the floor, as in rond de jambe en l'air (one foot) or tour en l'air (both feet).

**Line**   The sculptural shape formed in space by a dancer's limbs and body. Good line is one of a dancer's most valued attributes. It is produced by a combination of flexibility, disciplined training in the positioning of the body, and the naturally beautiful shape and proportion of body parts according to the ideal of classical ballet (highly arched feet and long, straight legs being particularly desirable).

**Lunge**  A wide-open (i.e., legs apart) stance on two feet in 4th position, in which one leg (usually the front) is bent and the other straight. It is often used as a preparatory position for pirouettes.

**Manège, en**  A term used to describe a series of steps (usually turns or turning jumps) performed while traveling in a circle around the periphery of the stage or studio. In classical ballet, turns en manège are usually performed as part of the coda, or conclusion, of a virtuoso male or female variation.

**Mark**  To suggest movements, to dance without doing all movements "full out." Dancers often mark a series of steps in a rehearsal in order to save energy or to quickly indicate movements to another dancer. Marking is a kind of dancer's shorthand.

**Oppositon, in**  Refers to positions in which the opposite arm from the working leg is lifted in 1st or 5th position. For instance, if the right leg is lifted in attitude croisée devant and the left arm placed overhead in 5th en haut, the position is referred to as "attitude in opposition."

**Ouvert** (*fem.*, ouverte)  Open, as in cabriole ouverte, a jump finished on one leg with the other held aloft (i.e., the legs are apart from each other, or open).

**Parallel position**  Not turned-out; usually used to refer to 6th position, in which both feet are placed together facing straight front, parallel to each other. Also frequently used to refer to the angle of the lifted leg in relationship to the floor; i.e., a leg at 90 degrees is parallel to the floor.

**Par terre**  On or along the floor, as in the movement rond de jambe par terre, in which the working foot inscribes a circular shape on the floor.

**Pas**  A step. Used to refer to any single movement in the ballet vocabulary.

**Pas de deux**  Literally, "steps for two." A dance for two people, usually a man and a woman—for example, the famous Black Swan pas de deux from *Swan Lake*. The traditional structure of a classical pas de deux is (1) an entrada for both dancers in which the man partners the woman, followed by (2) a male solo variation, (3) a female solo variation, and (4) a coda in which both perform individual feats of virtuosity, then dance together at the conclusion.

**Penché** (*fem.*, penchée)  Inclined. Usually refers to arabesque penchée, a position in which the dancer tilts forward from the hip, directing the torso and head toward the floor, and lifting the foot of the extended back leg up toward the ceiling.

**Petit** (*fem.*, petite)  Small. A term describing small movements that are not performed high in the air, such as petits assemblés. It can also refer to the height of the working leg (i.e., not far off the floor), as in petits retirés.

**Piqué**  Literally, "pricked." 1: A movement in which the strongly pointed toe of the lifted and extended leg sharply lowers momentarily to hit the floor, then immediately rebounds upward. Used synonymously in some ballet syllabi with the term "pointé." 2: Adjective describing a movement in which the dancer transfers the body weight from one leg (in plié) to the other by stepping out directly onto pointe or demi-pointe with a straight leg; for example, piqué arabesque.

**Pirouette**  A turn on one leg on demi-pointe or pointe in any pose.

**Placement**  The alignment of the parts of the body and the distribution of body weight over the feet. Correct placement is essential to the successful execution of all movements in classical ballet.

**Pointé**   A movement in which the strongly pointed toe of the lifted and extended leg sharply lowers momentarily to hit the floor, then immediately rebounds upward. Used synonymously in some ballet syllabi with the term piqué.

**Pointe, en**   The position of the foot in a pointe (or toe) shoe, in which the heel is raised with the foot pointed vertically, and the dancer stands balanced on top of her toe(s).

**Pointe work**   Movements or exercises performed in pointe shoes en pointe.

**Port de bras**   Movements or positions of the arms.

**Preparation**   The musical phrase that acts as a lead-in for the dancer; also, the movements that a dancer executes in preparation for beginning a dance phrase. At the barre, the preparation is usually two or four counts of music, during which the dancer lifts his or her arm to the position from which the exercise begins.

**Prima ballerina**   The top-ranked female soloist in a ballet company. This title is usually reserved for only a few world-class ballerinas.

**Promenade**   A slow rotation of the body in adagio exercises, in which the dancer, maintaining a pose on one leg with the other raised off the ground, executes many little pivots of the supporting heel in order to turn the body around on the whole foot. In the Soviet syllabus, this movement is called "tour lent," and the term "promenade" is reserved for a variation of the same movement in partnering, or pas de deux, work, in which the man supports the woman, pivoting her around while she is poised on one leg en pointe.

**Pronated**   Same as "beveled."

**Pulled-up**   A term used by dancers to indicate that the muscles of the torso and/or legs have been correctly engaged, or contracted, with the result that the weight of the body seems to be lifted away from the floor. It is impossible for a dancer to maintain correct stance or to be technically accurate without being pulled-up.

**Quatrième, à la**   In the 4th position.

**Raccourci**   Describes a leg action in which the dancer bends the knee from an extended position, sharply bringing the foot in toward the supporting leg.

**Relevé**   Describes a position of the supporting foot in which the heel has been raised from the floor, and the dancer is balanced on the ball of the foot (or on the toes, if en pointe). Also, the combination of a demi-plié followed by the raising of the heel(s) from the floor.

**Repertoire**   The works of choreography, or ballets, that are performed by a dance company.

**Reverse, in**   Refers to the repetition of an exercise "in reverse," in the following manner: Every step initially begun with the front foot now begins with the back foot. All movements initially performed dessous (under) are now performed dessus (over). All movements initially performed en dehors are now performed en dedans. All movements that traveled forward now travel backward, and all movements that traveled sideways toward the front foot now travel sideways toward the back foot. For example:

| Initial form of exercise | Exercise in reverse |
| --- | --- |
| Pas de bourrée en tournant en dehors | Pas de bourrée en tournant en dedans |
| Petit jeté derrière (dessus) | Petit jeté devant (dessous) |
| Coupé dessous | Coupé dessus |
| Tombé croisé en avant | Tombé croisé en arrière |
| Assemblé croisé derrière | Assemblé croisé devant |

**Rolled in, rolled over** An incorrect position of the supporting foot or leg in which the weight is allowed to drop forward onto the inside of the foot or leg.

**Romantic period** The early- to mid-nineteenth century period in the history of ballet, in which ballets such as *Giselle* and ballerinas such as Marie Taglioni were in vogue. The typical plot for a Romantic ballet concerned the romantic involvement (usually with tragic results) of an earthly male hero and an un-earthly, supernatural female heroine (i.e., the struggle between flesh and spirit).

**Rond, en** In a circular shape. Usually refers to the spatial pattern of execution by the arms or working leg during a movement such as port de bras en rond or grand battement jeté en rond.

**Sauté** Jump.

**Seconde, à la** In the 2nd position. A movement in which the arm or leg is extended to the side of the body is said to be performed à la seconde.

**Sickled** An incorrect position of the foot in relationship to the ankle, in which the dancer overextends the outside of the foot by turning the foot inward from the ankle toward the inside of the leg.

**Soviet syllabus** The method for training classical ballet dancers as used in the U.S.S.R. today. It is based upon the principles developed by the great Russian teacher Agrippina Vaganova, but has been considerably modernized in recent years.

**Spotting** The technique of turning the head during pirouettes so as not to become dizzy. When spotting, a dancer quickly whips the head around and re-focuses the eyes with each turn of the body (see p. 38).

**Stance** The posture of the body when standing upright. Correct stance is essential for the development of a strong ballet technique (see p. 5).

**Supporting leg** The leg that is supporting the weight of the body.

**Sur la place** In place; without traveling.

**Sur les pointes** En pointe. Standing on the toes.

**Terre, à** On the floor.

**Terre à terre** Close to or along the floor. Jumps that are terre à terre are low, with minimal elevation.

**Tire-bouchon, en** Literally, "like a corkscrew." Usually refers to a type of en dedans pirouette in which the leg is initially extended to the side in the preparation, then quickly brought to a high position in retiré at the side of the knee as the dancer relevés and turns. Also refers to an adagio type of renversé (see p. 214).

**Tour** A turn of the body.

**Tournant, en** Turning.

**Transfer of weight** To step from one foot onto the other.

**Tucked under** An incorrect position of the pelvis in which the buttocks are pressed forward, forcing the pelvis to tilt and throwing the hips out of proper alignment.

**Turn-out** Rotation of the legs outward from the hip joints so that the kneecaps and toes face outward away from the center of the body. All traditional movements in classical ballet are performed turned-out.

**Upbeat** Every musical measure is composed of beats; for example, in 4/4 time there are four beats to a measure, in 3/4 time, three beats. The upbeat is the beat that immediately precedes a strong musical count or downbeat (i.e., "+

1" with "+" being the upbeat). It is important to hear the upbeat because it often "leads" the dancer into movement.

**Upstage**   The part of the stage that is closest to the backdrop and farthest away from the audience. The term is derived from the period of the sixteenth and seventeenth centuries in European theatrical history, during which all stages were slanted, or raked, at an angle downward toward the audience in order to give them a better view. Dancers often use the term to indicate their location or direction of movement on a stage.

**Vaganova, Agrippina** (1879–1951)   The great Russian teacher who in the 1930s developed the system for teaching ballet upon which the Soviet syllabus is now based. She was a graduate of the St. Petersburg Imperial Ballet School, a ballerina of the Maryinsky Theater, and later a much-revered teacher at the Leningrad State Ballet School. In 1934 she became director of the Leningrad Choreographic Technicum and published her famous textbook, *Fundamentals of Classic Dance.*

**Variation**   A solo dance choreographed primarily for the purpose of displaying a dancer's technical prowess—for example, the variations for each of the six fairies in the prologue of *The Sleeping Beauty*, choreographed by Petipa.

**Virtuoso**   Highly skilled. A virtuoso dancer is one who displays dazzling technical prowess, one whose ability is far above that of the average dancer.

**Warm-down**   The practice of ending a session by executing a series of small, less taxing movements immediately after having executed larger, more strenuous ones. The purpose of warming down is to slowly bring the heart rate back to normal after performing a tiring, demanding group of movements at top energy level. Dancers often warm down with small jumps after completing the grand allegro exercises in class.

**Warm-up**   The practice (common to all forms of athletics) of beginning a session by gradually exercising and stretching out the muscles of the body until they are able to function at optimum levels. A dancer whose muscles are "cold" from inactivity must warm up, usually by performing movements at the barre in combination with stretching and/or floor exercises. The warm-up is essential in order to be able to dance with optimum speed, flexibility, and technical accuracy, without danger of injury.

**Whole foot, on the**   Standing on the supporting leg with the entire sole (ball and heel) of the foot flat on the floor.

**Working leg**   The leg that is performing (as opposed to the supporting leg, upon which the dancer is standing). In rond de jambe en l'air, for instance, the working leg is the one executing the circles in the air.

# Selected Bibliography

Baryshnikov, Mikhail. *Baryshnikov at Work*. Edited by Charles Engell France. New York: Alfred A. Knopf, 1978.

Grant, Gail. *Technical Manual and Dictionary of Classical Ballet*. New York: Dover, 1967; 1982.

Hamilton, William G. "The Best Body for Ballet." *Dancemagazine* (October 1982): 82.

———. "Physical Parameters of High-Level Ballet Dancers." Paper delivered at the Sixth Annual Symposium on Medical Problems of Dancers and Musicians, Cleveland Clinic and Aspen Music Festival, Aspen, Col., July 31, 1988.

———. "Physical Prerequisites for Ballet Dancers." *Journal of Musculoskeletal Medicine* (November 1986).

Hardaker, William G., Jr., Lars Erickson, and Martha Myers. *Pathogenesis of Dance Injury*. Champaign, Ill.: Human Kinetics Publishers, 1986.

Karsavina, Tamara. *Classical Ballet: The Flow of Movement*. London: Adam and Charles Black, 1962.

Messerer, Asaf. *Classes in Classical Ballet*. Translated by Oleg Briansky. Garden City, N.Y.: Doubleday and Company, 1975.

Puretz, Susan. "Psychomotor Research and the Dance Teacher." In *Science of Dance Training*, ed. Priscilla Clarkson and Margaret Skrinar. Champaign, Ill.: Human Kinetics Publishers, 1988.

*Additional Recommended Reading*

Arnheim, Daniel D. *Dance Injuries: Their Prevention and Care*. 2nd ed. St. Louis: C. V. Mosby Company, 1975; 1980.

Ashley, Merrill. *Dancing for Balanchine*. New York: E. P. Dutton, 1984.

Bruhn, Erik, and Lillian Moore. *Bournonville and Ballet Technique*. New York: Macmillan, 1961.

Clarkson, Priscilla M., and Margaret Skrinar, eds. *Science of Dance Training*. Champaign, Ill.: Human Kinetics Publishers, 1988.

Dunn, Beryl. *Dance! Therapy for Dancers*. London: Heinemann Health Books, 1974.

Featherstone, Donald E. *Dancing without Danger*. South Brunswick and New York: A. S. Barnes, 1970.

Fitt, Sally Sevey. *Dance Kinesiology*. New York: Schirmer Books, 1988.

Gregory, John, and Alexander Ukladnikov. *Leningrad's Ballet*. London: Robson Books, 1981.

Howse, Justin, and Shirley Hancock. *Dance Technique and Injury Protection*. New York: Theatre Arts Books/Routledge, 1988.

Kostrovitskaya, Vera. Translated by Oleg Briansky. *One Hundred Lessons in Classical Ballet*. Garden City, N.Y.: Doubleday, 1981. Also available translated by John Barker, published by John Barker, 1979.

———, and A. Pisarev. *School of Classical Dance*. Moscow: Progress Publishers, 1978.

Laws, Kenneth. *The Physics of Dance*. New York: Schirmer Books, 1984.

Lawson, Joan. *The Teaching of Classical Ballet.* New York: Theatre Arts Books, 1974.

————. *Teaching Young Dancers: Muscular Coordination in Classical Ballet.* New York: Theatre Arts Books, 1975.

Mara, Thalia. *The Language of Ballet: A Dictionary.* Princeton, N.J.: Princeton Book Company, 1987.

Paskevska, Anna. *Both Sides of the Mirror: The Science and Art of Ballet.* Brooklyn, N.Y.: Dance Horizons, 1981.

Ryan, Allan J., and Robert Stephens. *The Dancer's Complete Guide to Health Care and a Long Career.* Chicago: Pluribus Press, 1988.

Shell, Caroline G., ed. *The Dancer as Athlete.* Champaign, Ill.: Human Kinetics Publishers, 1986.

Shook, Karel. *Elements of Classical Ballet Technique.* New York: Dance Horizons, 1977.

Silver, Daniel. *Handbook on Dance Injuries.* Los Angeles: Daniel Silver, 1986.

Solomon, Ruth, and Sandra Minton, eds. *Dance Injuries.* Reston, Va.: AAHPERD, 1989.

Sparger, Celia. *Anatomy and Ballet.* New York: Theatre Arts Books, 1949; 1970.

Tarasov, Nikolai Ivanovich. *Ballet Techniques for the Male Dancer.* Garden City, N.Y.: Doubleday, 1985.

Vaganova, Agrippina. *Basic Principles of Classical Ballet.* 1946. Reprint. New York: Dover, 1969.

Vincent, L. A. *Competing with the Sylph: Dancers and the Pursuit of the Ideal Body Form.* Missim, Kansas: Sheed, Andrews, and McMeel, 1979.

————. *The Dancer's Book of Health.* Missim, Kansas: Sheed, Andrews, and McMeel, 1978.

Watkins, Andrea, and Priscilla M. Clarkson. *Dancing Longer, Dancing Stronger: A Dancer's Guide to Improving Technique and Preventing Injury.* Princeton, N.J.: Princeton Book Company, 1989.

Woolliams, Anne. *Ballet Studio: An Inside View.* New York: Merriweather Press, 1978.

Wright, Stuart. *The Dancer's Guide to Injuries of the Lower Extremity: Diagnosis, Treatment, and Care.* New York: Cornwall Books, 1985.

**Cynthia Anderson** is from Pasadena, California, where she studied with Evelyn LeMone. She became a member of the Joffrey II Dancers in 1974 and joined the main Joffrey company in 1976, remaining with them until 1982. She performed with the Washington Ballet from 1984 to 1986. In the summer of 1986, she was invited to join American Ballet Theatre as soloist.

**Theodore Brunson** is from San Diego, California, where he studied with Jacquelyn Hepner and Jillana. After receiving additional training at the American Ballet Theatre School under the direction of Patricia Wilde, he was invited to join American Ballet Theatre II. He joined the Pennsylvania-Milwaukee Ballet in 1984 and was promoted to soloist in 1987.

**Cynthia Harvey** is from San Raphael, California. She studied with Christine Walton in northern California and David Howard in New York City. She joined American Ballet Theatre in 1974 and was promoted to soloist in 1978 and principal dancer in 1982; she is particularly grateful to the ballet masters and mistresses of ABT for the training she received during her years with the company. In the fall of 1986, at the invitation of Anthony Dowell, she joined England's Royal Ballet as a principal dancer. She has performed with Fernando Bujones in Japan, Alexander Godunov in France, and for several seasons with Baryshnikov and Company.

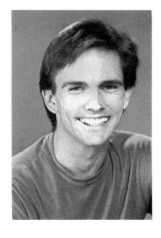

**Robert Hill** is from Merritt Island, Florida, where he studied at the Dussich Dance Studio. He received additional training at the School of American Ballet and the Philadelphia College of Performing Arts. He first danced with the Atlantic Contemporary Ballet, then in 1982 was invited to become a member of American Ballet Theatre. He was promoted to soloist in 1985.

**Carrie Hobart** is from Los Angeles, where she studied with Daniel Job, Nicole Sowinska, and Stanley Holden. She joined American Ballet Theatre in 1981, after studying in New York at the American Ballet Theatre School.

**Susan Jaffe** is from Washington, D.C., where she studied with Hortensia Fonseca, Roy Gean, and Michelle Lees. After performing with American Ballet Theatre II for two years, she was invited to join the main company in 1980. She rose quickly through the ranks, becoming a soloist in 1981 and a principal dancer in 1983. She is also a member of ABT's touring troupe, Baryshnikov and Company.

**Ellen Krafft** is from Evanston, Illinois, where she studied with Larry Long, at the Evanston School of Ballet, and at the Ellis-Duboulay School. She became a member of ABT II in 1978 and joined American Ballet Theatre in 1979.

**Valerie Madonia** is from Buffalo, New York, where she trained with Maria Battaglia. She attended the National Ballet School in Toronto from 1975 to 1979 and joined the National Ballet of Canada in 1979. She returned to the United States in 1981 to dance with American Ballet Theatre, studying in New York with Maggie Black and Elena Tchernichova. After five years with ABT, during which time she performed with the touring troupe, Baryshnikov and Company, she joined the Joffrey Ballet in 1987.

**Magali Messac** is from Toulon, France, where she studied with Olga and Henry Taneff. In 1969, she joined the ballet company of the Hamburg State Theater in Germany. She was promoted to principal dancer in 1974 and remained with the company until 1978, when she came to the United States to join the Pennsylvania Ballet as principal dancer. She was invited to dance with American Ballet Theatre in 1980 and performed with them as principal dancer for six years. Her teacher in New York was Maggie Black. In the fall of 1986, she joined the Pacific Northwest Ballet in Seattle as principal dancer.

**Rachel Moore** is from Davis, California, where she studied with Marguerite Phares. She joined American Ballet Theatre II in 1982 and became a member of the main company in 1984. She studies with Maggie Black in New York City.

**Andrew Needhammer** is from Bloomingdale, New Jersey. He was trained in New York City by Richard Thomas and Barbara Fallis. He danced with American Ballet Theatre II from 1981 to 1984, spending the summer of 1983 dancing with the Pantomime Theater at Tivoli in Copenhagen. In 1984 he joined the National Ballet of Canada.

**Johan Renvall** was born in Stockholm, where he received his training at the Royal Swedish Ballet School and with Constantine Damianov. He danced with the Royal Swedish Ballet in 1977, then came to the United States in 1978 to join American Ballet Theatre. He was promoted to principal dancer in 1987.

**Patricia Renzetti** was born in New York City and received her initial training from William Christensen, Mattlyn Gavers, and Bene Arnold in Salt Lake City, Utah. She then joined Ballet West, where she became a soloist. During the 1970s, she was principal dancer with the Dortmund Ballet in West Germany, the Scapino Ballet in Amsterdam, the Israel Ballet, and the Iranian National Ballet. In 1981 she joined the London Festival Ballet as senior artist. In 1983 she moved to Florida to become the principal ballerina of the Tampa Ballet.

**Amy Rose** is from Glenview, Illinois. She studied on scholarship at the Ruth Page Foundation, the Chicago City Ballet School, the American Ballet Theatre School, the David Howard Ballet School, and a Joffrey Ballet Workshop. She has been a guest with the Universal Ballet Company and the Ballet Philippines. She joined American Ballet Theatre in 1979 and was promoted to soloist in 1987.

**Hilary Ryan** is from Potomac, Maryland; she studied with Mary Day at the Washington School of Ballet. She danced with the Washington Ballet in 1980 and joined American Ballet Theatre in 1981.

**Robyn Simmons** is from Merritt Island, Florida. She studied with Ludmila Factor in Paris and with Barbara Riggins and Russell Sultzbach while on scholarship as a apprentice with Southern Ballet Theatre in Winter Park, Florida. She has attended summer workshop programs with the Joffrey Ballet, the San Francisco Ballet, and the North Carolina School of the Arts. At the time the photographs for this book were taken, she was a dance major at the University of South Florida, Tampa.

**Carla Stallings** is from Sacramento, California, where she studied with Marguerite Phares. She received additional training from Bill Martin-Viscount, the School of American Ballet, and the American Ballet Theatre School. She first danced with the predecessor of ABT II, Ballet Repertory Company, then joined American Ballet Theatre in 1977. She was promoted to soloist in 1984. In 1987, she joined the Boston Ballet as principal dancer.

**John Turjoman** is from Tucson, Arizona. He studied with Richard France and at the Joffrey and ABT schools in New York City. He became a member of ABT II in 1981 and joined American Ballet Theatre in 1983.

**Cheryl Yeager** is from Washington, D.C., where she studied with Hortensia Fonseca at the Maryland School of Ballet. She joined American Ballet Theatre in 1976 and was promoted to soloist in 1981 and principal dancer in 1986. She is also a member of the touring troupe, Baryshnikov and Company.

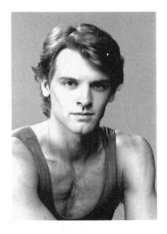

**Ross Yearsley** is from Bainbridge Island, Washington. He studied with Frank Bays, the Cornish Institute, and Maggie Black in New York City. He was first a member of ABT II, then was invited to join American Ballet Theatre in 1984.

The author wishes to thank additional models from the University of South Florida Dance Department, including William Adams, Vanessa Austin, Karen Burns-Taylor, Kelly Darr, Dana Gauntlett, Julia Jones, Tracy Kramer, Karrie Pfeiffer, Sandra Robinson, Cheryl Sunier, Eric Wolfram, Jay Magner, Jennifer Shannon, Richard Sullivan, and Mary Devine; from the School of American Ballet, Erin Tait, Codie Elizabeth Bayer, Amy Arlene Groos, and Jennifer Fuchs; and Diana Warren from Robert Fitzgerald's studio in New York and Michael Glennon from the Graham School.